DATE DUE			

WAR, BATTERING, AND OTHER SPORTS

society / religion

religion / society

Series Editor

ROGER S. GOTTLIEB

Published

WAR, BATTERING, AND OTHER SPORTS
JAMES McBRIDE

Forthcoming

THE CULTURE OF EXTINCTION
FREDERIC L. BENDER

WHY ALTHUSSER KILLED HIS WIFE
GERALDINE FINN

A FEMINIST COSMOLOGY
NANCY HOWELL

WAR, BATTERING, AND OTHER SPORTS

THE GULF BETWEEN AMERICAN MEN AND WOMEN

JAMES MCBRIDE

HUMANITIES PRESS
NEW JERSEY

First published in 1995 by Humanities Press International, Inc.,
165 First Avenue, Atlantic Highlands, New Jersey 07716

©1995 by James McBride

Library of Congress Cataloging-in-Publication Data

McBride, James.
   War, battering, and other sports : the gulf between American men
and women / James McBride.
      p. cm. — (Religion/society/society/religion)
   Includes bibliographical references and index.
   ISBN 0–391–03882–6. —ISBN 0–391–03881–8 (pbk.)
   1. Men—Psychology. 2. Masculinity (Psychology) 3. Abusive men.
   4. Football—Social aspects. 5. War and Society. 6. Man-woman
   relationships. I. Title. II. Series.
HQ1090.M395   1995
155.3'32—dc20   94–39404
                                                                      CIP

A catalog record for this book is available from the British Library

Printed in the United States of America

Serious sport has nothing to do with fair play. It is bound up with hatred, jealousy, boastfulness, disregard of all rules and sadistic pleasure in witnessing violence: in other words it is war minus the shooting.

—George Orwell

I MYSELF AM WAR.
I imagine human movement and excitation, whose possibilities are limitless: this movement and excitation can only be appeased by war.
I imagine the gift of an infinite suffering, of blood and open bodies, in the image of an ejaculation cutting down the one it jolts and abandoning him to an exhaustion charged with nausea.
I imagine the earth projected in space, like a woman screaming, her head in flames.

—Georges Bataille

The intellectual structure of feminism encourages us to be intelligent skeptics, to investigate beyond the superficial images constructed for us by the media. In all its varieties, feminism views interconnection as important: war, incest, pollution, racism, poverty and how men treat women are not separate from each other, but integrally linked in a larger value system.

—Kay Leigh Hagan

CONTENTS

ILLUSTRATIONS

ACKNOWLEDGMENTS

IN ITS ORIGINAL FORM, the idea for this book was sketched out in a paper that I presented before the "Women and Religion" section of the American Academy of Religion's annual meeting in Kansas City, November 1991. I was delighted at the time by the overwhelmingly positive response I received from many of my colleagues in the audience, including those who had worked in the battered women's movement. I especially remember one female colleague, married to an ex-football player, who confessed that she had always intuited a relationship between domestic violence and such male activities as war and contact sports but that male friends had offhandedly dismissed the association. She was convinced that the paper voiced what many women have long suspected. I also am indebted to the leaders of that section who saw merit in the original paper proposal and urged me to undertake the writing of a full-length manuscript—Ellen Umansky and, particularly, Naomi Goldenberg, whose work has inspired many of us in the area of psychology and feminist theory.

In terms of research on the physical and emotional battering of women in the United States, I would like to thank the staff at the National Clearinghouse for the Defense of Battered Women in Philadelphia, whose materials proved to be an invaluable resource for this book, as well as the staffs at the National and State Coalitions Against Domestic Violence throughout the country. I spent countless hours in phone conversations with shelter workers, administrators, and organizers who were too numerous to acknowledge individually here but who were very generous with their time. These are the individuals who must confront daily the appalling toll misogynist violence takes on women and children. In a society whose esteem for sport figures and war heroes eclipses all others, I believe it is these committed individuals, struggling with male supremacist ideologies as well as frequently unresponsive state agencies and legislatures, who truly deserve public acclaim. And I would be remiss if I did not mention Chris Merser who founded and administers the Women's Resource Center of Manhattan—a wellspring of information for those doing research on feminist issues in New York.

In addition to reading stacks of books written by (or ghost-written for) former professional quarterbacks, linemen, coaches, etc., I found two books extremely helpful in exploring the rhetoric of football: *Sports Quotations: Maxims, Quips and Pronouncements for Writers and Fans,* edited by Andrew

J. Maikovich (Jefferson, NC: McFarland & Co., 1984) and *Football's Greatest Insults,* compiled and written by Kevin Nelson (New York: Putnam, 1991). My thanks also goes to Mary Caplan—a therapist, feminist, friend, and sometime football fan—who made it possible for me to observe the New York Giants firsthand and who spent many an afternoon in a Broadway café with me, analyzing the Superbowl and feminist theory. The chance meeting with Bob Markey and Julie Ortner on Superbowl Sunday, 1993, in Grand Central Station was especially fortuitous in light of the subject of this project, and I would like to acknowledge his gracious permission to use the photograph of his work on domestic violence and football in this book. His unstinting dedication to the political responsibilities of the artist bears with it the hope that someday violence against women will no longer be a common occurrence in America.

In regard to the research on various models of interpretation, it would have been difficult to negotiate the twists and turns of French psychoanalytic and feminist theory without the assistance of my colleagues in our faculty study group at Fordham's College at Lincoln Center, most notably Anne Hoffman, Patricia Clough, Eva Stadler, Len Cassuto, Louise Mirrer, and Frank Boyle. A number of my former and current students also helped by providing information and insights on domestic violence and by discussing feminist psychology, particularly Luce Irigaray's work, including Melanie Green, Stephanie Vader, Trish Preston-Roberts, Carolyn Jacoby, Amy Weintraub, Julian Carter, and, especially, Kate McHale. My thanks goes to Bradley Ball for bringing Paige duBois's work to my attention. And I am also thankful for the discussions with Teresa and Pepe Longo in Paris and Pisa about Jean Baudrillard's reading of the Gulf War. But I am most indebted to my former colleague at the College of Wooster, Elizabeth Castelli, whose brilliance as a scholar is grounded in her appreciation of the nuances and subtleties of contemporary discursive constructions. Although the faculties of Johns Hopkins, the University of Chicago, and the Graduate Theological Union/ University of California at Berkeley were all influential in shaping my intellectual life, she has done more to revolutionize my own thought and that of my students than anyone else.

I am grateful to Lee Riffaterre who helped to expedite the permission of the *New York Times* to use the "Descent of Man" cartoon depicted in chapter five. And I would also like to acknowledge the support of those friends who have sustained me during the research and writing of this book, including David and Garris Gregory, Lisa Bergeron, Otto Krause, Ilana Gavin, Tom Deluca, and Therese Walsh. Keith Ashfield of the Humanities Press deserves an extra special thanks for his extraordinary patience, particularly with the unavoidable delays I had to weather in completing the manuscript. Most of all my heartfelt gratitude goes to Joyce Bartle whose love and encouragement buoyed my spirits throughout these past four years. And finally I'd like to dedicate this book to my parents, Louise and Eugene McBride, who showed me that there is an alternative to violence for this and future generations.

PREFACE

MANY AMERICANS ARE OFFENDED by the very concept of "blood sports": intentional bloodletting for "fun" seems cruel and shameful. Animals are deemed innocent and the look of terror in their eyes rends the heart. Even neglect is considered inhumane, but ironically here in the United States, the wealthiest country in the world, there are more shelters for animals than for battered women. Women are the victims of men who take pleasure in exercising power over them both emotionally and physically. As male practices that brutalize the "Other," war, football, and battering are all "blood sports" which many men enjoy either vicariously or directly. To be sure a cursory look at war and football as male territorial games suggests that they have little to do with women—most enemy soldiers, like opposing football players, are male. But what seems most peculiar is that the rhetoric of war and football frequently genders the opponent female as a psychological prerequisite to conflict. Even though the bodies be male, construing the enemy as female taps into a withering hostility drawn from the construct of what it means to be a man in a patriarchal culture. Oftentimes men rhetorically unman their opponents before attempting to dominate them. In the world of male braggadocio, the conquered foe confirms what the rhetoric alleges; the enemy did not measure up. Misogyny is written in the blood of the vanquished.

As a sport taken seriously by both players and fans, the "game" of football mimes male "reality," whether it be war on the battlefield or the "war between the sexes." Men's adversaries may be found in many locations, for example, across the line of scrimmage in the totemic play-acting of professional football, on the other side of the globe in the guise of a foreign dictator and his armies, or across the dining room table in the person of a female partner. The enemy as female, metaphorically inscribed in these male practices, sometimes has its nightmarish realization in the widespread occurrence of rape on battlefields abroad and in the near epidemic emotional and physical abuse of women here at home. But it is not only women who suffer but all those who are depicted in a "womanly," that is, submissive, position, as is evidenced by the tens of thousands of Iraqi casualties during the Gulf War and by the increasing prevalence of gay-bashing. This book attempts to explore the relationship between these male territorial games and violence against women (or those construed as such) by examining various theoretical rubrics, including the classic "Authoritarian Personality" model, René Girard's theory of scapegoating, Georges Bataille's depiction of male sexuality, and Luce Irigaray's post-Lacanian critique of androcentrism.

Although these models are drawn from various disciplines—sociology, psychology, anthropology, philosophy, literary theory, and psychoanalysis, all of them address the concerns of social ethics. Whereas ethics has always been regarded as a subdiscipline of philosophy and has largely been devoted to personal decision making, social ethics is a field that examines the explicit and/or implicit normative claims of collectivities, for example, professions, political parties, universities, businesses, religious movements, governmental bureaucracies, etc. It therefore draws upon the disciplines of the social sciences and humanities to make explicit the presuppositions that underlie the policies of social institutions and the behaviors of social groups. These presuppositions sometimes are evident in codes of ethics or in public policy statements, but frequently these codes and/or statements screen an underlying dynamic of which the group may or may not be aware. Where written guidelines are absent, the values that inform behavior are most often tacitly understood by members of the group. Either they need no articulation or they are repressed because their expression may jeopardize group consciousness and solidarity. The study of the relationship between what is articulated and unarticulated, what is seen and unseen, suggests that there is an intimate relationship between *ēthikē* and *psychē*. In the context of war, battering, and football, misogynist violence—either figuratively or literally expressed—reflects a particular configuration of the male psyche in which these social practices embody a culturally constructed psychological need to abuse women for the sake of a male identity recognizable to the homosocial community. Although the rules of war, like the rules of the game, do not specifically describe the enemy as woman, the discursive construction of the opponent as female bears witness to its prevalence in the male imaginary.

I refer to this particular configuration of symbolic and imaginary dimensions as the masculinist psychic economy. Some may question why I would use the neologism "masculinist" rather than what appears to be the perfectly good term "sexist." Sexism signifies the domination of women by men, but, because these male territorial games victimize not only women but also men, construed as women in the male imaginary, the term sexism seems inappropriate. It sounds somewhat odd to describe the symbolic castration and penetration of a male opponent as being sexist. Heterosexist may be closer to the truth, but misogyny (although largely practiced by heterosexual males) is not unknown in the gay male community, as many lesbians might attest. The masculinist psychic economy therefore strikes the right balance between male hegemony, on the one hand, and the victim gendered female, although s/he may be of either sex. Averring the temptation of biological reductionism, it also acknowledges the cultural origins of misogyny. Clearly not all men think this way, and it implies that there is the possibility for a cultural shift in the way men regard women.

In the description of this masculinist psychic economy, I have made recourse to Freud. Although there are many feminists who would like to exorcise the manes of this father of fathers once and for all, I believe that Freud is still very relevant. As the French feminist psychoanalyst Luce Irigaray has argued, Freud, like his latter-day incarnation Lacan, may be of little use in describing women ("the Other of the Other"), but both the Freudian and Lacanian models have great expository power in accounting for the psychological dynamics that underlie an androcentric social order. Castration anxiety and the imagery of phallic penetration seem to play obsessive compulsive roles in male activities like war and competitive sports. But unlike Freud who traced male *Angst* to Oedipal fears of the father, Irigarary postulates the origin of misogyny in the desire for revenge against the mother. And whereas Lacan's semiotic rendition of the model sheds Freud's nineteenth-century biologistic assumptions, it does little to articulate an alternative to the masculinist psychic economy. That requires a new semiotics: a utopian dream and eschatology based on a female imaginary that has far more revolutionary potential than the old Marxist vision. Irigaray has increasingly devoted her work to theorizing the proleptic glimpses of that future. Unfortunately her work has been misunderstood here in America and attacked by a number of feminists over the past twenty years. It is argued that her consistent reference to "woman" rather than "women" is ahistorical, mythological, and Eurocentric. Moreover many take great offense at her metaphoric identification of woman with the labia, fearing that Irigaray is as biologically reductionistic as Freud. These criticisms seem to me to be ill-considered. Women have suffered the emotional and physical tribulation of patriarchal social orders throughout the world, especially in those societies marked by Western influence. The term "woman" symbolizes the residue that has eluded masculinist control and bears the hope of a new language, freed from a masculinist psychic economy.

Although some readers may question the use of Freud, Lacan, and/or Irigaray in analyzing the aetiology of misogynist practices, I think that others will deem this book controversial for far different reasons. As the most popular organized sport in the United States, surpassing even the national pasttime of baseball, football is considered sacrosanct by men throughout the country. The bone-shattering violence on the field is justified for many reasons, from its alleged character-building traits to its boisterous endorsement as just plain fun. To examine the role of football in the construction of gender—and particularly its misogynist consequences—challenges the heartfelt love that most men feel for the game, so it is not only sports commentators and football athletes but most likely countless football fans who will find this analysis of the "gridiron" almost sacrilegious. I discovered that many men, even those who have more liberal or progressive political attitudes, become almost incoherent with rage over the thought that this cherished male ritual has anything to do with violence against women. The rhetoric of the game suggests otherwise. And the very reaction that the analysis elicits has personally convinced me that there is more than an element of truth in the conclusions presented herein.

I expect that in some quarters this book will be met with *ad hominem* arguments: that the author knows nothing of the game and therefore distorts its benign intentions; that he obviously disdains physical sport and therefore has a not-so-hidden agenda; that, because he doesn't exhibit the requisite deference to football, he must not have "red blood" in his veins. When intellectuals begin to question those beliefs and practices which are closest to the heart of American male identity, for example, patriotism and sport, the response is often one of visceral anger. Of course, anti-intellectualism is one of the preferred stances by demagogues of the right, but it is sometimes employed as a tactic by mainstream male commentators who disguise it under the name of "realism." Although admittedly an academic, I have been isolated from neither the culture-at-large nor the male bonding that so typifies America's Capraesque ideology of the "common man." I was raised in a working-class steel town in Western Pennsylvania that revered football, and over the years I have become well versed in its subculture through the camaraderie that marks gatherings of (largely) male football fans in living rooms and bars across the country. I am intimately aware of both its phenomenological and existential meanings to men, manifest in the excitement that the game engenders. A number of critics may argue that I take football's rhetoric of castration and phallic penetration too seriously, that these expressions are merely figures of speech, but we can no longer naively assume that such figures of speech are irrelevant to the images that we have of ourselves or to the distribution of power in our society. And just because I am critical of the way bodies—be they male or female—are construed in contemporary America, it does not evidence any hostility toward physical culture itself. On the contrary our society cries out for a healthy, nonmisogynous, resurrection of the body. But transforming our bodies requires transforming our minds.

That transformation demands that we look at the underlying psychological impetus for male territorial games. Although most assuredly there were reasons for the recent United States involvement in the Middle East, they are in my opinion inadequate and not merely on political and economic grounds. As President Bush himself asserted, the war was a working through of America's "Vietnam Syndrome," which had allegedly undermined American self-confidence in general and cast doubts in the minds of many about American masculinity. In this respect, the selection of Saddam Hussein and his consequent demonization as a new Hitler served a psychological purpose, quite exclusive of the political and economic realities of the Gulf. Although historians may argue over whether the United States had a genuine interest in going to war against Iraq, American intervention as a gender performance fit the need of an androcentric culture to reconfirm its masculinity. Building on the successes of the Reagan years in the invasions of Grenada and Panama, President Bush found in Saddam Hussein a convenient target to unleash the awesome military force accumulated during the Cold War. But had it not been Saddam Hussein, it most certainly would have been another hastily designated enemy. I am sure that defenders of the Gulf War will be particularly incensed by the analysis of Saddam Hussein as a scapegoat for the anxieties over American manhood. It has been argued that Saddam Hussein is a monster; most assuredly his human rights record is abysmal. He openly defied international law. But neither the violation of human rights or international law has stood in the way of the United States supporting dictatorial regimes in the past. The difference between Saddam Hussein and other tyrants is one of timing: the invasion of Kuwait coincided with the long-simmering crisis in American masculinist identity.

Finally there are those who have embraced the so-called "men's movement" in the United States as an alternative approach to resolving "male hysteria." The leaders of this movement—men like Robert Bly and Sam Keen—have opposed war as an unwarranted sacrifice of men and a senseless exercise in violence. A number of male commentators (and a few female) see in the men's movement the potential to revolutionize relations between men and women. Bly suggests that men need to redirect their "warrior energy" which has been expended in the histrionics of war abroad and the abuse of women and children at home. To some the men's movement seems to be a hopeful sign that men are capable of change. Pursuant to this suggestion, I have become involved in the men's movement over the past two years, attending men's groups, men's workshops, and men's weekends (even the proverbial drumming ceremonies). My commentaries on its potential to change American androcentrism are therefore based on firsthand experience as well as the theoretical writings that drive the movement. Although I have taken pains in this book to respect the privileged character of conversations with other men, I have drawn freely on my general impressions. The suspicions of many women about the men's movement are well placed. Misogynist views are frequently articulated, and its isolation from women does nothing to abate them. It holds little hope for change unless its participants, like men across the country, begin to attend to women's voices.

My hope is that this book will initiate discussion on the links between misogynist practices and androcentric mass consciousness. My intent is not to show that competitive sport "causes" war or that either "causes" the battering of women. It seems to me that all three are associated expressions of something that lies in common. I invite the reader to explore those associations and origins with me and to reconsider the far-reaching social changes recommended by other feminist theorists in this new light.

Chapter One

FROM BAGHDAD TO BATTERING:
MALE TERRITORIAL GAMES AND THE ABUSE OF WOMEN

Ain't you got a drink in the house?
Not before breakfast dear.
I didn't ask ya for any lip. I asked ya if ya had a drink.
Gee, I wish. . . .
There ya go with that wishin' stuff again. I wish ya was a wishin' well
so I could tie a bucket to ya and sink ya.

—*Public Enemy* (1931)

SUBSEQUENTLY SMASHING A GRAPEFRUIT into her face, James Cagney
portrayed the mobster Tom Powers who humiliates his "moll" (Mae Clarke)
in what was to become a classic American movie scene. The film helped to
establish Cagney as the archetypal "tough guy" of Hollywood films during
the depression. Warner Brothers boxed the film's beginning and ending with
statements roundly condemning gangsters and the social conditions that produced their kind; however, there can be little question that the producers'
moral protests were somewhat disingenuous. As the first of the immensely
popular and profitable mobster films of the 1930s, *Public Enemy* excited its
audiences with scenes of violence, including the emotional and physical
abuse of women. It was made apparent that their wishes were completely
irrelevant in a "man's world." Some sixty years later, Cagney's image may
appear to us to be an anachronism—a caricature of male egotism unrecognizable in contemporary American society. But as foreign as this image
appears to be, it is not as dated as it might seem. For in the homes of
America, behind closed doors, the practice of domestic violence continues
unabated. Somewhere in this country at this very moment a woman is being beaten by her husband or boyfriend. Perhaps it is the first time, but
more likely than not it is but one in a whole series of beatings. Perhaps she

1

will survive the emotional humiliation, the bruises, the burns, the cuts, and broken bones. But perhaps not. Four women are killed by their male partners every day in the United States.[1] Sixty years later, America's "Public Enemy" remains at large.

Upon encountering the issue of domestic violence during the Gulf War in 1990–91, I had to admit my shock. To be sure I was aware that in this country's past the abuse of women had been fairly widespread and a commonly accepted practice; however, the second wave of feminism that had broken over this country in the 1960s and 1970s had seemingly revolutionized American society. Remarks about "slapping around" women or "teaching them a lesson" no longer were acceptable in mixed company. Television "sit-coms" no longer chided the long-suffering and endlessly patient wife with taunts like "some day, Alice, some day, pow! zoom! to the moon!" Even though Ralph Kramden always evidenced his sorrow for threatening Alice by assuring her "baby, you're the greatest," those lines from *The Honeymooners* today ring hollow and seem neither funny nor heartwarming. Instead they conjure up the twisted image of domestic "bliss" from an antediluvian era—an era that supposedly bears little resemblance to America in the 1980s and 1990s.

I was not unaware of the fact that "wife-beating" still existed, but I suppose I assumed that it was relatively rare, subsisting on the margins of society in poverty, ignorance, and the frustrations that both generate. Perhaps it was in part because I came from a household where any sort of physical or emotional violence was simply anathema to my parents. And although I was dimly aware that other fathers in the neighborhood beat their wives and children, I always sympathized with the victims as those unfortunate few who could not avoid the "old man's wrath." As a twelve-year-old, I remember seeing one of the neighborhood kids, a large ham-fisted boy, finally standing up to the father who had whipped him regularly all his life. And with my friends, I cheered when, on the street corner in front of the schoolyard, the boy turned the tables on his father and beat him mercilessly. In retrospect I now wonder whether that boy-child uses his fists on his female partner and on a whole new generation of children. Today I count myself lucky, for I realize that the domestic environment of mutual respect and love that I experienced is far from being the norm in this country. Domestic abuse is alive and well, and although attempts are made by female victims as well as their male batterers to hide the violence (either out of fear or shame), the evidence drawn from emergency rooms, police reports, court arraignments, and women's shelters all point to a problem of almost epidemic proportion.

BATTERING IS FUNDAMENTALLY ABOUT EXERCISING POWER AND CONTROL OVER ANOTHER PERSON

The relationship between domestic violence and other forms of aggressive male behavior was first pointed out to me in January 1991 after the "hot war" had commenced in the dramatic aerial bombardment of Baghdad. I had been talking to a couple of friends who were workers in battered women's shelters—one in the District of Columbia and the other in New York's rural Hudson Valley—and discovered their mounting concern over developments in the Middle East. It was not only the war itself that produced their anxiety; it was the fear that the war would be accompanied by a marked increase in the number of battering victims. Although, typical of most such facilities in the United States, her shelter was already operating at full capacity, the DC battered women's advocate expressed her deepest concern. Like her colleague at the rural shelter she had noticed that, since August 1990 (when the Gulf crisis had begun), "things seemed more violent" and that there were "more incidents" than usual. The number of calls made a dramatic surge with the outbreak of war on January 16, and they feared the worst for the following weekend was Superbowl Sunday.

The association between the Superbowl and domestic violence has been a point of controversy in both the press and the battered women's movement for a number of years. As Anne Menard, the Director of Connecticut's Coalition Against Domestic Violence reported in *Ms.*, "Our shelters have known for many years that hotlines are going to be heavy on Super Bowl Sunday."[2] Numerous shelter workers from across the nation have confided in me that they, too, share Anne Menard's suspicions. On the other hand, some advocates, like Meg Ross of the Louisiana Coalition for Domestic Violence, have suggested that there is no more a link between domestic violence and the Superbowl than there is with the appearance of the full moon—an assumption popularly held by shelter workers for a number of years and disproven in a study conducted jointly by the domestic violence coalitions in Alabama and Louisiana. Other advocates for battered women have questioned the link between domestic violence and football by suggesting that the upsurge in reports of battering, rape, and incest during the month of January is attributable to other factors. For example, it is proposed that many victims of domestic violence endure these assaults during December in order to keep the family together for the Christmas holidays and then seek assistance after the season is over. Some who are more amenable to the model of domestic violence based on male stress levels claim that January is a month in which the bills from Christmas arrive, making the explosive behavior of male partners more likely. The decline of domestic violence reports in February is sometimes attributed to the receipt of tax refunds, thereby mitigating the stress on the batterer. And some advocates fear that this emphasis on the Superbowl will be damaging to the battered women's movement itself—an emphasis that could be read as implying that domestic violence is a seasonal phenomenon and therefore a temporary aberration in domestic relationships. On the contrary, they warn, domestic violence occurs year-round.

Although she recognizes this possibility for misinterpretation, Lenore Walker, author of the acclaimed book *The Battered Woman* and one of the preeminent spokespersons for the battered women's movement in America, nonetheless argues that "there is a 'very strong relationship' between contact sports and battering."[3] In one 1988 study she reported dramatic increases in hot line calls to shelters after the defeat of the Denver Broncos by the Washington Redskins in Superbowl XXII. "The game may not cause violence directly," reported one article in *Mother Jones* in 1987, but it can be a contributing factor to battering.[4] Some advocates trace the cause of battering to the pressures experienced by male partners, be they financial or emotional. When increased levels of stress overwhelm their ability to handle them, men frequently may lash out at those closest to them—their wives, girlfriends, or children. For these advocates, football games may so overstimulate men with violent images that women become convenient targets. Hence it shouldn't be unexpected when violence on the television screen is reprised in the living rooms of America. "A big football game on television," concluded Robert Lipsyte, a sports reporter for the *New York Times,* "invariably becomes the Abuse Bowl for men conditioned by the sports culture to act out their rage on someone smaller."[5] But many battered women advocates disagree with this stress model of domestic violence. To be sure, viewing football may well be associated with the physical or emotional abuse of women, but it is not because men are so overly stimulated that they have lost control. Domestic violence is no accident. Football, like war, is a form of male aggression, consciously played out in a variety of cultural practices. As Esta Soler of the Family Violence Project (San Francisco, CA) told Rachel Lurie in an article that appeared in the *Village Voice* during the Gulf War, "[b]attering is fundamentally about exercising power and control over another person. And so is football."[6] Whether in the context of war, sports or battering, violence is something many men—even ostensibly educated, "well-adjusted" men—enjoy. One study, published in 1981, examined the effects of watching football on seventy six college students, evenly split between men and women. Whereas there was no difference in the amount of pleasure experienced by male and female subjects watching football plays of low or intermediate levels of violence, gender played an important role in determining response to highly violent plays. Males demonstrated significantly more pleasure from watching these plays than did their female counterparts.[7]

This relationship between football and domestic violence was dramatically underlined in a work designed by the sculptor/performance artist Robert Markey and exhibited at the Grand Central Station Concourse on Superbowl Sunday, January 31, 1993. Politically active in the peace and justice movements, he had long focused his work on the conflicts in Central America and its victims, for example, his sculptures "Children of Hope, Children of Sorrow." Becoming increasingly sensitized to the issue of domestic violence in this country, Markey resolved to call media attention to this epidemic by building a piece for public display that would dramatize the association of football and the victimization of women and children. He constructed a large scoreboard, miming that which stood over the Tampa football stadium, with appropriate lines for the competing teams: the Dallas Cowboys and the Buffalo Bills. But whereas the typical scoreboard marks only the results of the manifest violence on the field, Markey added a third line that tracked its latent corollary, male violence against women, most often hidden from public view behind the closed doors of American homes. By continually augmenting this line during the course of the game (reflecting the statistic that one woman is battered in the United States every fifteen seconds), Markey brought to light the frightening relationship between the violence of sport on the field and the sport of violence in the home (See Figure 1.1). "The changing of the team scores will seem a rare interlude to this constant changing of the 'battered women' scores."[8] The apparent association of battering and football led NBC—the carrier of Superbowl XXVII—and the National Football League itself to sponsor a pregame thirty-second public service announcement on Superbowl Sunday 1993 urging viewers to call shelter hotlines if domestic violence threatened or occurred. But neither was willing to admit any direct association between the game and the battering of women. The suggestion seemed to be that any association was incidental and represented an aberration from accepted masculine norms, responsibly exercised through "character-building" leisure activities like football. But by revealing what had remained officially repressed—the relationship between male violence and the abuse of women, Markey demonstrated that the final score of the Superbowl—Dallas Cowboys 53, Buffalo Bills 17, Number of Women Battered Since Opening Kickoff 843—was certainly no cause for celebration. Markey confessed that he had no definitive explanation as to why battering increases on Superbowl Sunday.

It may have to do with the fact that men drink more on this day and much violence is alcohol related. It may have to do with frustration because of one's team's losing. It may have to do with an increase in testosterone watching big men slam their bodies against each other. It may be something else entirely.[9]

FIGURE 1.1   The "Battered-Women Scoreboard" created by artist Robert Markey
and photographed by Paul Franz appeared in Grand Central Station,
New York. Greenfield Recorder. Reprinted by permission.

But whatever its cause, Markey's work suggested that different forms of
male violence are intimately associated with one another.

January 1991's Superbowl XXV therefore only intensified the dangers to
women that some workers in the battered women's movement felt were
manifest during the Gulf War. But empirical evidence to substantiate these
claims state by state was difficult to obtain for a number of reasons. To
what extent were increases in hotline calls attributable to the war itself? Or
to increased awareness through press coverage about the dangers of battering? Or to new outreach programs of domestic violence coalitions? Or to
the opening of new shelters? Or the establishment of new hotlines? Or to
more efficient reporting procedures? Or to changes in the way calls were
classified? In some cases, as in Texas, the 1990 figures were lost by the
state agency responsible for maintaining records, and so a statistical comparison of 1990 through 1992 was impossible. Indeed how could increases
in requests for shelter be accurately assessed when most shelters already
run at full capacity, and many women and their children cannot be accommodated? As in the controversy over the Superbowl, some state coalitions
even expressed concern about stressing the relationship between the Gulf

conflict and battering, fearing it would detract from their argument that domestic violence is a systematic rather than incidental problem.

Yet despite these obstacles to gathering evidence, calls to some state co-alitions against domestic violence and individual shelters across the United States supported the conclusions made by those friends who had first drawn this issue to my attention. One shelter in northern Utah reported a 56 per-cent increase in calls during January 1991 over the previous January. An-other in Concord, New Hampshire, noted a 39 percent increase during the first week of the hot war. And although Marcia Seals, the current director of the New Jersey Coalition for Battered Women, recalled an eerie lack of hotline calls at her shelter during the first week of the war, she remem-bered quite vividly that "all hell broke loose" during the second week. Statewide the New Jersey Coalition reported an increase in hotline calls of some 20 percent during January and February of 1991 over the previous year, attributable in her reckoning to the Gulf War. Other shelters in the vicinity of military bases not surprisingly reported substantial decreases in hotline calls during the Gulf conflict (due to the transfer of batterers along with other armed forces personnel to the Middle East) and marked increases after the return of the troops from Desert Storm. As Carol Gundlach of the Alabama State Coalition asserted to me in a telephone conversation, "many men came back batterers who were not so before." They brought home more than the glory of war.

Teaching Her a Lesson

In Western, androcentric, predominantly white societies whose media are obsessed by terrorism and the vulnerability of its innocent civilians to mur-derous attacks, the eye is drawn to the margins of that world order: Third World countries—Libya, Syria, Iraq, Iran—which allegedly harbor these heinous criminals. Danger appears in the sound of the foreign tongue, the guise of the immigrant, the practitioner of an alien religion, particularly Islam, as in the cases of Pan Am Flight 103 or the World Trade Center bombings. Yet this gesture, which simultaneously locates the source of danger outside the Eurocentric mainstream and validates an androcentric American culture of militant vigilance, disguises a very disturbing phenomenon. In America, terror begins at home.

In a society that intoxicates itself with violence—television, films, music videos, books and magazines (not to mention the world's most powerful military establishment), brutality in the home should come as no surprise. It is here that the *bellum domesticum* rages. Yet there seems to be little awareness of the extent to which domestic violence has become ingrained in American families, regardless of race, class, occupation, religion, or education. "Domestic disputes," as they are sometimes euphemistically called, are most often assaults by men against women. Although, particularly with the advent of the men's movement, some men have complained that they too are victims of battering, the statistics compiled by the U.S. Department of Justice indicate that 95 percent of all victims in these "disputes" are women. By and large battering is a gender-specific, misogynist practice that seeks to punish, humiliate, and terrorize women. Although many unreformed batterers have suggested that their violence is directed toward "disciplining my woman," this excuse of "teaching her a lesson" thinly veils a deeper, more complicated desire to inflict pain upon the woman or women to whom he is closest.

The extent of physical injuries resulting from domestic incidents is truly appalling. Women regularly sustain black eyes, bruises, fractured skulls, cuts, severe burns, puncture wounds, internal bleeding, broken noses, jaws, limbs, and teeth, and hearing and visual impairment. Women are sometimes assaulted by their male partners or ex-husbands and ex-boyfriends with belts, straps, wrenches, crowbars, screwdrivers, knives, pistols, and even automobiles, motorcycles, and off-road vehicles. Rape is a fairly common practice in a battering household. From one third to one half of all battered women have been raped by their male intimates who sometimes even force various foreign objects into the vaginal and anal openings of their female partners' bodies. Compared to the nonabusive household, rape is anywhere from five to nine times as frequent in abusive relationships. Some studies of battered women have elicited testimony of rape in almost 80 percent of the cases. Of course, the weapons listed above are not the weapon of choice. Most batterers prefer to use their hands and feet in slapping, shaking, punching, kicking, and slamming women's bodies.

In the Bureau of Justice Statistics 1991 study on "Female Victims of Violent Crime," government researchers found that of the reported crimes of domestic violence over four fifths were classified as assaults, one tenth as robberies, and only 3 percent as rapes. (The victims most often do not even report rape to the authorities because, due to their intimate history with the rapist, both the police and the courts will not take it seriously.) Of the 85 percent that were assaults, one quarter were aggravated. According to the Department of Justice, which maintains these records, aggravated assault is an

[a]ttack or attempted attack with a weapon, regardless of whether or not an injury occurred, and attack without a weapon when serious injury results. Serious injury includes broken bones, lost teeth, internal injuries, loss of consciousness, and any injury requiring two or more days of hospitalization.[10]

Whereas these aggravated assaults are classified as felonies, three quarters of the attacks were categorized as misdemeanors. Here the department describes simple assault as an "[a]ttack without a weapon resulting either in minor injury (for example, bruises, black eyes, cuts, scratches or swelling) or in undetermined injury requiring less than two days of hospitalization."[11] Although, as a misdemeanor, simple assault seemingly is a far less serious crime, Patrick A. Langan and Christopher A. Innes found in their 1986 study that half of these misdemeanor assaults resulted in more extensive injury to the female partner than in over 90 percent of the cases of aggravated assault.[12] Hence the predominance of misdemeanor assaults in domestic violence cases cannot be construed as evidence that only a minority of instances involve a high level of violence. As Angela Browne reported in her book *When Battered Women Kill,* one study showed that women are more likely to be killed literally at their male partner's hands than by virtue of a weapon. One should not be deceived by the terminology: what begins as simple assault has the potential to be just as deadly.[13]

Many of these women are victimized repeatedly; some are beaten monthly, sometimes even weekly. The 1986 Langan and Innes study indicated that one third of all women who initially are battered are victimized again within the next six months. The work of Stark and Flitcraft suggests that women married to batterers are physically beaten on average at least three times every year.[14] Victims of serial battering are particularly in danger because of the escalation of violence common to this pattern of abuse. In *Terrifying Love: Why Battered Women Kill and How Society Responds,* Lenore Walker noted that, in the majority of cases in her study, as the number of battering incidents increased so did the intensity of physical intimidation and violence. Each year it is estimated that between fourteen and seventeen hundred women are murdered by their male partners. Although women constitute only one quarter of the total number of murder victims annually, 30 percent were killed by their husbands, estranged husbands, boyfriends, ex-boyfriends or former spouses. The *Journal of the American Medical Association* reported that there exists a troubling connection between domestic disputes and the phenomenon of murder-suicides in this country. It estimated that between one half and three quarters of all such cases concerned distraught males who took the lives of their female partners and then killed themselves.[15]

As if the physical abuse and deaths of women by their "loved ones" were not enough, battering has other casualties as well. In most cases children are witnesses to the emotional and physical abuse of their mothers by their fathers or stepfathers. It undoubtedly makes a lifelong impression upon the child who must struggle with the legacy of a dysfunctional family in her or his adulthood. Most will have to work through a very skewed understanding of what it means to be female; unfortunately some may perpetuate the image of the terrorized subject either in themselves or in the way they treat women when they grow up. But it is not only their psychological welfare that is at risk.

Children are physically in danger in homes where domestic abuse is prevalent. "Children in homes where domestic violence occurs," reports Sherry Ford in her article "Domestic Violence: The Great American Spectator Sport," "are physically abused or neglected at a rate of 1500 percent higher than the national average."[16] Sometimes children are literally caught between the batterer and the female partner and suffer domestic "collateral damage"; sometimes they are the direct target of the batterer's anger. Physical beatings of children may occur in nearly 50 percent of the homes where a batterer resides; sexual abuse has been reported to be in as many as 30 percent of these homes. Most often the child's tormentor is the batterer himself, but in some cases the child is beaten by the batterer's victim—the child's mother or stepmother. Many women find it difficult to sustain calm with the children when they are under such duress from their male partners. They strike out at their children, either believing it legitimate as a result of acquiescing to their own fate or as a release from the terror that has become such a part of their daily existence. As Lenore Walker noted in her analysis of the "battered woman syndrome," physical and emotional abuse by a woman's male partner has the potential to poison her life and distort her view of the world, even jeopardizing her relationship with those she wants to protect: her own kids. Many shelter workers have noted that bringing women together with their children out of the homes where they have been victimized frequently stops child abuse in the family, not only by the male partner but also by the mother or stepmother.

One strategy to counter the violence of the male partner has been to take abuse seriously, to see it as criminal behavior, that is, simple or aggravated assault, and to arrest the perpetrator. Historically police have been hesitant to intervene in domestic altercations. More often than not they saw themselves basically as interlopers whose basic job was to restore calm and then leave. At best some police officers undertook the responsibility of mediating the "dispute," but many officers believed themselves out of their depth because mediation spoke more to social work than law enforcement. As a consequence, arrest was a rarity unless the severity of the attack reached the threshold of aggravated assault or police were actually on hand to witness the attack. Lenore Walker has reported that in the past convictions of batterers for incidents reported by their victims were practically nil.

Taking the batterer into custody, however, would have the advantages of putting a halt to the immediate violence that victimizes both women and children, and it was hoped interrupting the spiral of violence which in many cases led to the battering deaths of women. Because about one third of all local calls for police assistance throughout the nation involves domestic conflicts (frequently requiring repeated visits by law enforcement officers), arresting the perpetrator had the added benefit of reducing the number of calls from these households. This strategy both reduced the risk to the battered victim and augmented the time that police could allocate to the investigation of other crimes. Moreover it provided mostly male police forces with a more comfortable rubric to interpret these domestic "disputes." Although it was felt by many workers in the battered women's movement that the police tended to be unsympathetic with battered women, the mandate to arrest the perpetrator reframed the situation for the police. The batterer was no longer seen empathetically as a man trying to assert his authority but rather as a lawbreaker who was the very opposite of the police officer. The results of this approach however have been mixed.

First initiated in a Minnesota police experiment, batterers were divided into three categories: those who were warned by the police against using violence; those removed from the household in order to "cool off"; and those arrested. In each of the first two groups, one third of the batterers assaulted their victims again. But among those who had been arrested less than one fifth repeated their attacks. Although the statistics here make the strategy of arrest look promising, other studies have indicated that these conclusions may be unwarranted. Researchers consistently have found that the rates of recidivism reported to them by battering victims are always much higher than the police statistics indicate.[17] The reasons are numerous: many cases do not reach the threshold of a crime in the opinion of investigating officers, despite a definition of assault that includes verbal threats; many repeat cases are not reported by the victim who fears revenge by her male partner for calling in the police. (In the Minnesota experiment, for example, police did not need the female victim to press charges in order to arrest the batterer. Hence, even calling the police risks the arrest of the male partner—a development that the victim may not want to hazard.) And the Bureau of Justice Statistics itself suggested that the rate of recidivism among those arrested may have more to do with the personality profile of the batterer rather than the arrest itself. It has been proposed that perhaps these batterers are those who do not threaten retribution and therefore the battering victims feel more secure in having them arrested. The worst offenders—those who threaten to kill the victim or kidnap the children if arrested—remain free.

ONE FIFTH TO ONE THIRD OF ALL WOMEN
WILL BE PHYSICALLY ASSAULTED BY THEIR
PARTNER OR EX-PARTNER DURING THEIR LIFETIME

Conservative estimates indicate that at least 2.1 million women are physically abused each year (National Crime Survey, 1978–82). The *Journal of the American Medical Association* concluded that these statistics are most likely too low because they do not include those who are institutionalized, indigent, incarcerated, or who do not speak English. Estimates by the American College of Obstetricians and Gynecologists double the figure of those battered to over 4 million, but even so these estimates represent only those women who have turned to some agency—be it law enforcement, medical, or social work—for assistance. And perhaps that figure could be doubled again. "Despite 20 years of empirical research," concluded one team of specialists in the field, "estimates of the number of women abused by their partners each year vary greatly, ranging from 2.1 million to more than 8 million."[18] Although serial victimization of battered women is a pronounced problem, the prevalence of domestic violence throughout society belies the myth that it is a problem limited to a narrow population. In its June 17, 1992 issue, which sounded the alarm to physicians about the seriousness of the problem, the *Journal of the American Medical Association* concluded that domestic abuse is frequently misdiagnosed by medical practitioners in hospital emergency rooms and physician's offices. In reviewing studies of emergency care, its Council on Ethical and Judicial Affairs found that whereas physicians had formerly come to the conclusion of domestic violence in only one in thirty-five cases, the studies pegged the figure as closer to one in every four cases! As a consequence, the Council reported that a survey of abused women indicated less confidence in physicians than in the police who have been widely criticized over the years for their insensitivity to victims of domestic violence.[19] The *Journal* concluded that "one-fifth to one-third of all women will be physically assaulted by a partner or ex-partner during their lifetime."[20] Workers within the battered women's movement place the estimates even higher. Lenore Walker, whose work has been a cornerstone of the movement, argues that nearly one half of all women in the United States will be battered by an intimate partner at some time in their lives.

The difficulty in obtaining consensus on the numbers of victims is in part empirical and in part definitional. The shame and fear that haunts the everyday life of domestic abuse victims prevents many from seeking the assistance they need to extricate themselves from the situation. And when they do receive medical treatment, some victims mask the true cause of their condition. Falling is the leading cause of death among women examined in hospital emergency rooms. The surgeon general of the U.S. Health Service reports that the highest rates for falls were among women between the ages of twenty-five and thirty-four—not among elderly women as would be expected.[21] It has not gone unnoticed by the surgeon general that injuries sustained in battering are consistent with those resulting from falls. Many younger women simply seek to mask the true origins of their injuries, attributing them to a clumsiness that the statistics would lead one to believe recedes with age! Even when women forthrightly state the cause of their injuries, physicians too often dismiss the victim's explanation.

Although the Reagan Administration made addressing the problem of terrorism a high priority during the 1980s by assigning then Vice President Bush to chair a Presidential Commission on the topic, the government continues to keep terrorism at home a low priority. The resources allocated by the government are simply inadequate for the dimensions of the problem. With only thirteen hundred battered women's shelters available nationwide, it is believed that only one in every four victims finds some refuge from this atmosphere of domestic terror. The president of the American College of Obstetricians and Gynecologists, Dr. Richard F. Jones, III, has reported that abused women are apparently a lower priority in the United States than abused animals because more money is spent on shelters for the latter than the former.[22] And because nearly one half of all battered women who flee their homes find their income reduced to below the poverty level, up to one third are compelled to return to the domestic situations from which they had fled. Terror is therefore systematically maintained by the neglect of the state—a neglect that has nothing benign about it. Is it any wonder that many disillusioned victims suffer in silence?

But the controversy over the numbers of victims is not just a result of disputes over gathering techniques; it also reflects disagreement as to what constitutes domestic violence. Some would limit its definition to forms of physical assault, but other battered women's advocates have long depicted physical violence as an inseparable piece of a larger whole that includes emotional battering.[23] Lenore Walker argues that a battered woman is one "who is repeatedly subjected to any forceful physical or psychological behavior by a man in order to coerce her to do something he wants her to do without any concern for her rights."[24] It might be argued that whereas emotional abuse almost always accompanies physical assaults, physical violence is not necessarily the outcome of emotional battering.

Although the insistence of women's advocates' upon the inclusion of emotional battering may seem to some overly broad and too intrusive into the private lives of couples, the emotional terrorism commonly cited is hardly the stuff of innocuous domestic spats. The domestic bully does more than bluster about the house. He employs strategies that demean, degrade, and control the life of his female partner. He ridicules his partner both at home and in public, making her intensely feel the shame of being a woman or that she could never meet his standards of what it is to be a woman or the mother of his children. She frequently is caught in a double bind, forced to assume the role of a sexual object, yet at the same time berated sexually for either not being his sexual ideal or being a "whore." He adopts tactics that separate her from her family and friends, particularly from contact with any other males. He follows her and spies on her every move. She is not to be left alone. If she thinks to elude his panoptic control for even a brief period of time, he threatens to beat her. His insecurity and jealousy sometimes result in forbidding her to use the telephone. In some cases, men have even ripped the phones out of the wall. In an effort to ensure his control over her, he frequently takes away her payroll or government assistance check to use as he deems fit. She has very little, if any, right to make decisions on how money is to be spent. And she certainly risks bodily harm if she dares criticize him. To live with a batterer is most often to be walking on eggshells. The children are frequently held hostage, so that by threatening to harm the children, he can compel her obedience. And sometimes he makes graphic demonstrations of the violence to which he will subject her and her children. These demonstrations include such actions as kicking in doors, punching out windows and walls, wielding knives, cleavers, hammers, crowbars, and the like, waving pistols at the wife and/or children, and even tormenting, maiming, and killing family pets to get his point across. He fails to take responsibility for his own behavior, frequently blaming others for his own problems and even his own feelings. Most often he argues that his victim is to blame for making him feel badly about himself. Therefore she "deserves what she gets." And if the female partner threatens to resist or to leave with her children, he trumps her move by warning that he will take away the children himself or will portray her as an unfit mother to the police and the courts. When all else fails, the batterer can escalate the emotional abuse (which lamentably characterizes the "good times" during such relationships) to physical/sexual violence.

Emotional and physical abuse are therefore two sides of the same coin. Threatening physical abuse and the threat of continued physical abuse generate a coercive environment in which a woman, living in terror, must be careful not to elicit the wrath of her tormentor. Of course it may be argued that whereas physical violence endangers the very health and sometimes even the lives of women and their children, emotional battering does not necessarily do so. Yet cases of emotional battering where a woman is threatened with a weapon by her male partner, even if no physical injury occurs, are classified as a felony. But whether or not specific instances of emotional battering are indictable under the category of aggravated assault, who can judge whether the pain caused by physical beatings and torture is more severe than the terror and humiliation resulting from emotional abuse?

THE REALITY OF GENDER IS CREATED
THROUGH SUSTAINED SOCIAL PERFORMANCES

Both sociologists and social psychologists have attempted to fathom why battering female partners has become such a widespread practice in the United States. Certain factors have frequently been cited as "causes" of battering: class, lack of education, lack of employment, generational transmission, and the use of alcohol and drugs. By isolating and weighing these factors, it has been hoped that researchers could identify the configurations of contributory and dispositive factors that result in this pattern of domestic terror. And perhaps with that information, public policy planners could recommend changes which would not only interdict the spiral of violence in the home but eliminate it altogether.

The image of a battered woman's body—arms and face bruised and lacerated, eyes swollen shut, nose bloodied—is so disturbing that many Americans assume it could never happen in polite company. Surely men who assume the mantle of responsibility, who are men of substance, would never strike their wives or girlfriends. It is an assumption that many Americans, both conservative and liberal, entertain. For the former battering is simply a matter of "breeding." As one upper-class woman put it to me, "One simply doesn't *do* that." For the latter it is presupposed that domestic violence is a product of despair and therefore exists on the very margins of America as a middle-class society. Changes in social structures and working toward the establishment of social justice, rather than "breeding," would eliminate this plague upon the underclass in urban ghettoes and working class in ethnic neighborhoods and suburbs. But whether conservative or liberal, both share the common assumption that battering is a problem of the lower classes of all races, caused by poverty and lack of education.

Some studies, however, have indicated that domestic violence is not necessarily tied to class. For example, the National Woman Abuse Prevention Project in Washington found that police received as many calls involving domestic disturbances among intimate partners in Montgomery County, Maryland—one of the richest suburbs in the United States—as in Harlem in New York City. One Harris Poll even reported that overall 20 percent of Americans approve of slapping one's partner, but though only 16 percent of those who did not receive a high school diploma agreed, 25 percent of the college-educated approved.[25] These disturbing figures indicate that, far from being unknown among the middle and upper classes, battering can be found here, too. New York City police have noted that in one recent fifteen month period over 1200 incidents of domestic violence were reported in Manhattan's exclusive Upper East Side. Although middle- and upper-class males may not suffer the same pressures or lack of education as those of the under- or working-classes, their relative affluence is no hedge against the anxieties that their social standing produces nor does it shelter them from androcentric expectations in their relations with women. In many instances the pressures of economic status and social conformity may be even higher than that of the lower classes. Recently the work of Stark and Flitcraft has challenged this conclusion, citing other studies that indicate domestic violence among the working- and under-classes at three times the rate of the middle- and upper-classes. In examining the data they suggest that the conflicting results from these and other studies comparing the relative frequency of battering in different socioeconomic groups are inconclusive. Yet as the National Woman Abuse Prevention Project noted, women from middle- and upper-class homes may seek private assistance through their physicians or therapists to deal with such abuse. And in instances where women do not work and have domestic help, these victims may even be able to hide themselves—and their mortification—from public view. Hence they are less likely to come to the attention of the police and social service agencies. But whether or not class is a factor in the *degree* to which domestic violence is prevalent, it is clear that battering is a respecter of neither class nor racial lines. Women—black, white, Hispanic, Asian, etc.—from all class backgrounds—be they rich, poor, or somewhere in between—are substantially at risk from violence by their domestic male partners.

As some of the studies cited above note, the number of years of education is not a reliable predictor of the occurrence of battering or its severity. In educational institutions still very much infused with androcentric values, men may not necessarily learn that the use of force is undesirable. On the contrary, as shocking as it may sound, some men use their acquired knowledge to legitimate their violence. Yet, in a culture steeped in the philosophy of *bellum omnia contra omnes,* only the naive could assume that education would never be used for ulterior purposes. And one 1990 study of spouse abuse showed that batterers with more years of schooling than their victims actually used *higher* levels of violence than did abusers with an equal or fewer number of years of schooling.[26] "The point, therefore," claim the authors of one widely respected study, "is not that better educated men . . . are less likely to beat their wives, but that they are more likely to recognize that they have a problem and need help."[27] Education in and of itself does not prevent violence against women: in some cases, it reflects a man's desire to take control of his immediate environment, including the women who populate it. However, it does offer the *possibility* that a man *might* entertain moral arguments against such violence, but there are no guarantees. As the vehicle for social change preferred by both conservatives and liberals alike, investment in the country's educational resources does not *necessarily* reach the source of the problem.

Likewise many commentators assume that violence throughout this society is based on joblessness which leads to despair. Women and children therefore become the convenient target of men who, if employed, might otherwise channel their energies. The frustrations that underwrite battering, it is contended, could be eliminated through economic revival and full employment. Yet here again, joblessness is at best a very limited contributing factor to battering; most domestic assaults are committed by abusers who have jobs.[28] Providing the unemployed batterer with a job will not necessarily stop the violence.

Whereas neither education nor employment are dispositive factors in battering, some researchers have argued that the theory of "generational transmission" is. This theory assumes that by observing the male partner's abuse of his mother and sometimes even suffering abuse himself, the boy-child will mimetically appropriate this behavior as the proper way to treat women and children. There is ample statistical evidence to bear out some relationship between being raised in a battering household and becoming an adult abuser. Massachusetts studies reported in hearings before the U.S. Senate Judiciary Committee and *Self* magazine in 1992 suggest that childhood witnesses of violence in the home have a 74 percent greater chance of commiting violent crimes than did children from nonviolent homes. Another study which appeared in *Deviant Behavior* in 1988 confirmed a positive correlation between batterers and their histories of being abused as children.[29] Some researchers have concluded that generational transmission is the key to unlocking the aetiology of battering.[30] As Philip G. Ney has argued, "children seek revenge when they grow up," most likely verbally abusing their partners and children and less often engaging in actual physical abuse.[31] Yet other respected theorists in the field fear that the link between generational transmission and battering will be distorted. Although it is true that boys raised in violent environments are more likely to become batterers than those from nonviolent backgrounds, the overwhelming majority of children from violent homes (80 percent to 90 percent) do not become perpetrators of domestic violence.[32] Hence, although generational transmission seems to make a stronger case than class, education, or unemployment as a cause of battering, it, too, must be seen as a contributing but not a dispositive factor.

Far more often, drugs and alcohol are depicted in the print media as being the source of domestic violence. The scenario runs something like this: men come home late from the bar or drink with their buddies at home and simply lose control. Likewise, crack, PCP, cocaine, and other drugs are cited as evidence of the role that drug abuse plays in spouse abuse. Numerous studies point out a significant correlation of battering with both alcohol and drugs.[33] A 1991 study of "explosive rage" indicated that in over four fifths of the incidents alcohol was present.[34] In a different 1991 investigation of twenty incidents where domestic disturbances ended in murder, nearly three quarters of the perpetrators had consumed alcohol.[35] Yet a statistical review by Stark and Flitcraft indicates that alcohol plays a role in fewer than 8 percent of the incidents in which police are called upon to intervene.[36] Moreover it is relatively clear to many battered women advocates that alcohol consumption does not "cause" battering. Although binge drinkers, for example, tend to be far more violent than nondrinkers, alcohol functions as the alibi for the violent behavior. The male partner can therefore both express his anger and frustrations in brutality against women and children and yet still redeem himself the next day. But the suggestion that "it wasn't him; it was the alcohol talking" has been a naive assumption that has long been held by desperate women in the hopes that their partners do not really harbor such hatred for them. Battering allegedly becomes more "comprehensible" when it is performed under the influence. It was certainly the litany of the temperance movement which believed "demon rum" to be responsible for the beating of women and children in the nineteenth and early twentieth centuries. But neither prohibition nor abstinence is the cure-all for battering. As batterers can attest, alcohol and other drugs are merely two alibis among many which may be employed to excuse a frightening violence.

The focus of attention on the abuse of alcohol in research on battering highlights a widely held assumption: batterers are men who cannot restrain themselves. As peculiar as it sounds in a society that devotes much of its intellectual and physical resources to designing and manufacturing weapons of increasing efficiency and destruction, violence is assumed to be *irra*-tional. Hence, many persons presuppose that abusers lack the proper socialization (education, class, upbringing) or are physically or psychologically impaired (drunk, high, temporarily insane). In either case battering is a product of passions that have gotten out of hand. Yet battering is no more out of hand than is war on the battlefield. Like war, battering is an outlet for aggression, but aggression is not undirected. Battering, like war, is purposeful. It not only aims to control women and their children through intimidation and physical beatings, it is a means by which a man may express his misogynistic inclinations. In other words violence is not only a means to an end (control), it is an end in itself. Although many reformed batterers regret the toll their behavior has taken on their female partners and children as well as on themselves, some have admitted the relish with which they undertook their course of action. They actually felt good about it while they were terrorizing their victims.

Although certain factors contribute to the configuration of circumstances that surround the issue of battering, it is clear that brutality against women and children is not "the booze talking." Nor can it be attributed solely to the frustrations of poverty, unemployment, or lack of education. "[A]part from age [victims tending to be under 30]," conclude Stark and Flitcraft, "no factors have been consistently found to increase a woman's risk of abuse. Race, income, occupation, alcohol, an inheritance of violence, isolation and status inconsistency are frequently cited as risk factors, but their importance remains ambiguous."[37] Batterers are not only the poor and uneducated; they are also wealthy and part of the educational elite. They are not only the intoxicated; they are also the sober. They are not without redeeming attributes. Many can be kind and generous, courteous and sophisticated. Many are not neanderthals; many are physically very attractive and mentally astute. And many are even loveable—at least in the eyes of many of their victims. So it is not that batterers "don't know any better," as if they are ignorant of proper restraints or have been overwhelmed by outside forces. On the contrary, they know exactly what they are doing. And what they are doing makes them "feel like a man." In this respect, battering is a sport—a male territorial game that tests the power and mastery of a man over those in his immediate environment. As some psychologists note, at least one of the aims of sport is enjoyment, and there is little doubt that batterers enjoy their sport, even their notoriety. For among those who seek help through private religious and therapeutic counselors or through social service agencies, the reputation of the batterer enhances his standing as a dangerous and, above all, virile individual—if not in the eyes of some women, at least in the eyes of many men. He is someone who cannot be overlooked or dismissed. He is a man to be reckoned with.

Just as the aetiology of battering cannot be attributed solely to any of the factors listed above, neither can domestic violence be reduced to football and war. Although a case can be made that viewers learn violent behavior by appropriating mimetically the images depicted on the television screen and in movie theaters, it seems to me that domestic violence is associated with football and war because all three are forms of male territorial games which express a cultural image of male domination. Assuredly domestic violence is not limited to either the football season or wartime; however, it may well have occurred in many instances during the course of Superbowl Sunday or the Gulf War as a spillover from these expressions of male aggression. According to Stark and Flitcraft, the only reliable predictor of battering is male violence itself. Those who have been violent in the past or who enjoy watching violent acts are most likely to be violent. For those men who are batterers and even for those who are not, violence is a defining characteristic of what it means to be a man. Manhood becomes a reflection in the eyes of the victim, in the fear they exhibit, in the signs of domination that they wear upon their bodies—the bruises, lacerations, and broken bones. Violence is the signature that unifies the male psyche in a culture that is predicated on male dominion over women.

The cultural construction of male gender was metaphorically represented a number of years ago in the 1980 film *Tattoo,* featuring Bruce Dern and Maude Adams. In the film Bruce Dern plays a tattoo artist (Karl) who lives in an apartment over his storefront business in Hoboken, NJ. Although seemingly well liked by his patrons, he is a very quiet and private man. His pristine apartment and fastidious preparation of food bear witness to the struggle to control both himself and his environment. A former U.S. serviceman in Japan, he comes to admire the aesthetic which enhances the surface of the body. One day an assistant for a modeling agency arrives to enlist his assistance in a fashion magazine shoot. Upon introducing herself, she is taken aback to see that he is engraving the image of a naked woman, legs spread apart, under a man's armpit—his underarm hair serving as the woman's pubic hair. Called upon to paint rather than engrave tattoo images on the bodies of a group of models, the artist becomes fixated on Maude Adams (Maddie) whom he invites to dinner.

Although the incident in the storefront reflects a certain vulgarity, the artist is more than respectful to the model. He is in fact controlling, vowing to kill an old boyfriend who makes a drunken pass at her in the restaurant. Like someone mesmerized by the movement of the cobra, she is fascinated by his art which transforms the bodies of others into a canvas for his imagination. Although the artist's subjects include both male and female bodies, it is clear that in his own mind his art defines a special relationship to women.

> *Maddie*: Do you ever do women?
> *Karl*: Yeah.
> *Maddie*: What kind?
> *Karl*: Oh, usually they're women who are ready to be identified.
>   Ready to belong. Women who need the mark in order to
>   exist. It's nothing new. It's actually been going on for
>   centuries.
> *Maddie*: Why do you call it the mark?
> *Karl*: Because that's what it is.
> *Maddie*: I thought you did tattoos to be funny, decorative, sexy.
> *Karl*: No, it's much deeper than that.

Maddie's response indicates her understanding that the tattoo is superficial, that it does not undermine the autonomy of the woman, that she freely chooses to enhance the surface of her body. But Karl insists the tattoo has a deeper meaning. It is a mark that transforms a woman into a creation of the male imaginary. Her reality is contingent upon and derived from the tattoo—the mark of the man. Maddie flinches at the thought of the needle, because it is evident that the mark of the man is not laid upon the surface but is infused under the surface of the skin and penetrates the female body. How long does the tattoo last, she inquires? Seductively, lovingly, yet with almost a sinister inflection he replies, "Forever." The transformation from woman into the creature of the male imaginary is irreversible.

Entranced by his quiet exposition, she has dinner with him in the apartment, but she discovers, much to her horror, that he regards women as property to be exchanged and controlled by men. He turns down her amorous overtures because she still "belongs" to another man. And yet he is obsessed by her and dreams of placing his mark upon her forever. His incessant calls terrify her. He resorts to drugging and kidnapping her, and takes her to a secluded house on the shore where her screams cannot be heard. There he methodically begins the work of engraving her body. Upon awakening to discover that her breast has already been tattooed, she yells in anguish, "Why me?" He chillingly replies, "Because I love you." In order to save her life, she is compelled to submit to him, to his will, to his work, which covers her body completely. Maddie is transformed into his creature. She is mesmerized by its beauty and allows him to consummate his desire for her; yet, at the moment of climax, when she is to lose herself forever, Maddie picks up the engraving needle and stabs her rapist in the back. Like the women who kill their batterer-rapists in self-defense, the protagonist decides that she has no other choice if she is to survive.

What may seem incomprehensible to some may be why the victim felt pity as well as terror for this man, why she sought at times to comfort him, why she almost bent to his will. In this society, the pattern of female victimization is so enculturated among many women as to almost feel "natural." One 1990 study comparing battered and nonbattered women concluded that battered women feel themselves to have fewer "masculine" attributes than did nonbattered women.[38] As disturbing as it might seem, in America battering makes many women feel more "womanly": powerless, dependent, and victimized. Likewise violence against women makes many men feel more "manly." His self-identity is invested in his control of women; without violence he is less than a man. Like Karl in *Tattoo,* his self-worth is contingent upon a relationship with women by which he can transform them into creatures of the male imaginary. The bruises on her body signify his mark which overwhelms the resistance of an autonomous human being and penetrates the surface of her body in order to make her his own. She has no life apart from him.

Yet even the batterer knows this conclusion to be a lie. For even when he succeeds in terrorizing her, he always suspects her "infidelity," that is, her "lack of faith" in his superiority as a man. He suspects her desire—though in his distorted world of the male imaginary, he translates the desire for autonomy into the desire for another man. In what can be called the masculinist psychic economy, woman apart from man is an impossibility. He frets about the impossible possibility: the fear that she is not contingent. And so battering becomes the means by which he substantiates his masculinist identity—an identity that androcentrically conceives the power of existence itself. Masculinity and femininity are neither genetic nor preconceived social roles. Instead, as Denski and Sholle have suggested in another context, "the reality of gender is created through sustained social performances."[39] Batterers are men because they "act like men." It is a continual process of revalidation, caused by male insecurities that they never "measure up." In the masculinist psychic economy, that social performance is intimately tied to violence.

To Beat It Out of Her

For many batterers, beating their female partner is more than expressing rage, more than exercising control, and even more than savoring the sadistic pleasure of inflicting pain. He feels that *his* woman's infidelity will lead to his own undoing, and to prevent his own dissolution as a man he seeks "to beat it out of her." Yet, because all too often her infidelities are imagined, what is it that he wishes to beat out of her? The truth? But then again it is his imagined truth—a truth that has nothing to do with her, a truth that has everything to do with him. Many observers are repulsed by the very idea of associating truth with beatings. It seems so patently false, so unjust, so disgusting, so medieval. And yet, as Page duBois has demonstrated in her work, the relationship between the production of truth and physical brutality is one that plays a central role in the male imaginary of Western patriarchal culture.

In her book *Torture and Truth,* duBois excoriates those who would venerate the Western philosophical tradition for the elevation of truth to transcendent nobility. The Hellenic nobility of *aletheia* is founded upon the torture of the body. The body of truth in this case is that of the slave. The body serves as a *basanos* or touchstone for the truth. Although the male citizens of Athens were expected to tell the truth freely, the validity of their word could only be extracted from the body of the slave who, under torture, would confirm or deny her or his master's testimony. As human beings they could apprehend yet could not fully comprehend the truth, and as slaves it was assumed that they would not freely give evidence against their owners. Hence truth was buried in the body which had to be compelled under torture to surrender its secret. The recovery of truth (*aletheia*)—

that which was once known but now forgotten (*lethe*) and which lay be-yond the reach of uncoerced inquiry—was therefore contingent upon physical abuse. The testimony of free men was tested against the touchstone of the slave's body to determine its value. The marks on the body signified a truth—a truth not meaningful to the slave but rather a truth that had mean-ing only in the eyes of the torturer. The welts, open wounds, and scars all bore testimony to the culture's creation of truth.

The intimate relationship between truth and blood, truth and torture, truth and bodily sacrifice is a theme that runs throughout a Hellenized Western Christian culture founded on the cruciform image of Jesus' broken body. For just as the truth of Christianity rests in the physical agony of the cru-cified Christ, so, too, is it assumed that truth is made manifest in and through the suffering of the human body. Underlying this principle is the presuppo-sition that, while the body itself is not the truth, it is the repository of truth. The body does not lie. Persons do, but when the body is put to the test, that is, torture, and the will consequently broken, truth is evident as the involuntary response of the body. This Hellenic conception describes truth as that which always remains hidden, elusive, out of the grasp of men who must compel its appearance. But whereas the probing of the body for truth was limited in Athenian society to slaves and barbarians, Christendom expanded the category of torturable bodies to all human beings. Ironically the literal torture of the human body was authorized to secure the purity of the metaphoric Body of Christ. It was designed to save the accused from themselves when, through their own ignorance and in contradiction to the dogma of the church, they had chosen otherwise (Gk. *hairesis*). Although the Cyprianite principle *salus extra ecclesiam non est* was directed toward heretics, it implied a certain self-consciousness of the church. If salvation outside of the church were possible, the church as the Body of Christ would not be the truth. The concept of heresy therefore structured the conscious-ness of the church as a continually threatened totality. Although depicted as being outside the church, the heretic embodied the fissure within the edifice of the dominant ethos. In *De cultu feminarum,* Tertullian argued, *"Timor fundamentum salutis est"*; yet, in the context of the Christian in-quisitions, is the fear essential to salvation the fear of the heretic or the fear of the torturer? Although fear is usually read through the eyes of the victim, the fear exhibited has more to do with the torturer's fear for his own truth. Hence the purpose of the *inquisitio* was therefore not only to search for deviance from the preestablished norm but also to reaffirm the truth of that norm through the subjugation of the victim's body.

It is interesting to note that, in Augustine's legitimation of the Roman Church's campaign against the Donatist heretics in the fourth century C.E., he compared ecclesiastical schism to a domestic dispute. Like the *paterfamilias,* the church authorities had the responsibility to admonish (*correptio*) and correct its dependents.

> And if any member of the family interrupts the domestic peace by diso-
> bedience, he is corrected either by word or blow, or some kind of just or
> legitimate punishment, such as society permits, that he may himself be
> the better for it, and be readjusted to the family harmony from which he
> had dislocated himself.[40]

Members of the household who challenged paternal authority questioned the father's truth which, without its defense by violence, threatened to un-ravel. Seen as necessary for the well-being of the household, his world and his truth, like that of the medieval church, were at stake. The benevolent intentions of the father, which allegedly underlay the domestic abuse of women and children, thereby served as an analogy to justify the paternal interest of the church in persecuting heretics, even if that meant physical coercion was to become a key social practice of the church during the Middle Ages.[41] In what seems to be almost an Orwellian example of doublethink, benevolence demanded the infliction of *poena* (L. pain, punishment) on the heretic for two reasons: to compel the body to give voice to and recant its Otherness and to punish the body for its deviance from the truth of the Body of Christ. Empowered by the church, inquisitors methodically pun-ished tens of thousands of victims throughout Europe.

During certain periods and in some locales, the inquisitors were even permitted to withhold knowledge of the charges and the witnesses' names from their victims. One particularly disturbing example comes from the records of the Spanish Inquisition in 1568, about a woman who was tortured on the *potro*. Stripped nearly naked, the victim's body was placed on the rack and looped with cords which were tightened by the torturer whenever a satis-factory answer was not forthcoming. That was virtually guaranteed because the victim was denied the right to know what her alleged crime was. Hav-ing refused to eat pork and having changed her bedding on Saturdays, she was suspected of being Jewish.

> She was ordered to be placed on the *potro*. She said, "Senores, why will
> you not tell me what I have to say? Senor, put me on the ground—have
> I not said that I did it all?" She was told to tell it. She said, "I don't
> remember—take me away—I did what witnesses say." She was told in
> detail to tell what the witnesses said. She said, "Senor, as I have told
> you, I do not know for certain. . . . Senor, you know the truth—Senores,
> for God's sake have mercy on me. Oh, Senor, take these things from my
> arms—Senor, release me, they are killing me." She was tied on the *potro*
> with the cords, she was admonished to tell the truth, and the garrotes
> were ordered to be tightened. She said, "Senores, do you not see how
> these people are killing me? I did it—for God's sake let me go."[42]

Asking the accused to confess to charges that are withheld from her seems the height of absurdity—a monstrous and sadistic act; yet, in this and similar cases, the point of torture was not to elicit the victim's truth from her body but to inscribe the torturer's truth on the body of the victim. In a sense it was irrelevant whether the victim admitted to her deviance. The body as tortured and broken was considered *prima facie* evidence of the truth of the torturer, even in cases when the will of the victim remained intact. Under the system of judicial torture in early modern France, judges could convict the accused on the basis of suspicion alone, that is, *avec réserve des preuves en leur entier,* even if the latter did not confess under the most heinous instruments of torment.

It would seem therefore that torture in and of itself is a social practice that proves the truth of the torturer. It is a truth about themselves that can be read on the surface of the bodies of their victims in ancient and modern times alike, tattooed in the marks of torture on the slave or heretic's body or in the bruises, lacerations, and broken bones of battered women. Violence is therefore a writing on the body, which makes visible what has been hidden; yet, the locus of its hiddenness does not lie in the body of the victim but in the imagination of the torturer. The torturer therefore seeks to reveal something about himself, to know his own truth. Like the victims of the Hellenic *agon* or the medieval inquisitor, the bodies of the victims of battering bear the signs of torture. They, too, have suffered the physical and emotional terror which their forerunners have endured.

As duBois points out, woman *qua* woman is constructed in Western culture as the paradigm of an interiority which shelters truth from the gaze of men.

> The female is analogous to the slave. The slave's body and the woman's body are marked off as property of the master; the subject of history in the ancient city, the Greek male citizen, ruled over his subordinates, animals, barbarian slaves, and women, who were seen as like one another in their subordination. Like slaves' bodies, tattooed with signs of ownership and origin, women's bodies were metaphorically inscribed by their masters. The veiled citizen woman, who conceals her true nature with cosmetics and drapery, remains an other, full of potential truth, uncannily resembling the slave, male and female, who awaits torture, who conceals truth.[43]

What truth does woman's body hide about a man? Why does he feel compelled to abuse *a woman* to find out something about himself? As duBois notes elsewhere, a woman's body is *tabula rasa* in Western culture—an empty slate on which is inscribed the master's mark.[44] The metaphor does not countenance the appearance of her own writing. She is the material foundation out of which he can create his own identity. The marks on her body can be read as the inscription of male power. She is the mirror in which he can visualize his own essence—an authenticity recorded in the terror in her eyes, the fearful shortness of breath, the ways in which her body and spirit give way to his fists and his voice. About herself she is as silent as the dead. To the torturer, a woman's screams belong to him; yet, what can be heard in those screams? He futilely listens for something missing, for that which is missing is produced by the screams and agony of the victim. He seeks his own truth. She embodies the elusiveness of self-knowledge and her cries echo his own anguish of not knowing. Although the mystery of what it means to be a man remains hidden, his position as batterer at least produces the knowledge that he is the subject of that mystery, whatever it may be. Battering, like torture, is a comfort in the midst of ignorance. It makes the victimizer feel better about himself.

In the modern era that has liberated Western societies from the stigma of slavery and state religion, the locus of truth has narrowed. Women and their children now stand alone where they once were accompanied by slaves, barbarians, and heretics in ancient and medieval societies. Women are therefore read as the site of truth, compelled into the open, compelled to be opened up, through the use of force. The "helpmeet" of Western culture's phylogenesis is revealed to be more than an appendage to man. Instead, woman is the embodiment of the self-alienation of men. She therefore represents the sign of male unhappiness and is duly the subject of male resentment and anger. She is a constant reminder of his inadequacy. To the batterer and rapist, it is her autonomy that is so infuriating—an autonomy that he cannot gain except through theft. By stealing her autonomy, he can divest himself of his own dependence and impose his own state of self-alienation upon her being. Yet the transaction is never complete because this vicarious possession of autonomy, once-removed, is never secure. She may be unfaithful, that is, not believe in his own illusion, and because his own resolution of self-alienation is contingent upon the theft of her autonomy, her "infidelity," either real or imagined, is unbearable. He hates her for it. Misogynous feelings and actions therefore flow from jealousy, but not necessarily the jealousy of the cuckold. Rather, in the male imagination, he is jealous of what she symbolizes but what he cannot have, even if he has exclusive control over her body. Misogyny fuels the desire for domination which is inevitably inadequate to his task, for like the victim on the *potro* the battered woman is ignorant of his desire—the secret which eludes him. His own truth, embodied in woman, will ultimately not yield to violence and hence, as frustration mounts, so, too, does the level of violence.

Within the masculinist psychic economy, a "true" woman is veritably produced via domination. "Real" men control "real" women—those who are culturally female by virtue of their biology and/or behavior. This construction of gender countenances two cultural taboos—females who "resist their natures", that is, act "mannishly," and males who assume "unnatural" roles, that is, act effeminately. As a sign of domination in an androcentric social order, battering as praxis produces "women." The physical abuse of women, children, and even other men establishes both the "femininity" (the weakness and submissiveness) of the victim and the "masculinity" (dominance) of the batterer. This protological act in the creation of "woman" in Western culture most often culminates in rape. As Catherine MacKinnon aptly observed, "To be rapable, a position that is social, not biological, defines what a woman is."[45] Frequently regarded as emotional, irrational, and childlike, women are depicted as naturally dependent beings, although their dependent status is either enculturated or enforced. Children share in their mothers' fate by virtue of their powerlessness. Some adult men, like women and children, may also be rapable. As a product of masculinist self-creation, the rapability of all three establishes the frontier beyond which lies the truth of the batterer-rapist himself, hidden in the minds and bodies of his victims as conceived by his own imagination.

Although many heterosexual males may not consider themselves homosexual, they nonetheless enact sublimated or even actual acts of rape through the domination and terrorizing of gay men or those perceived to be gay. In this context the fear of women and what they symbolize doubles back on itself. For whereas biologically identified females embody the truth that remains so elusive to the batterer-rapist, male homosexuals in the eyes of homophobic men embody their own fear of permanent self-alienation. This construction is based on the isomorphic identification of homophobes with gay men who are caricatured as the dominated partner in sexual relationships. Male homosexuals are regarded as effeminate "sissies"—a label that virtually every boy in this culture is taught to fear. To be a sissy is to be a fraudulent male—one who does not define himself by the domination of women. Homophobes evince a deep anxiety that, because their bodies are the same as gay men, they too might be gay. And inasmuch as to be dominated means to lose the possibility of compelling truth's appearance from a woman's body, to be homosexual is to be "less than a man." Because the presence of gay men is a reminder of that innermost fear, homophobic men seek to eliminate that presence, particularly in homosocial environments like the military, through the removal of either avowed or suspected homosexuals, for example, dishonorable discharges, gay-bashing. Hence both verbal and physical violence against gay men stems from the desire to efface the very possibility of being in a woman's position. The disdain with which a homophobic masculinist culture regards gay men reflects the disgust that a misogynist culture has for women.

The relationship of homophobia and misogyny suggests that the subject of masculinist hatred is the metaphoric woman, whether present in male or female bodies. The batterer is resolved therefore "to beat the truth out of her," to tell him what he neither knows nor understands. And it is this lack of knowledge that creates fear at the very core of his being and produces a deep sense of alienation from who he is. Battering as a social practice therefore seeks to unite what has been separated, for he believes that, like the Hellenic torturer, he can come to know himself through the abuse of the Other. Batterers think that the more violence employed, the more "truth" can be produced, but the elusiveness of this truth is frustrating and infuriating. He no more understands himself after battering "women" than before; he feels lost and empty, as if the victim's pain could fill him up. But even though her pain does not alleviate his own, violence itself becomes a compensation for his own self-alienation. If she is conceived as the source of the truth about himself and yet, like the victim on the *potro,* she does not yield that truth, she is transformed into the cause of his pain. In his own mind, the victim torments the victimizer: she is to blame for his pain. And, therefore, he simply wants "to beat the shit out of her."

The configuration of the body, woman and filth is a commonplace in the history of Western culture which stigmatizes women simultaneously as the physical object of both desire and repulsion. Under the sign of menstruation, the vaginal opening is tabooed and reviled and yet remains an object of fascination. As the paradigmatic penetrable body, woman is the locus of orifices, by "nature" a creature pierced, dominated, and bloodied. To the batterer she appears a prisoner of her own biology, inscribed by excretion of bodily fluids and wastes. She is what she excretes—blood and feces. Her body is not clean, but filthy, and sex with her is dirty when it is good and even more so when it is not. She is shit. To beat the shit out of her is her undoing. It is to destroy her and affirm the batterer himself. His actions confirm that he is not shit. In the masculinist psychic economy, the act of battering as a social practice therefore produces woman as shit. Implied is the normative judgment that juxtaposes the production of shit with the production of truth. To beat the shit out of her (or those in "her" position) is to compel the appearance of the truth. These metaphors present an interesting juxtaposition. Both are hidden in the body, and yet both are objects of fascination. The desperate relationship between torture and truth echoes the scopophilia of anal compulsion. The body of the victim is made to surrender what is so viscerally important to the abuser. Excrement as truth reflects the sensual and cognitive dimensions of his own psychic reality. It tells him something about himself as a man. The "shit" here is not hers, but rather his own "shit," his own violence, whose goal—to overcome his own self-alienation—remains unreachable as long as he is violent and disappears when he is not. The "cause" of violence therefore remains elusive to the batterer. It is common to hear batterers say that they do not understand what comes over them.

Although the rational rewards of battering—the material and sexual gains derived from the victim's acquiescence—are explicable, batterers cannot explain fundamentally their compulsion to batter. Rationalizations may be offered by referring to childhood upbringing or to their violent "natures," but rarely is battering explained as a ritual of manhood in a misogynist culture. Conceived philosophically battering is not merely a social practice that establishes gender identity; it is a heuristic means to "discover" what it means to be a man in an androcentric culture. For the batterer, the truth of male identity lies in his performance, not in the coerced excuses or pleas for mercy from the victims of violence. In the end, it doesn't matter what she says.

Various studies of battering suggest that this configuration of violence and truth is bound together by the abuser's obsessive libidinality. Stark and Flitcraft, for example, have reported that '[b]attered women are 13 times more likely than nonbattered women to be injured in the breast, chest and abdomen, and 3 times as likely to be injured while pregnant, an injury pattern suggesting the sexual nature of domestic violence."[46] Coupled with the high incidence of rape, the sexual character of these attacks implies that what the batterer seeks to know is intimately bound up with his own sexual identity. Particularly disturbing is the obsessive interest in women's breasts which, as signs of female gender identity, are subject to a deep-seated hostility. The synecdochal expression of rage toward female breasts suggests an unresolved tension between the batterer and his mother which has been carried over into adulthood. Moreover, targetting the abdomen, particularly of pregnant women, confirms the batterer's fear of what lies hidden in the woman's body. "Mere notification of pregnancy," declared the Supreme Court in *Planned Parenthood* v. *Casey* (1992), citing expert testimony before the District Court, "is frequently a flashpoint for battering and violence within the family. The number of battering incidents is high during the pregnancy and often the worst abuse can be associated with pregnancy."[47] Studies indicate that among the general population, between 15 percent to 25 percent of women in general are battered by their intimate partners during pregnancy. That figure jumps to 40 percent to 60 percent among pregnant women who have been battered at some time previously.[48]

Whether consciously or unconsciously, to be intent on causing a miscarriage presents an odd but powerful juxtaposition evident in the mind of the batterer. "Beating the shit out of her" and causing a miscarriage identifies the fetus with excrement. This association is reminiscent of Freud's description of infantile sexuality wherein the child assumes that "the baby, we know, is supposed to live inside the mother's body (in her bowel) and to be born through the intestinal outlet."[49] It implies that the batterer's violence is linked to a libidinal anality which, in his mind, embodies the secret to his own existence lying hidden in the victim's body. Pregnancy is suggestive of both the replication of his own origin and his own expulsion from the mother's body into an alien world. The very existence of the fetus, or even its potential existence, implies that he has been displaced and his estrangement is permanent. The reaction of the batterer is multifaceted. On the one hand, the fetus embodies the recapitulation of his own birth and reminds him of his ambivalent feelings toward a mother whose body, which he once shared as a self-sufficient and secure totality, is lost to him. He was once one with her. They shared a common identity. In the world of infantile sexuality where he identifies himself with feces, he mimes the act of birth by offering his feces, himself, to his mother. This gift of himself is to be cherished and treasured. And just as he identifies himself with feces so, too, does he identify it with his mother. But often the mother rejects this "gift" just as she has rejected him by expelling him into a foreign environment. To treat the woman-mother "like shit" is an ambivalent gesture which simultaneously inscribes his own identity as feces in the flesh of the woman-mother and yet manifests the anger of the child for suffering rejection. On the other hand, the fetus displaces him as the primary focus of the woman's attention. Her pregnancy proves her "infidelity" to him, not by seeking solace with another man, but by replacing him with another infant. He is no longer unique. As the source of gratification, she is no longer exclusively his—a prospect he can little abide. But whether he feels rejected or replaced, she becomes the subject of a withering anger by men who cannot forgive the mother-woman for her "betrayal." To "beat the shit out of" a pregnant woman therefore is to destroy that which reminds him of his own rejection or which threatens to replace him altogether. It is to destroy a truth that displaces his own, that is, his own identity, which remains precariously elusive despite his best efforts to exercise control over his immediate environment.

War, Battering, and Other Sports

As the mass of statistics gathered by researchers in the area of domestic violence shows, battering is not an anomaly in American society. On the contrary it is a piece of a much broader phenomenon of violence—a violence that many men believe, consciously or unconsciously, is necessary to prove their own manhood. Like battering, football and war are social performances which continually reinscribe gender identities on and in the bodies of men and women. Although violence on the football and battle fields is associated with battering, it is not evident that they "cause" the abuse of women. On the contrary, battering seems to be linked to football and war as associated *symptoms* of a masculinist psychic economy. Both football and war are male sports whose enjoyment is predicated on the use of violence against an Other. And whereas the rules of war, like the rules of football, have prevented women from full participation in these male sports, it is evident from the language employed that these games—at times deadly ones—are heavily gendered social performances. The rhetoric of football and war suggests that the enemy—this Other—frequently is depicted in language reminiscent of the positioning of the female, victimized by a male aggressor. If "woman" is defined socially, rather than biologically, as the dominated in androcentric culture, then there seems little doubt that the rhetoric used in these male territorial games seeks to transform male enemies into "women," largely through the use of castration and rape metaphors. The coincidence of battering, war, and the Superbowl, evidenced by the testimony of women's shelter's workers, therefore reflects a spillover of male violence against "women," metaphorically perceived, to actual female partners and vice versa. Victory on and off the (battle/football) field proves to these men that they are neither what they desire or fear: women.

NOTES

1. Karen Stout, "Intimate Femicide: A National Demographic Overview," *Violence Update* 1, no. 6 (February 1991): 3.
2. Gene Ruffini, "The Super Bowl's Real Score: 'Are these the ingredients for Woman-Bashing?'", 11, no. 3 *Ms.* (November/December 1991): 93.
3. Ruffini, "The Super Bowl's Real Score," 93.
4. Laura Fraser, "Super Bowl Violence Comes Home," *Mother Jones*, XII, no. 1 (January 1987): 15.
5. Robert Lipsyte, "Violence Translates at Home," *New York Times,* January 31, 1993, S5.
6. Rachel Laurie, "Unnecessary Roughness: The Super Bowl and Wife Beating," *Village Voice,* January 29, 1991, 132.
7. Jennings Bryant, Paul Comisky, and Dolf Zillman, "The Appeal of Rough-and-Tumble Play in Televised Professional Football," *Communication Quarterly* 29 no. 4 (Fall 1981): 256–62.
8. Robert Markey, Artist's Statement, Superbowl/Domestic Violence Performance Piece, Grand Central Station, New York, January 31, 1993, n.p.
9. Markey, Artist's Statement, n.p.
10. Bureau of Justice Statistics, Office of Justice Program, U.S. Department of Justice, *Criminal Victimization in the United States, 1991* (A National Crime Victimization Survey Report: NCJ-139563), 154.
11. Bureau of Justice Statistics, *Criminal Victimization,* 156.
12. Patrick A. Langan and Christopher A. Innes, *Preventing Domestic Violence Against Women* (Bureau of Justice Statistics, Office of Justice Program, U.S. Department

of Justice, Special Report) 1986, 3.
13. Angela Browne, *When Battered Women Kill* (New York: The Free Press, 1987), 11.
14. Evan Stark and Anne E. Flitcraft, "Spouse Abuse," in *Surgeon General's Workshop on Violence and Public Health Source Book* (Leesburg, VA: Surgeon General's Workshop on Violence and Public Health, October 1985), 19.
15. "Violence, Values, and Gender," *JAMA (Journal of the American Medical Association)* 267, no. 23 (June 17, 1992): 3194.
16. Sherry Ford, "Domestic Violence: The Great American Spectator Sport," *Oklahoma Coalition on Domestic Violence and Sexual Assault* (July/August 1991): 3.
17. Vide, David Hirschel, Ira Hutchison, and Charles Dean, "The Failure of Arrest to Deter Spouse Abuse," *Journal of Research in Crime and Delinquency* 29, no. 1 (February 1992): 7–33.
18. Hirshel, Hutchison, and Dean, "Failure of Arrest," 8.
19. Council on Ethical and Judicial Affairs, "Physicians and Domestic Violence: Ethical Considerations," *JAMA* 267, no. 23 (June 17, 1992): 3191.
20. Council on Scientific Affairs, "Violence Against Women: Relevance for Medical Practitioners," *JAMA* 267, no. 23 (June 17, 1992) 3185.
21. "From the Surgeon General, US Public Health Service," *JAMA* 267, no. 23 (June 17, 1992): 3132.
22. Teri Randall, "ACOG Renews Domestic Violence Campaign, Calls for Changes in Medical School Curricula," *JAMA* 267, no. 23 (June 17, 1992): 3131.
23. Vide, Kathleen Ferraro, "Physical and Emotional Battering: Aspects of Managing Hurt," *California Sociologist* 2, no. 2 (Summer 1979): 134–49.
24. Lenore E. Walker, *The Battered Woman* (New York: Harper & Row, 1979), xv.
25. Sue E. Eisenberg and Patricia L. Micklow, "The Assaulted Wife: 'Catch 22' Revisited," *Women's Rights Law Reporter* 3, no. 3–4 (Spring-Summer 1977): 142.
26. Jacalyn A. Claes and David M. Rosenthal, "Men Who Batter: A Study in Power," *Journal of Family Violence* 5, no. 3 (September 1990): 215–24.
27. Anson Shupe, William A. Stacey, and Lonnie R. Hazelwood, *Violent Men, Violent Couples. The Dynamics of Domestic Violence* (Lexington, MA: Lexington, 1987), 31.
28. Martin D. Schwartz, "Work Status, Resource Equality, Injury and Wife Battery: The National Crime Survey Data," *Free Inquiry in Creative Sociology* 18, no. 1 (May 1990): 57–61.
29. Jack Carter, William A. Stacy, and Anson Shupe, "Male Violence Against Women: Assessment of the Generation Transfer Hypothesis," *Deviant Behavior,* 9, no. 3 (1988): 259–73.
30. Gerald T. Hotaling and David B. Sugarman, "An Analysis of Risk Markers in Husband to Wife Violence: the Current State of Knowledge," *Violence and Victims* 1, no. 2 (Summer 1986): 101–24.
31. Philip G. Ney, "Transgenerational Triangles of Abuse: A Model of Family Violence," in *Intimate Violence: Interdisciplinary Perspectives* ed. Emilio C. Viano (Washington, DC: Hemisphere, 1992): 16.
32. Stark and Flitcraft, "Spouse Abuse," 17, and Evan Stark and Anne Flitcraft, "Woman-Battering, Child Abuse and Social Heredity: What Is the Relationship?" *Sociological Review* (1985): 31, 147–71.
33. Vide, Albert Roberts, "Substance Abuse among Men Who Batter Their Mates: The Dangerous Mix," *Journal of Substance Abuse Treatment* (1988): 5, 2,

83–87, and Glenda Kaufman Kantor and Murray A. Straus, "The 'Drunken Bum' Theory of Wife Beating," *Social Problems* 34, no. 3 (June 1987): 213–30.

34. David Wesner, Chandu Patel, and John Allen, "A Study of Explosive Rage in Male Spouses Counseled in an Appalachian Mental Health Clinic," *Journal of Counseling and Development* 70, no. 1 (September 1991): 235–41.

35. Michael Slade, Lynton J. Daniel, and Candace J. Heisler, "Application of Forensic Toxicology to the Problem of Domestic Violence," *Journal of Forensic Sciences* 36, no. 3 (May, 1991): 708–13.

36. Evan Stark and Anne Flitcraft, "Violence among Intimates: An Epidemiological Review," in *Handbook of Family Violence* ed. Vincent van Hasselt et al. (New York: Plenum Press, 1988), 309.

37. Stark and Flitcraft, "Violence among Intimates," 307.

38. Christine Mattley and Martin D. Schwartz, "Emerging from Tyranny: Using the Battered Woman Scale to Compare Gender Identities of Battered and Non-Battered Women," *Symbolic Interaction* 13, no. 2 (Fall 1990): 281–89.

39. Stan Denski and David Sholle, "Metal Men and Glamour Boys: Gender Performance in Heavy Metal," in *Men, Masculinity and the Media* ed. Steve Craig (Newbury Park, CA: Sage, 1992), 47.

40. *St. Augustin's City of God and Christian Doctrine. A Select Library of Nicene and Post-Nicene Fathers of the Christian Church* (Grand Rapids, MI: William B. Eerdmans, 1973), 2: 412.

41. Augustine was sometimes invoked to legitimate the use of force against heretics, for example, the arguments of Hernando del Pulgar, the royal secretary to Spain's Queen Isabella at the close of the fifteenth century. Vide, Henry Kamen, *The Spanish Inquisition* (London: Weidenfeld & Nicolson 1965), 51. It should be noted, however, that Augustine himself objected to the use of torture unto death. But rather than oppose it on grounds of human cruelty, he considered it a futile practice that reflected the fallibility of human judgment. "And when he has condemned and put to death, the judge is still in ignorance whether he has put to death an innocent or guilty person, though he put the accused to the torture for the very purpose of saving himself from condemning the innocent; and consequently he has both tortured an innocent man to discover his innocence, and has put him to death without discovering it."*St. Augustin's City of God,* 2: 404.

42. Henry Charles Lea, *A History of the Inquisition of Spain* (New York: Macmillan, 1906–8), 3: 25.

43. Page duBois, *Torture and Truth* (New York: Routledge, 1991), 90.

44. Page duBois, *Sowing the Body: Psychoanalysis and the Ancient Representation of Women* (Chicago: University of Chicago, 1988), 130–66.

45. Catherine A. MacKinnon, *Toward a Feminist Theory of the State* (Cambridge, MA: Harvard, 1989), 178.

46. Stark and Flitcraft, "Spouse Abuse," 21.

47. *Planned Parenthood of Southeastern Pennsylvania, et al.* v. *Robert Casey, Governor of Pennsylvania,* No. 91–744 (1992), 47.

48. Vide, Richard Gelles, "Violence and Pregnancy: Are Pregnant Women at Greater Risk of Abuse?" *Journal of Marriage and the Family* (1987): 1337–9; Jacquelyn Campbell, *Nursing Assessment for Risk of Homicide with Battered Women* (Community Health Nursing Department, Wayne State University College of Nursing, 1986); Stark and Flitcraft, "Violence among Intimates"; Lenore Walker, *The Battered Woman Syndrome* (New York: Springer, 1984).

49. Sigmund Freud, *The Genital Organization (An Interpolation into the Theory of Sexuality), The Standard Edition of the Complete Psychological Works of Sigmund Freud* ed. and trans. James Strachey (London: Hogarth, 1974), XIX: 145. Cf. Freud, *On the Sexual Theories of Children, Standard Edition,* IX: On page 217: "The baby must be evacuated, like a piece of excrement, like a stool."

AMERICA'S WAR IN THE GULF:
PHALLIC AND CASTRATION IMAGERY
IN THE RHETORIC OF COMBAT

One thing you can't call Schwartzkopf is a sissy.

—Col. Harry Summers, U.S. Army (ret.)

AT THE CLOSE OF the Baghdad summit on May 30, 1990, Saddam Hussein announced to representatives of his fellow Arab neighbors that the Iraqi economy was at the breaking point. Exhausted by its eight-year war with Iran, which cost the Iraqis some three hundred fifty thousand lives and $102 billion, Saddam's regime was heavily dependent upon the recovery of oil prices in order to repay its war loans, repair the damage to its economic and physical infrastructure, and sustain its enormous military establishment. Demobilization threatened both economic and political instability. Saddam feared that, as in the past when international oil prices dropped precipitously to $7/barrel due to overproduction, some of his OPEC partners might abandon a united front for either economic or political gain. "Therefore, we would ask our brothers who do not mean to wage war—I am now speaking only as far as Iraqi sovereignty is concerned—I say to those who do not mean to wage war on Iraq: This is in fact a kind of war against Iraq."[1]

In a July 15, 1990 letter to the secretary general of the Arab League, Chedli Klibi, the Iraqi Foreign Minister Tariq 'Aziz specifically outlined the grievances of his government by alleging that Kuwait was not only cooperating with the West in forcing down international oil prices but had also been slant-drilling oil wells under the Iraq Kuwait border in order to steal Iraqi oil from the Rumaylah desert. Between January and July of 1990, the price of oil plummeted from $19/barrel to $13/barrel, well below the officially agreed-upon OPEC price of $18/barrel at the time of 'Aziz's letter.[2] Every $1 drop in the price translated into a $1 billion annual loss to an Iraqi economy heavily dependent on oil revenues. Moreover the Kuwaiti practice of slant drilling allegedly had cost the Iraqis an additional $24 billion. 'Aziz warned that Kuwait's behavior was "not less effective than military aggression."[3] Kuwait could resolve the crisis, the Iraqis argued, either by cancelling the Iraqi debt of some $30 billion, which it had borrowed from Kuwait during the Iran-Iraq war, or by backing Iraq's demands for higher international oil prices. But what seemed reasonable to the Iraqi regime took on the appearance of blackmail in Kuwaiti eyes.

Making good on Saddam's implied threat at the Baghdad Conference that "we can no longer withstand the pressure,"[4] two Iraqi armored divisions and helicopter assault troops poured across the Iraq-Kuwait border on August 2, 1990. The invasion succeeded in a matter of hours, and tempted by the riches of Kuwait, Saddam chose to augment his original demands by setting up a puppet government and later announcing the annexation of the country as Iraq's nineteenth province. Seemingly caught off guard by the Iraqi invasion, the American government responded by sending elements of the 82nd Airborne division to Saudi Arabia on August 7, 1990. As the world's leading consumer of oil (28 percent of worldwide production), the United States sought to forestall any attempts by Iraq to extend its control of oil production by seizing Saudi oil fields.

Although the economic consequences of the Iraqi invasion threatened U.S. interests in the Middle East, President Bush argued in a speech to the American people on August 8, 1990 that it was a matter of "U.S. principles." These principles included support for international law, opposition to aggression, the right of peoples to self-determination, and the protection of American nationals abroad. In what has been recognized as the high point of the Bush administration, the president managed to orchestrate the support of the United Nations, including the then-Soviet Union, for a series of UN resolutions condemning the invasion and annexation of Kuwait. Moreover he formed a coalition of military forces from twenty-eight nations, numbering some five hundred fourty thousand (including military personnel from among Arab countries whose relations had been notably strained), in order to defend Saudi Arabia and compel Iraqi withdrawal from Kuwait. The war lasted six weeks, from the initiation of the air war on January 15, 1991 to the culmination of the one hundred hour ground war on February 28, 1991. The Coalition's casualties were remarkably low as America tuned into the world's first conflict of the postmodern age—a Nintendo war in which brutality took on the hyper-real aura of Hollywood cultural fiction. The popularity of the president soared to an over 90 percent approval rating, and the country celebrated in one of the biggest ticker tape parades in history, headed by Generals Colin Powell and Norman Schwartzkopf, down New York's great White Way.

The support for Operation Desert Shield/Storm, however, was not unanimous. On January 26, 1991, over two hundred fifty thousand Americans marched on Washington to stop the war. Haunted by memories of Vietnam, these Americans feared that the conflict with Iraq would reiterate the mistakes the United States had made in getting involved in an Asian ground war a generation earlier. The echo of Vietnam bore witness to the dark side of what George Bush had called the American tradition of "[s]tanding up for our principles." The ghosts of Vietnam, which had haunted American politics and American consciences, still lived in the films that compulsively refought the war (*Rambo, Platoon, Jacob's Ladder, Born on the Fourth of July*) and in the obsessive persistence of the POW/MIA movement. The president resolved that Iraq would not be another Vietnam and that America would not fight this war with "one hand tied behind our back."

But as the figures for Iraqi casualties rolled in—conservatively estimated at one hundred to one hundred fifty thousand Iraqi soldiers (over one third of all Iraqi armed forces) and five to fifteen thousand civilians killed, the memories of carpet bombing and free-fire zones in Southeast Asia returned. The military assured the American public that the air war used "surgical strikes," most often accompanied by "smart bombs"—radiation and laser-guided explosives; yet, of the two hundred fifty thousand bombs dropped on Iraq and Kuwait, less than 7 percent were "smart bombs" and 10 to 20 percent of those actually missed their targets. The remaining 93 percent— the so-called "dumb bombs"—missed their targets 75 percent of the time.[5] As one military commentator noted, the phrase "surgical strike" is something of a misnomer because it is analogous to operating on the body more with a hatchet than delicate and precise instruments. It creates extensive damage in the area surrounding the intended target. Yet, although the political language of the Oval Office and the Pentagon attempted to reflect the principle of noncombatant immunity, the authorized military targets included those elements of Iraq's economic infrastructure that could, in any way, support its military. There seems to be little question that Iraqi-fortified positions, communications and command centers, military bunkers and arsenals were legitimate targets, but what about food convoys from Jordan, water purification plants, power plants that supplied electricity to Baghdad homes and hospitals, canneries, and bottling plants? Targeting these facilities violated the internationally recognized code of conduct in war.[6] In its postwar study "The Impact of War in Iraq: Report to the Secretary-General," UN inspectors concluded:

> The recent conflict has wrought near apocalyptic results upon the economic infrastructure of what had been, until January 1991, a rather highly urbanized and mechanized society. Now, most means of modern life support have been destroyed or rendered tenuous. Iraq has, for some time to come, been relegated to the pre-industrial age.[7]

Torn by civil war, the Iraqi population suffered the consequences of Operation Desert Storm not only in the numbers killed and wounded but also in the lack of food and medicines, the destruction of the communications and power generating systems, the absence of proper sewage treatment and the pollution of water supplies. Iraqis by the tens of thousands faced terror, famine, disease, and death.

The high cost of the war to both the Iraqi military and Iraqi civilians was legitimated by the president's claim that it was to be the test of a "New World Order," forged from the ashes of the Cold War—"a world where the rule of law supplants the rule [sic] of the jungle."[8] Although the president's message to American pilots on January 16, 1991 laid claim to a "just cause," the appeal to the rule of international law by the administration did not ring true because the U.S. government during the Reagan/Bush era accepted international authority only where it saw fit. Although Iraq was urged to comply with a series of UN resolutions (Security Council Resolutions 660, 661, 662, 664, 665, 666, 667, 670, 674, 677, and 678) demanding its withdrawal from Kuwait, the American government had no such qualms about the enforcement of UN Resolutions 242 and 338 demanding Israeli withdrawal from the Occupied Territories. Moreover, the United States used its Security Council veto to stop the passage of a resolution condemning the Israeli invasion of Lebanon in 1980. Likewise the Reagan/Bush administrations had brushed aside UN General Assembly Resolutions condemning the American invasions of Grenada and Panama respectively and chose to ignore the World Court's 1986 decision against the United States for the mining of Nicaraguan harbors.[9] Of course, all good Kantians know that rules which admit exceptions are no rules at all. The U.S. government denounced the puppet regime established by Baghdad in Kuwait City on the grounds that it violated not only Kuwait's sovereignty but also the principle of self-determination, yet President Bush had been a part of an American government that had sought for almost a decade to overthrow the popular Sandinista revolutionary government of Nicaragua. And while the president opposed the annexation of Kuwait by Iraq, the United States still exercised jurisdiction over its own "commonweath," Puerto Rico, the last of America's colonial possessions. Despite the administration's appeal to the principle of self-determination, the powerful al-Sabah family was restored to the throne in Kuwait. Thus, the president's solemn invocation of the "rule" of international law was ironic, to say the least, and may be cynically read to function as an ideological veil for some other purpose, most notably the economic interests of the United States.

Actions on behalf of those interests might well be justified by teleological argument if the good to be gained outweighed the harmful consequences of the war. Although the "preservation" of international law was won and the Iraqi withdrawal from Kuwait was secured, the alleged perpetrator of the invasion still remained in power in Baghdad. Moreover the war cost the lives of over one hundred fifty thousand Iraqis, combatants and noncombatants, many of whom were to die in the civil strife and devastation of postwar Iraq. The ecological damage was severe, due in part to Iraq's setting fire to 85 percent of Kuwait's 550 oil wells and in part to the Persian Gulf oil spill, conservatively estimated at 1.5 million barrels or approximately six times the size of the Valdez disaster in Alaska. Kuwait itself stood in ruins, sustaining billions of dollars in damage; the country would take years to recover.

The war itself cost over $50 billion, not including the $7 billion in debt forgiveness offered Hosni Mubarak for pledging Egypt's support for the UN Coalition. In addition, the United States and its allies had a long list of IOUs due in return for international support for the Coalition, for example, a $140 million loan to the Chinese from the World Bank and support for most favored trading status (despite Tiananmen Square), $7 billion in assistance to the Soviets including food aid, and a $4 billion foreign assistance package to Israel in return for its promise to refrain from military action. Ironically, by the early spring of 1991, the United States favored propping up the price of oil to $22/barrel, $2 more per barrel than the price demanded by Iraq during the spring of 1990—a price that the United States had deemed too high, resulting in pressure on Kuwait to keep oil prices down and precipitating the Iraqi invasion. If military force had been used ostensibly to secure certain economic advantages for the United States, the war seemed patently counterproductive.

From both the deontological perspective ("the rule of international law") and the teleological perspective (the harmful consequences listed above), the decision to go to war seemed to be ethically flawed. Even though the president claimed in his address to the nation on January 16, 1991 that the "war could wait no longer," it was apparent that many Americans could. While 46 percent of those polled backed a U.S. decision to engage in combat, 47 percent still wished to avoid war by urging the continued support of economic sanctions against the Iraqi regime. Although the controversy continues over whether the Bush administration was actually involved in the arming of Iraq during the late 1980s and even whether the U.S. Ambassador April Glaspie tacitly, but mistakenly, gave the wrong signals to Saddam on the eve of the invasion,[10] the debate over the wisdom of Operation Desert Shield/Desert Storm will become a matter for historians. Yet, as President Bush described it, U.S. intervention meant more than a debate over principles and policies; it became a test of the American character. Measured by the intensity of confrontations between the war's supporters and antiwar demonstrators in the large cities and small towns throughout the country, the rhetoric of the war was heavily invested with emotion. It wasn't just a battle in the Middle East; it was a war for the soul of America.

In his "State of the Union" address on January 29, 1991, the president declared, "The conviction and courage we see in the Persian Gulf today is simply the American character in action."[11] Operations Desert Shield and Desert Storm evoked a neopatriotism that had been long dead in an America torn apart by the Vietnam War. Fascinated by the array of futuristic new weapons used by Coalition forces, most Americans vicariously participated in the war, many thrilling to the drama of the kill in the Nintendo-like camera shots of weapons destroying their targets. Its surrealistic character and the virtual absence of American casualties redeemed the country from the legacy of the past and restored a sense of dominion and almost invincibility. The Reagan era of "peace through strength" had borne fruit. "By God," declared the president, "we've kicked the Vietnam syndrome once and for all."[12] This discursive configuration of the Middle East conflict shifted the rhetoric of war from political principles and economic interests to a psychological rubric: a "working-through" of the "Vietnam syndrome" through the collective participation in a cathartic confrontation. In this respect the choice of Saddam Hussein as enemy seemed incidental to a deeper concern: that Americans test their mettle in order to rediscover and reassert their self-confidence. As one professional man stated to me at a forum on the war at Fordham University, New York City, in February 1991, "I really don't know about all these ethical arguments. All I know is: the war makes me feel good."

"Feeling good" about the war attested to its nature as a form of moral virtue in the classical sense, *vir,* that is, the affirmation of certain "manly" attributes such as courage and fortitude. It should not be surprising then that the rhetoric of combat during the Gulf War was heavily cathected with the language of a virile asceticism, replete with images of the castration and phallic penetration of the enemy. Thus, the model of character ethics summoned forth by the president, his advisors, and the mass media alike—a model that distinguishes between "us" and "them"—reflected a compelling need to "gender" the moral discourse of war in order to reaffirm the dominant, masculine identity of America as the world's one remaining superpower.

This Is What We're Fighting For

Although President Bush eventually won the support of Congress and the nation for his efforts against Saddam Hussein, it was a small group of advisors who shaped the strategies, tactics, and language by which the war would be waged. The chairman of the Joint Chiefs of Staff, General Colin

Powell, urged the president "to draw a line in the sand." The president chose to make a stand at the Saudi border, but during the first few weeks of the war, he had little except bravado to stop Saddam Hussein if the latter chose to invade the Saudi kingdom as well. The schoolyard metaphor fit George Bush's depictions of Saddam Hussein which were reminiscent of the bully whom adolescent boys fight for territorial dominance. "When we win, and we will," the president assured the American people, "we will have taught a dangerous dictator, and any tyrant tempted to follow in his footsteps, that the United States has a new credibility and that what we say goes."[13]

Framing the conflict in terms of adolescent aggression complemented the gendered way in which the invasion of Kuwait was described. Initially the president alluded to the stereotypic attributes of "a powerful Iraqi army [which had] invaded its trusting and weaker neighbor."[14] Although the purpose of the United States was allegedly to stand up for American principles (regarded as being synonymous with civilized behavior), the descriptions of the invasion took on a more blatant sexual tone as the conflict intensified. The victim of Saddam's bellicose and overwhelming assault, Kuwait, was depicted as being female.

In his speech to the nation of January 16, 1991, launching Operation Desert Storm, the president described Saddam Hussein as a man who had "systematically raped, pillaged and plundered a tiny nation."[15] Although it is highly unlikely that General Norman Schwartzkopf had had the opportunity to review the president's remarks before drawing up his own statement to the troops on January 16, he reiterated the president's sentiments almost word for word. "Iraq must cease its rape and pillage of its weaker neighbor and withdraw its forces."[16] The expression "the rape of Kuwait" became so common in television commentaries, news articles, and political speeches that it was almost an obsessive compulsive component in any discussion of the crisis. The currency of the image in both official and popular discourse was encouraged by the flooding of American bookstores with Jean Sasson's propagandistic *The Rape of Kuwait*—a compilation of atrocity stories—in the fall of 1990. Of the 1.2 million copies printed, some two hundred thousand were sent by the Kuwaiti Embassy in Washington to American troops in Operation Desert Shield. In light of these efforts, it is no surprise that these images would appear in the president's "State of the Union" message given before Congress on January 29, 1991: "Saddam Hussein's unprovoked invasion, his ruthless, systematic rape of a peaceful neighbor, violated everything the community of nations holds dear."[17]

Echoing the Allied propaganda images of the rapacious Hun during the First World War, the representation of Saddam Hussein as a rapist shifted the emphasis in the discursive construction of the conflict from the economics of oil to the sexual politics of terror. And this shift certainly served the president's purpose, either consciously or unconsciously, for in the living rooms of America, the president's invocation of this imagery domesticated the threat that was half a world away. Manipulating gender stereotypes, the president was to champion the weak and the defenseless, the female, against the unwanted intruder, whose assault was unprovoked. The political and economic rationale for the invasion was dismissed out-of-hand, for the aggressor was beyond the pale of the law and of civilized humanity. The undertone of the president's call to arms indicated that it was not for mundane political purposes but rather for the defense of womanhood. One correspondent for the *New York Times* later captured this sentiment in action when he quoted a company commander about to board an assault helicopter for the invasion of Iraq, "'And this is what we're fighting for,' he added, whipping a pair of women's black silk underwear from inside his helmet."[18]

The denunciation of the "rape of Kuwait" simultaneously was accompanied by the identification of the instrument of rape: the Iraqi army. From the outset of the crisis, the president consistently emphasized the size of the Iraqi armed forces, the fourth largest in the world. The phallic thrust and penetration of the Iraqi military were conceived to be an extension of Saddam's own personality. As George Bush emphasized in his September 17, 1991 speech to the American people, " the United States has no quarrel with the Iraqi people. Our quarrel is with Iraq's dictator and with his aggression."[19] Throughout the Gulf crisis, the president employed a turn of phrase that depicted Iraqi capabilities as the personification of Saddam himself, for example, "Saddam Hussein's nuclear bomb potential," "Saddam's artillery and tanks," "his chemical weapons," "Saddam's vast military arsenal."[20] And hence the resolution of the crisis was adamantly placed in terms of an ultimatum: either the voluntary withdrawal of Saddam's army/phallus from its ravaged neighbor, Kuwait, or its destruction. The rhetoric of political, military, and even mass media figures became infused with the vehemence of indignant males who threaten their enemies with castration.

In a rhetorical gesture that one reporter termed "military bravado" at the January 23, 1991 Pentagon Briefing, General Colin Powell warned the Iraqi leader, "First we're going to cut it off and then we're going to kill it"[21]— an expression so suggestive that the *New York Daily News* chose to drape it over the front page of the newspaper. Powell dwelt on the image by extending the metaphor of the body to the entire Iraqi military establishment wherein the Iraqi army served as the phallus and the military command center in Baghdad functioned as the brain. The attack against the body of the Iraqi military, headed by Saddam Hussein, would proceed by "deaden[ing] the nerve endings" in Baghdad and then "intensify[ing] the cutting off process" in Kuwait.[22] As if to underline his point, General Powell participated in a bomb-signing ceremony at Dhahran air base in Saudi Arabia by inscribing one explosive with a message addressed to Saddam, "You didn't move it. Now you'll lose it."[23]

Resonances of the castration theme could also be found in the imagery used by the field commander, General Norman Schwartzkopf. In his personification of the Iraqi military, the enemy airforce was conflated with "the ability to see." The success of Saddam's military was predicated on this oculocentrism; hence the attack against Iraqi airfields was the attempt to eliminate the sine qua non for effective military action. Yet Schwartzkopf's expression was more than a mere blinding—it was a deocularization of the enemy. "Once we had taken out his eyes," declared the general, "we did what could best be described as the Hail Mary play in football."[24] The dramatic and dangerous maneuver of Coalition forces that outflanked the Iraqi army necessitated the elimination of Saddam's intelligence-gathering capacity (that is, his gaze). Given the Freudian model in which the eyes serve as a surrogate for the phallus,[25] the elimination of Saddam's gaze served as the means toward his humiliation (that is, his castration). In Schwartzkopf's estimation, Saddam was "neither a strategist nor is he schooled in the operational art nor is he a tactician nor is he a general nor is he a soldier. Other than that, he's a great military man—I want you to know that."[26] In this assessment the field commander's derisive comments posited a "cause" to the enemy's defeat: Saddam must have been inadequate to this great test of manhood. The Schwartzkopf news conference therefore simultaneously took credit for eliminating the threat that Saddam represented and asserted, ex post facto, that Saddam was never really a threat to begin with. Yet Saddam's inadequacy, hidden beneath political braggadocio, could only be revealed by "hardened" military professionals under whose gaze, according to ABC's Sam Donaldson, Saddam "folded like a banana."[27] In his characteristically blunt language, Richard Nixon declared Saddam "militarily castrated," and Schwartzkopf concluded that "there's not enough left of him to be a regional threat."[28]

In some respects the underlying discourse of castration and combat as a performance of male sexuality embodies a reduction and simplification of the politics of war to an almost adolescent level of gender construction. It should not be surprising therefore that the crisis in the Gulf appealed to the producers of one of the most influential vehicles in the production of adolescent male sexuality: comic books. In her work on mass culture, Norma Pecora has gathered empirical data demonstrating that most comic book consumers are adolescent males. Viewed through the lens of superhero comics, the world is a white culture wherein women are most often depicted as victims, frequently threatened by nonhuman, nonwhite, and/or socially deviant, if not outright evil, characters.[29] Although the Gulf War prompted one publisher, Apple Comics, to produce a new series entitled the *Desert Storm Journal*, (See Figure 2.1), perhaps the most intriguing war-related issue starred one of the five most popular superheroes in the comic world: The Punisher.

Marvel Comics published two issues of *The Punisher*, #47, "Caught in a Desert Storm" and #48, "Next Stop: Baghdad," in April and May of 1991, respectively, which illustrated the sexual politics of the war. With the properly WASP name Frank Castle, the protagonist has been victimized by faceless criminals who murdered his family, and he now seeks revenge in the guise of "The Punisher"—a superhero who specializes in high-tech warfare. Although the invention of the crime mystifies the origins of adolescent male anger, its legitimation is played out through the Punisher's one-man war against criminals. In thinly veiled references to the controversy over Iraq's attempt to secure a "supergun" from European arms merchants in 1990, issues 47 and 48 detail the Punisher's attempt to destroy the supergun obtained by the "President of Trafia"—Saddam Hussein of Iraq—who secured the weapon from a Western inventor and arms merchant to assist in his war against "Zukistan" (Iran). In "Next Stop Baghdad" the Punisher recounts how he had saved the arms merchant from an assassin only to discover that the inventor had built "the world's largest gun" for Trafia. "Now Trafia's waving the #$@# around and threatening the Middle East."

Making a spectacle of the weapon registers as a shock to the male psyche and illustrates the underlying discursive construction of the arms race. The almost caricatured phallomorphic image of the "big gun" is deemed not only a threat to other Middle East countries but also an affront to the Punisher. As Freud argued in the "Medusa's Head" (1922), "[t]he erect male organ also has an apotropaic effect.... To display the penis (or any of its surrogates) is to say, 'I am not afraid of you. I defy you. I have a penis.' Here, then, is another way of intimidating the Evil Spirit."[30] The dynamic established by such phallic display causes the Punisher to project his most primal anxiety into the very words of his opponent, the head of "Trafia's security," Colonel Razir.

> The potential for humiliation. You see, you may have noticed we speak frequently of humiliation ... you could say we are obsessed with it. It is the driving force behind most Middle Eastern policies ... to humiliate our enemies and avenge past humiliation."[31]

The projection of the Punisher's innermost fear allows him both to anticipate the performative reiteration of his own masculine identity (if he is victorious) and to divest himself from humiliation (if he fails).

As a citizen of the First World, Frank Castle, the protagonist, is a practitioner of Western rationality, which allegedly has mastered these inner-

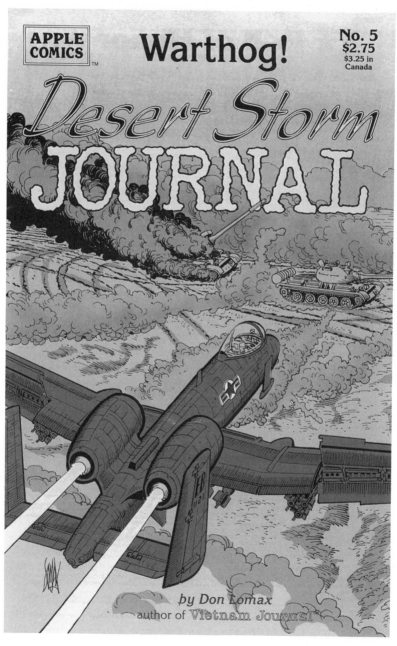

FIGURE 2.1   The *Desert Storm Journal* comic book cover no. 5, June 1992.
Reprinted with permission from Apple Press Inc., Greencastle, PA.

most fears—fears that supposedly still run rampant in the mysterious, dark, and threatening cultures of the Third World. The conflict within himself becomes a conflict between his alter ego, The Punisher, and the personification of Otherness, "my greatest enemy, Saracen." (The character Saracen therefore serves as a vehicle to express Western racial and religious stereotypes about Arabs and, derivatively, Muslims.) It is Saracen, having murdered and replaced Colonel Razir at the behest of the president of Trafia, also known as Saddam Hussein, who captures and tortures the Punisher, ultimately tying the superhero in cruciform to "the muzzle of the world's biggest gun."[32] Due to be martyred on this, Saddam Hussein's, phallus, the imagery is dramatically reversed when the Punisher escapes his bonds and, upon firing, the barrel of world's largest artillery piece explodes into pieces. In the after-math, sprawled in the debris, arms and legs akimbo, Saddam mutters, "My gun. . . . My Gun!!!"[33] The reversal is completed in the shift of the locus of braggadocio from the President of Trafia and his henchman, Saracen, to the Punisher, for it is the Punisher who rides victorious in this test of manly endeavor. As it had been just three months earlier, there was not enough of the President of Trafia/Saddam to be a threat to anyone, and in his place was the one "who carries justice on a gunbelt and leaves no survivors."[34] Or as Vice President Dan Quayle put it in his own inimitable way, it was "a stirring victory for the forces of aggression against lawlessness."

HITLER REDUX

As a foil for the reassertion of American masculinity, Saddam Hussein had to be depicted as both potent and evil. Moreover it had to be ensured that Desert Shield/Storm would not repeat the humiliation suffered by the U.S. military at the hands of the Vietnamese some twenty-five years earlier. In order to unwrite the trauma of Vietnam, it required the framing of a post-Vietnam War in a pre-Vietnam context. Thus, the rhetoric of the Gulf War did not allude to the jungles of Southeast Asia but to World War II. Seen from the hindsight of total victory and the unconditional surrender of the Allies' enemies, World War II symbolized the recovery of what had been lost: an American self-respect predicated on the admiration and fear generated in the hearts and minds of other peoples. As a member of the last generation of leaders to fight in World War II, George Bush exploited this nostalgia for *pax Americana* to reinscribe confidence in the American psyche. By drawing a parallel between the Gulf crisis and World War II, the president could both entice the public into a dramatization of the conflict between America and totalitarianism and also speak convincingly of a preordained result: the certain defeat of America's opponent. Yet a repetition of what

Studs Terkel once called the "Good War" necessitated a reinvention of the antagonist.

From the very outset of the conflict, the president seized control of the production of war rhetoric by depicting Saddam Hussein in the role of Adolf Hitler. Certain similarities worked to the president's advantage: the Iraqi armored assault on Kuwait and the invasion of Poland by Nazi Panzer divisions; the totalitarianism of the Bath'ist and National Socialist regimes; Hitler's anti-Semitism and Hussein's anti-Zionism. The president implied that identification in his first speech to the nation after the invasion: "Iraq's tanks stormed in blitzkrieg fashion through Kuwait in a few short hours." The president noted that the policy of the British government in 1939, which later became known as appeasement, "does not work."[35] As he was to suggest in his January 1991 "State of the Union" message, the United States faced "another defining hour" which would test the virile asceticism of the American will. And it was not long before Bush's rhetorical flourish infused the Washington scene with the haunting aura of the late 1930s. In this performative revival of World War II, America had to avoid the Scylla of isolationism and the Charybdis of appeasement. Indeed, Washington insiders noted Bush's obsession with not becoming another Chamberlain. The syndicated columnist Charles Krauthammer joked in December 1990 that, upon James Baker's return from Baghdad, the bags of Bush's envoy be checked for any evidence of umbrellas. And Senator Jesse Helms opined that if Franklin Delano Roosevelt had had to face the same opposition as Bush, "the French would be making their soup out of sauerkraut today."[36]

On October 15, 1990 George Bush finally made public policy what had hitherto been only stated by syndicated columnists: Saddam Hussein was another Adolf Hitler.

> Every day now, new word filters out [of Kuwait] about the ghastly atrocities perpetuated by Saddam's forces . . . of a systematic assault on the soul of a nation, summary executions, routine torture, newborn babies thrown out of incubators . . . dialysis patients ripped from their machines . . . Hitler revisited.[37]

The description of Saddam as "a Hitler" became a commonplace in the mass media, repeated in newspapers, news magazines, and local and national television programs and indeed seemed to generate a life of its own beyond the immediate control of the administration. At least two journalists allege that in the anti-Saddam hysteria, editors for the *New Republic* retouched a photograph of Saddam for its September 3, 1990 cover in order to trim the Iraqi's characteristic bushy mustache into one more reminiscent of the Hitler prototype.[38] The identification of Saddam with Hitler was assisted through the publication of atrocity stories, most notably the alleged removal of Kuwaiti babies from incubators by Iraqi soldiers. The charges were substantiated by testimony before the Congressional Human Rights Caucus by a young woman named Nayirah whose last name was withheld supposedly in order to protect her family in Kuwait from retribution. It was only after the war that it became known that this witness was a member of the ruling al-Sabah family and that her testimony was arranged by Hill & Knowlton, the public relations firm contracted by the ousted Kuwaiti government for a reported $6 millon. Nevertheless the associations of Saddam with Hitler and nazilike atrocities became deeply embedded in public's mind— an association that carried psychological as well as political connotations.

It is almost impossible to underestimate the power that the image of Hitler holds in popular culture. To the Western imagination Hitler is a metaphysical principle. Depicted as being larger than life, this charismatic figure, who mesmerized the people of Germany and orchestrated some of the most heinous crimes against humanity, embodied the incarnation of evil. The historian William L. Shirer described him as a man "possessed of a demonic personality, a granite will, uncanny instincts, a cold ruthlessness, a remarkable intellect, a soaring imagination, and—until the end, when, drunk with power and success, he overreached himself—an amazing capacity to size up people and situations."[39] As a man raised above the masses, this führer served as the ego ideal for the collectivity,[40] a quasi-divine figure or man-god, who exercised, in the words of Albert Speer, his architect and armaments minister, a "magnetic force."[41]

Speer confessed that the enthusiasm generated by Hitler, as the epicenter for this collective effervescence, was almost physical. Hitler seemed to be stimulated by the crowds who stood enraptured before him in a relationship akin to aural rape. One intimate reported that "[t]he last eight to ten minutes of a speech resembled an orgasm of words."[42] There seems to be little doubt that Hitler understood this power as a symbol of his sexual magnetism. In *Mein Kampf,* written during his imprisonment in the Landesburg prison for his participation in the 1923 Bavarian putsch, Hitler compared the masses to "the woman whose psychic state is determined less by grounds of abstract reason than by an indefinable emotional longing for a force which will complement her nature."[43] He reportedly once told Pauline Kohler, a young woman whom he apparently wanted to impress with his masculinity, that he could stand for hours, arm erect in the Nazi salute, at parades and party rallies; indeed he ridiculed Hermann Goering who, in his opinion, was too weak and soft to do so. "He is flabby," the Führer concluded. "I am hard."[44] And Speer noted that Hitler himself believed he exuded "a powerful sexual appeal to women."[45]

Yet it was not only his voice that would spellbind his admirers; it was also his gaze. Prime Minister Neville Chamberlain's ambassador to Germany, Neville Henderson, recalled that "[m]any Germans, women in particular, used to descant to me upon the radiance of his expression and his remarkable eyes. When I looked into the latter, they were generally hot and angry."[46] To men Hitler's gaze became a "castrating stare" (Speer) that simultaneously frightened and enthralled his audience. It was a power that he wished to preserve intact. For that reason Hitler believed he should never marry lest the suggestion of marital relations diminish his potency among the admiring throngs. His sexual liaisons seem to have been very few, most notably his relationship with his half-niece Geli Raubal, who committed suicide in 1931, and with Eva Braun. And even these relationships were kept well hidden from the public. Both Raubel and Braun remained invisible to the public eye during Hitler's political career, largely sequestered to their private rooms in Hitler's apartments and villas. To do otherwise would shatter the power that he exercised by virtue of his fidelity to the *Volk*.

As Klaus Theweleit has argued at the close of the first volume of *Male Fantasies,* "the Fuhrer's 'wife,' in that fascist ritual, was the unconscious of the masses who were pouring into block formations."[47] The thunderous cries of *"Sieg Heil"* amid the fields of red swastika flags bore witness to the absolute mastery of one man over the collective. As Deputy Führer Rudolph Hess cried out at the Nuremburg party rallies, *"Deutschland ist Hitler; Hitler aber Deutschland ist."* Yet it was not only in the context of domestic German politics that Hitler exercised such sexual prowess. Hitler's military aggression against Poland, the Low Countries, and France frequently was described in terms of a sexual assault. Symbolized by the figure of Marianne, France was deemed to be a victim of "rape." And from the Allied perspective Hitler's brutish sadism was particularly evidenced by his demonstrative glee over the capture of Paris in 1940.

In light of the power that Hitler embodied, it is not unexpected that interpretations of Hitler attempted to undercut the legitimacy of his authority. Biographies of the Führer evidence the suspicion that there was something alarmingly "unnatural" about Hitler's magnetism. Psychohistorians have used this suspicion to speculate that Hitler was in some way sexually "deviant," either psychologically or even physically. Some have suggested that his sadism and megalomania were compensated in private by an "ertogenic masochism." In his 1971 article "Hitler's Character and Its Development: Further Observations," Norbert Bromberg described scenes in which Hitler's infatuation with a young German actress took the form of "grovelling at her feet," pleading with the woman to kick and abuse him.[48] The 1943 report of psychoanalyst Walter C. Langer to the wartime Office of Strategic Services (the forerunner of the Central Intelligence Agency) alleged that Hitler could not achieve orgasm except by having a woman urinate or defecate on his face.[49] Bromberg concluded,

From what we have seen about the sources of Hitler's sexual anxieties and his characteristic defense mechanisms, it is not too difficult to trace the emergence of his perversions. In the first place, his intense castration anxiety and fear of the female genitalia readily account for his preference to see rather than to act. Indeed, seeing itself is sexualized in his case, since the organs of sight are substitutes for parts of his genital apparatus, the testicles.[50]

In Bromberg's construction of Hitler, the Führer's gaze was infused with sublimated sexual desire and authority, and it was this quality to which his followers responded. Yet Bromberg's psychohistorical explanation suggests that the idol of millions was seriously disturbed. These claims about Hitler's alleged perverse sexual practices were buttressed by speculation that Hitler's genitals themselves were malformed. In *"The Death of Adolf Hitler": Unknown Documents from Soviet Archives,* Lev Bezymenski cited the Soviet pathology report on Hitler's charred body which claimed that he suffered from monorchism, or the presence of only one testis in the scrotum.[51] The absence of the left testicle would also be explained by cryptorchism, the failure of the testis to descend into the scrotal sack. Although the problem of an undescended or missing testicle does not necessarily entail physical malfunctioning in sexual practice, speculation abounds that its absence had profound psychological consequences for Hitler. Numerous historians and psychoanalysts, including those consulted by the American OSS during World War II, have been tempted to explain Hitler's behavior, both political and personal, in light of the rumors that surrounded the Führer's mysterious sexual life. These speculations seem to suggest that Hitler was a monster because he was "less than a man."

Yet in the widely praised book by Leonard and Renate Heston, *The Medical Casebook of Adolf Hitler,* little reliable evidence is found either for the Führer's supposed masochism or monorchism/cryptorchism. The Hestons suggest that the alleged autopsy on the remains of Hitler conducted by Soviet physicians was tainted by political expediency: to be used to demonstrate that Hitler was a deviant, physically, psychologically, and therefore politically. The likelihood that these charred remains—if they were in fact those of Hitler—would be sufficient to determine whether the subject was malformed is highly questionable. Moreover Hitler's medical records kept by Dr. Erwin Giesing and Dr. Theo Morell indicate no such deformity. As to Hitler's alleged masochistic personality, the Hestons found no concrete evidence of psychiatric illness through the mid-1930s and attribute the increasing incidents of rages and physical degeneration to amphetamine toxicity, caused by the injections of Dr. Morell.[52]

On the other hand, the biographer Robert G. L. Waite reported that Norwegian and American dental specialists had confirmed through the study of

Hitler's dental records that the body examined by the Soviets was indeed the Führer's. Waite concluded that Hitler's personality fit the pattern of emotional disturbance among monorchid/crytorchid males: chronic castration anxiety, the compensation for the loss of the testicle by overly cathecting eyes and breasts, anal obsessiveness, and anti-intraceptive psychological tendencies to counter the fear of sexual inadequacy.[53] Although the scientific grounds for the allegations of Hitler's psychological and sexual deviance are open to dispute, the empirical basis for this controversy may be in one sense irrelevant to the role that the construction of the Hitler myth plays in the psychic economy of the West. In the popular imagination Hitler embodies an abnormal, primal, and charismatic authority, capable of great evil— a man who by definition stands above the mass as a symbol of absolute power, a political leader who stands apart from the civilized standards of restraint in the international community, and a personality whose origins are veiled in the irrational, the perverted, the deviant. From the postwar rereadings of the events of the late 1930s, the war with Hitler was a test of manhood. The policy of "appeasement" signified a relapse into fear and cowardice. In order to undermine Hitlerism as a form of libidinal politics, the mythologies of psychosexual and physico-sexual deviance proliferated as strategies of resistance. By marginalizing Hitler as a madman and deviant, it was possible to delegitimate and disempower him, and so Hitler remains inscribed in the consciousness of the West.

Hence the invocation of the appellation "Hitler" in reference to Saddam Hussein cannot exclude certain sexual connotations. Hussein's totalitarian regime, his anti-Zionism, his use of poison gas against the Kurds, his "rape" of Kuwait, even the ubiquitousness of the dictator's face in the cities and towns of Iraq, are conflated together in the reappropriation of Hitler's image whose libidinal authority makes the war a "defining moment" in the reassertion of American masculinity. The images of the Iraqi president surrounded by his generals reminded commentators of Hitler in his bunker or in the East Prussian "Wolf's Lair" where veteran officers cowered before a "ruthless and cold" leader accustomed to absolute obedience and the exercise of absolute power. And the Western media pointed out that viewers should be as suspicious of Saddam Hussein's supposed affection for children, shown during his meetings with the families of Western hostages, as they were of Hitler's displays of love for children and animals. But perhaps more than anything else, Saddam Hussein's "cult of personality" afforded commentators the opportunity to personify the enemy in one individual. Just as Adolf Hitler was identified in Nazi ideology with Germany, so, too, was Saddam Hussein considered synonymous with Iraq in American war rhetoric. As the phallic extension of Saddam's personality, the Iraqi army had to be "cut off" and killed. His male gaze, as a sign of domination, needed to be effaced, either metaphorically, through the elimination of Saddam's air force, or symbolically, through the destruction of his image, not only on dart boards, gun targets, T-shirts, and toilet paper at home but also in the portraits of the dictator that appeared on the walls of Kuwait City. I recall one image in particular on the morning of Kuwait's liberation from the occupying forces of Saddam's military, February 28, 1991. A television crew captured the act of a Kuwaiti guerrilla defacing a large wall portrait of Saddam Hussein. Beside the soldier were two cans of paint: one red and one black. The soldier had just finished painting rouge on Saddam Hussein's cheeks and was in the process of applying the *coup de grâce*— the black beauty mark.

The acts of metaphorical and symbolic castration, however, were no more than the reiteration or confirmation of what had been presumed in the popular imagination: that Saddam was already outside the community of men—or at least those considered "normal" and sane. And it was not only that he was frequently depicted in the "womanly" position in an economy of power. He was also depicted as being subhuman. This assumption underlay the popularity of yet another anti-Saddam T-shirt. Here the image of the Iraqi president's face was superimposed over the body of a tarantula. Belonging to the wolf spider family, the tarantula symbolizes extreme danger, even death, due to its venomous bite. In medieval folklore its poison reputedly produced a form of "madness" called tarantism, manifest in a compulsion to dance wildly. The conflation of Saddam Hussein with tarantism suggests that he embodies the threat of the abnormal to the well-ordered life of Western civilization. Indeed, Hussein was most often described by American politicians as being either a wild animal or a psychopath. Throughout the Gulf crisis, the president contrasted the West's "rule of law" with Saddam's "law of the jungle."[54] And as early as August 2, 1990, Senators Christopher J. Dodd (D-CT) and Trent Lott (R-MI) stated respectively that Saddam was a "madman" or "maniac" who made plain the need for continued possession of sophisticated weapons in a very dangerous world.[55] One psychohistorian even suggested that Saddam Hussein was the victim of a "Nebuchadnezzar imperial complex."[56] And, of course, it was not uncommon to hear the Iraqi leader referred to on the street as "Saddam Insane."

THIS SCUD'S FOR YOU

The great anxiety over Saddam Hussein was articulated as the fear of unreason which might spread like a contagion throughout the Arab Third World, carried largely by his Palestinian supporters and radical Muslim sympathizers. Power politics became transformed into the lust for oil and a lust for power, regarded as much the same thing: an irrational, uncontrollable and dangerous force. In his classic text *Madness and Civilization,*[57] Michel Foucault argued that Western culture constructed madness as a police matter—an aberration that necessitated confinement. Although Arab civilization has been Eurocentrically viewed as being outside Western culture, the legacy of colonialism encompassed the Third World in the net of international law drawn from the natural law theory of the Christian worldview. Hence, from the standpoint of the United States, operating under the auspices of the United Nations, Saddam's allegedly irrational invasion of Kuwait was ultimately a police matter, to be handled through force rather than negotiation. After all, it was argued, how can one negotiate with a madman?

Saddam's behavior called for his confinement—at the very least to within the borders of Iraq itself. Some Americans expected his ouster altogether, while others even at the highest levels of government advocated his extermination. Indeed, General Michael J. Dugan, the American Air Force Chief of Staff, was removed in July 1990 not only for revealing U.S. air strength in the Gulf but also for suggesting that Saddam be personally targeted. "If and when we choose violence," he reportedly stated,"[Saddam] ought to be the focus of our efforts."[58] And although Dugan was fired for suggesting that the United States do the same to Saddam Hussein as it had to Colonel Muammar el-Qaddafi in Libya in 1986, the U.S. Air Force apparently targeted Saddam on the very first day of the war.[59] Although the State Department officially denied that the United States sought to assassinate the Iraqi head of state, efforts continued in the destruction of suspected presidential headquarters, including the scandalous bombing of the civilian Al-Ameriyah bomb shelter in Baghdad on February 13, 1991 that claimed the lives of over four hundred men, women, and children. Even after the horror of the tragedy was revealed, the Pentagon continued to argue that it was a legitimate military target on the grounds that it was frequented by the highest Bath'ist party officials.

Yet it was not because of Saddam's alleged insanity that, according to George Bush, "the war could wait no longer." Rather the "rape" of Kuwait was perceived as being a threat to the United States—and not just in terms of economic loss if Saddam were to cross the border into Saudi Arabia. For by invading Kuwait, Saddam had chosen to challenge the reputation of the United States as the preeminent arbiter in the affairs of the Middle East. Would America be shamed and humiliated in the eyes of the world by the dictator of a Third World country? Would the United States ultimately be exposed as an impotent superpower? In his speech "Toward a New World Order" George Bush emphasized that "America [would] not be intimidated."[60] And as American armed forces began to take their positions in the Saudi desert and the Iraqis established and strengthened their fortifications in Kuwait, the rumors of war took on the language of a phallic rivalry. General

Colin Powell confessed his strategy in an interview with reporter Ed Bradley just four days before the air war was launched. "You're going to have to beat me—as they say in basketball—in my face." Thus, the president could explain in his "State of the Union" message on January 29, 1991 that Americans understood "instinctively" why the United States had gone to war. It was not a question of political judgment but rather one of American self-respect.

The war as a ritual of male identity was to be demonstrative proof of America's virile asceticism. The Reagan's era's ideal of "peace through strength," measured in microcosm in the invasions of Grenada and Panama, would now be tested to the fullest. Although American confidence was artificially buttressed by the parallel to World War II, America's victory in the Gulf was not a foregone conclusion. With a purported 1 million men under arms and over five thousand tanks, Iraq was neither a Grenada or Panama, and yet the very trepidation with which the president and his Joint Chiefs of Staff undertook Operation Desert Shield indicated the power of their anticipated victory. If they could defeat Saddam Hussein on the battlefield, America would be "back"—back to the post–World War II era of *pax Americana,* reconfigured under the guise of a "New World Order."

Thus, the war seemed inevitably entwined with conceptions of the male body and gender relations. For just as the "rape" of Kuwait entailed the penetration of the powerless victim, so, too, was the punishment of the "rapist" replete with images of phallic domination. If, as Freud suggested, conflict is constituted by male phallic display or its surrogates, the fetishes of war, that is, weapons, would be infused with sexual significance as well as destructive power.[61] A number of scholars have noted this characteristic in the discourse of nuclear weapons. In her book *Missile Envy,* Dr. Helen Caldicott, a physician and organizer of the nuclear freeze movement, was alarmed by the extent to which the nuclear arms race had become an ordeal of competitive virility—a virtual exercise in the comparison of phallic endowments. Its origins, reasoned Caldicott, must lie in some deep-seated psychopathology of patriarchal culture.[62] Following in Caldicott's footsteps, Carol Cohn has studied the language employed by defense intellectuals in their discussions on the development of nuclear strategies. During one session, she reported that

> lectures were filled with discussion of vertical erector launchers, thrust-to-weight ratios, soft lay-downs, deep penetration, and the comparative advantage of protracted versus spasm attacks—or what one military advisor to the National Security Council has called "releasing 70 to 80 per cent of our megatonnage in one orgasmic whump." There was serious concern about the need to harden our missiles, and the need to "face it, the Russians are a little harder than we are." Disbelieving glances would

occasionally pass between me and my ally—another woman—but no one else seemed to notice.[63]

In his book *Fathering the Unthinkable. Masculinity, Scientists and the Nuclear Arms Race,* Brian Easlea has described this phenomenon as evidence of a "compulsive masculinity." Modern arms designers produced the atomic bomb in their own image, unabashedly naming their creations as normatively male offspring, for example, "Fat Man" or "Little Boy."[64] In light of the prevalence with which phallic imagery was used during the nuclear arms race, it should not be surprising that such language would also appear in the discursive construction of the Gulf War. In a column that remarkably echoed this sentiment, William Raspberry of the *Washington Post,* inveighing against peace demonstrators, compared the war effort itself to the birth of a child. "An analogy comes to mind," he argued.

> You can warn your daughter to take every precaution against pregnancy. You can do what you can to help her understand the long-term implications of child bearing—how it would strain relations with her friends, limit her opportunities and options, and require the allocation of resources that might be put to other uses.
> But once the baby is born, warning against pregnancy makes no sense. Far better to do what you can to limit the damage and make sure the baby turns out well.[65]

To Raspberry, as to many other Americans, the war was "our baby" to be nurtured and loved. But if the hostilities against Saddam were the offspring of a masculinist psychic economy, then the weapons that brought us the war had phallic significance—no matter what their size.

In her widely heralded work *Against Our Will. Men, Women and Rape,* Susan Brownmiller cited the now familiar chant that marked the cadence of marching soldiers in boot camp:

> *This is my weapon, this is my gun*
> *This is for business, this is for fun.*

The association of the soldier's phallus with his rifle occurs in a context in which the soldier's identity as a man is stripped away. He is rhetorically castrated by the incessant badgering of drill instructors who variously call their recruits "ladies" or "girls." In this initiation into the warrior community, humiliated individuals are compelled to seek their manhood from the collective, embodied by the drill instructor. And it is he who gives the recruit back his masculinity in the form of a weapon, the infantryman's rifle. The soldier is nothing without his weapon, for it is this weapon that entitles him to his identity—an identity mediated by the collective. Because the weapon symbolizes his masculine identity and serves as a surrogate for his own phallus, the handling and shooting of the rifle is infused with sexual arousal. The recruit has always been urged to love and care for his weapon as if it were himself. And it was no different in the Gulf War where the ever-present threat of sand might impede its proper functioning. As one officer reportedly confessed in the interim between the launching of the air and ground assaults, "It is reassuring to clean your weapon. It's something you can do."[66] The GIs themselves started the practice of sliding condoms over their rifle barrels in order to keep out the sand.[67]

Yet it is not only that the weapon has phallic significance; the inverse is also implied. The phallus itself is deeply associated with the gun as an instrument of violence and domination. This identification suggests that the object through which sexual desire is manifested—women or men who appear or are made to appear in women's roles—is conceived as the enemy in a struggle colloquially described as the "war between the sexes." The inference presents itself that the construction "woman" is in some sense regarded as a threat which, at its most extreme, may necessitate a fight to the death; however, the power of the phallus as gun may be suffiicient to master these fears and control the threat. Hence self-confidence derived from phallic power ensures that the encounter with "woman" may in fact be "fun."

In the context of the Gulf War, the castration imagery used to emasculate Saddam Hussein effectively transforms the figure of the enemy into a woman.[68] Yet, from the psychoanalytic point of view, inscribed in the consciousness of each man is the presupposition that the mother was the possessor of the phallus—of power—which has been lost through her castration.[69] The woman in each mother, the mother in each woman, embodies a residue of danger, as both the once-proud possessor of the phallus and the living symbol of its loss. As the source of castration anxiety, woman must be mastered if man is to retain his self-identity, and that anxiety is allayed if the male can ensure that he, and not the woman, has control of the phallus. In Freudian terms, the weapon as a fetish or phallic surrogate "remains a token of triumph over the threat of castration and a safeguard against it."[70] The control of the phallus by the male as its exclusive possessor therefore must be displayed in acts of sexually-charged aggression.

Not surprisingly the rhetoric of the war against an unmanned Saddam Hussein is replete with allusions to various forms of rape. Saddam had threatened the Coalition forces with the "mother of all battles"[71]—a reference to a conflict of apocalyptic significance between believers and the infidel, the Third and First Worlds. Yet the reference was inverted in American popular discourse to indicate that if Saddam embodied the "mother of all battles," the American military would be "motherfuckers." As *Ms.* reported in its March/April 1991 issue, one Air Force officer commented, "Tell him Dad's coming to kick Mom's butt."[72] T-shirts began appearing in American streets with the logo "FUCK IRAQ." One reporter, Bryan Brewer from WFLA, a radio station in Tampa, FL, presented a similar T-shirt to General Schwartzkopf in Riyadh—one with a screw passing through the head of the Iraqi leader. "It's just my size," Schwartzkopf allegedly responded, " Extra Large."[73] It is open to question to what the general was referring. Perhaps the most vivid image of rape was presented on the floor of the U.S. Congress on February 12, 1991 by Representative Gary Ackerman (D-NY) who gave the following rendition of the rapist's cry "Slam, bam, thank you, m'am":

> *Slam, bam, thank you Saddam*
> *You should have took the letter*
> *Now take the loss, reverse the course,*
> *Because it ain't going to get no better.*

That same slogan—"Slam, bam, thank you, Saddam"—was scrawled on the sides of U.S. Army trucks carrying members of the 101st Airborne toward the Kuwaiti border on January 18, 1991.[74] And the *Washington Post* itself reported in words strangely reminiscent of the rape context that many Americans believed that Saddam Hussein got what he deserved—in short, he was "asking for it." These images of genital rape were frequently complemented by allusions to both oral and anal violation.

The confusion over the correct pronunciation of Saddam's name evidenced a parapraxis that conjured up images of violent sexual assault. News reporters and even the president frequently intoned the Iraqi leader's name as "Sodom" Hussein. The onus of illicit sexuality was associated with his very identity in virtually every reference. One tabloid even homophonically/homophobically boasted the headline "Saddam Has AIDS"—a particularly offensive invective since the image of anal penetration is linked to the homophobic association of homosexuality with AIDS. Saddam Hussein is doubly marginalized: not only as a practitioner of a "deviant" sexuality but also as a "disease carrier" who, though marginal to the New World Order, threatens to "infect" the Third World with his "deviant" politics. The implication is that Saddam Hussein, like homosexuals, ought to be stamped out. The headline neatly summarizes the sexual politics of the Gulf War: "deviant" politics begets "deviant" sexuality and vice versa.

The original sin, which lay at the foundation of Saddam Hussein's divergence from orthodoxy, both politically and sexually, lay in his transgressive behavior toward Kuwait. On the one hand, "Sodom" himself was viewed as a rapist who had invaded his "female" neighbor. On the other hand, his subsequent castration and transformation into "woman" in popular war rhetoric suggested his vulnerability to violation, both orally and anally.[75] One of my colleagues, a specialist in early Christianity, mentioned her alarm at watching on television one of the bomb-signing ceremonies at Dhahran air base during which an Air Force officer inscribed the following logo on his bomb: "Mrs. Saddam's Love Toy." The vulgar allusion to a dildo suggests its insertion into the anus of the Iraqi leader.[76] The proliferation of anti-Saddam T-shirts also reflected the themes of oral and anal rape. Emblazoned with the familiar image of America's favorite cartoon character Bart Simpson, one proclaimed the message of "Operation Desert Dude": "Saddam Sucks." Others that made the rounds in local New York stores included one entitled "Sodom-ize Hussein," showing the Iraqi being raped by a Patriot missile, and another depicted the anal penetration of Saddam Hussein by a SCUD missile with a variation of a popular beer slogan: "Hey Saddam. This Scud's for You!" And perhaps the most religiously offensive of all was the popular T-shirt, "Shiite Happens," despite the fact that the Shi'ite majority in Iraq had a tenuous relationship with Saddam Hussein and the Bath'ist party. The identification of Saddam with anal libidinality and human excrement reached its logical conclusion in the production of "Hussein's Insane" toilet paper by which the American public-at-large could enjoy the humiliation of their enemy. It was not only the desire to defecate on the Iraqi leader that came to the fore; it was also the wish to utterly destroy his face for by doing so Americans could efface his power. Toy gun and dart boards appeared with a bull's eye marking Saddam Hussein's face as a target. A popular T-shirt displayed the Iraqi leader's face with cross-hairs over his forehead and the logo "Do It!" One manufacturer exploited the war by issuing Desert Storm golf balls, each embossed with Saddam Hussein's face. The package asked, "Wouldn't you like to drive this face 300 yards?"

Although it might be argued that war is serious business and indeed people die in combat, it is also not uncommon for soldier and civilian alike to thrill to the intensity of warfare. In some cases American GIs were alarmed that the collapse of the Iraqi front lines was proceeding at such a pace that they would not have the opportunity to "get into the fun" of combat. The mass surrender of Iraqi troops to advancing armored units preempted the expression of military bloodlust that was sometimes candidly described in blatantly sexual terms. "Well, they surrendered too fast to kill a lot of them," confided one Marine captain. "Yes, we were disappointed. If you've ever got close to a girl hoping to get it and you didn't, it was about the same."[77]

Of course the practice of the veteran spinning war stories for family and friends has always been a part of the tradition of war, but now in the living rooms of America, civilians had the opportunity to vicariously participate in combat. Bush's address to the nation on January 19, 1991 announcing the commencement of the "hot war" drew more viewers than any other television event with the exception of John F. Kennedy's funeral in 1963.[78]

The president's speech set the tone for the Nintendo war in which millions of Americans tuned in to CNN and the three major networks day and night. And, although the dangers of massive casualties were always present, some viewers were remarkably casual. As one University of Oklahoma student put it, "I'm gonna pop some popcorn and watch the war." With video cameras attached to missile warheads, viewers experienced the war by zeroing and closing in on targets and witnessing their destruction. What had only been possible in arcades featuring video games like "F-15 Strike Simulator" and in the homes of America with game cartridges manufactured by Sega, Nintendo, and Genesis was now a virtual reality. Yet the hyperreal aspect of these aerial assaults dispelled both the danger of combat and its bloody consequences. It became an exercise in pure control, technological mastery, which nonetheless retained the pleasure of domination. It was as if what Paul Virilio and Sylvère Lotringer have called "the militarized part of their identity,"[79] previously unconscious in an economy dominated by defense industries, had become conscious. But it was not a cause for alarm. It was, for many, enjoyable.

The pleasures derived from the "Nintendo" war are rooted in the very structure of television viewing. On the one hand, as the vehicle for the transmission of information, television is the medium of the symbolic order. Indeed the figures of the fathers—be they generals or presidents—dominated the broadcasts. Much of television time during the war was devoted to "hard news" rather than entertainment, yet many Americans found the coverage of the war entertaining. Some commentators praised the American public for taking the business of the country so seriously and regarded it as a sign of American democracy's health. Such conclusions ignore the reasons why American viewers took pleasure in the war. Television is not only an instrument for the transmission of information; it is also a medium to enjoy a sense of totality. From the standpoint of the male imaginary, television feeds the viewer a series of images that bring immediacy, simultaneity, and wholeness into a male consciousness characterized by estrangement from the body politic in general and women in particular. The consumption of these fleeting images brings the viewer into a presence—as if "you are actually there"—which otherwise would escape. But, although television implies the promise of a return to wholeness, it rarely delivers its promise because, in an age where rapid cuts are the norm in commercial advertisements and programming, the images are rarely held for more than a few seconds. Television is a promise deferred—hence its addictive quality.[80] However what many viewers found fascinating about watching the bombing runs of American warplanes was the sustained image of the target, as if seen by the unblinking eye of an omniscient God. The outcome seemed inevitable from the outset, as indeed it was because the films were shown after the fact, chosen as dramatic records of American technological mastery. The viewer experienced the excitement of an uncertain immediacy with the certitude of success. The promise made was the promise delivered—a visual confirmation of the war rhetoric of American leaders. The libidinal anticipation of the bombing run was realized not only in direct hits, an almost physical sense of release, but also in the complete devastation of the target. Absolute dominion had been won. The totality had been totally consumed—or so it seemed—without a remainder to threaten either American masculinity or the symbolic "New World Order." Unlike Vietnam this televised war, with images carefully selected by the Pentagon, was deeply satisfying to most viewers.

Although many businesses, both small and large, used the war as a means to reap profit through the manufacture of patriotic merchandise, many Americans of all ages and classes happily participated in the consumption of hegemonic images. For the children stores offered not only Desert Storm comic books, but also Desert Storm toys, for example, guns, trucks, tanks, planes, and helicopters, a Desert Shield box game ("Gulf Strike" distributed by the Avalon Company), and Desert Storm collector's cards (See Figure 2.2). Adults had the opportunity to experience the ersatz thrill of war by dressing in combat fatigues and shooting each other with imitation M-16s that fired paint in "Skirmish," dubbed by its promoters as the "sport of the 90s (See Figure 2.3)." Nor did the phallic imagery of the Gulf War escape notice by entrepreneurs who produced "Patriot Condoms" ("Anything else . . . . . . is just a SCUD"), whose package displayed the drawing of a Patriot missile, and "Desert Shield Condoms" ("designed with the hardened veteran in mind"), whose box was covered with a drawing of an American tank and an American soldier, disarmingly similar to the phalliclike image of Camel cigarette's Joe Cool (See Figure 2.4).[81] Even the merchandisers to the upper-middle and upper classes were caught up in the enthusiasm. Steuben Glass manufactured an expensive glass version of the star-spangled banner; Ralph Lauren found a ready market for his Polo American flag sweaters; and Bloomingdale's promoted its 1991 Father's Day sale by marketing it in conjunction with the end-of-the-war parade up Manhattan's Broadway. Appearing among the photographs of returning veterans dressed in Bloomingdale's shirts and ties was the patriotic salutation:

This Father's Day, we salute dads everywhere [apparently with the exception of Iraq] with special emphasis on those who are returning from service in the Persian Gulf. In cooperation with Operation Welcome Home NYC and the world's largest ticker-tape parade on June 10th, Bloomingdale's celebrates the spirit of fatherhood.

In light of the castration and phallic imagery used in the discursive con-

FIGURE 2.2   The Topp's Desert Storm Collector's Cards created during the Gulf War Crisis. Reprinted with permission from the Topps Co., Inc.

FIGURE 2.3   The Skirmish Paintball brochure cover is a product of Skirmish U.S.A., Jim Thorpe, PA.

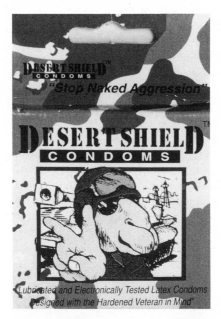

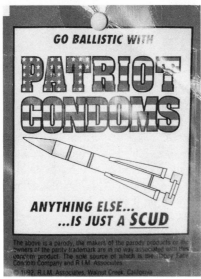

FIGURE 2.4   Desert Shield Condoms and Patriot Condoms were just two of the many products resulting from the Gulf War Crisis.

These are products of Big Star Concepts, Inc., Carmel, CA., and R.I.M. Associates, Walnut Creek, CA. Photograph by Jonathan Roberts.

struction of the war, the idea of "the spirit of fatherhood" takes on a different connotation than that implied by Bloomingdale's.

Nonetheless the collective effervescence of the war culminated in the June 10 parade that proceeded from Battery Park up the Great White Way to the cheers of tens of thousands of onlookers. A handful of antiwar protestors was safely ignored. The day of celebration ended with one of the largest fireworks displays in the history of New York City, but oddly it was a recapitulation of the war itself. The ecstacy of the pyrotechnic display and the joy that it brought spectators could only echo the memory of that which it had sought to suppress: the bombing of the Iraqi capital and the terror and misery that accompanied it. As one American Air Force officer commented on the first night of the air war, "I saw one of the most fantastic fireworks demonstrations. Baghdad was lit up like a Christmas tree."[82] With its appropriately phallic images of flags held high, the ritual of the parade sought to close the Gulf War as an episode in the reassertion of American strength and manhood; yet, the underlying psychological dynamic could not be so easily contained. If the enemy was Saddam Hussein not only as a phallic rival but also as castrated figure—a "woman," then the consequences of this discursive construction might not be so neatly contained within the theater of a foreign war, thousands of miles from American shores and far removed from the domestic front. There was one more act to be played out in the military context—only this time one much closer to home.

WHAT'S THE BIG DEAL?

In the fall of 1991, Linda Francke broke the story about the scandalous behavior of male aviators at a convention of retired and active Naval and Marine Corps officers. Held at the Las Vegas Hilton, September 5 through 7, just six months after the close of the Gulf War, the 35th Annual Symposium of the Tailhook Association[83] was promised as a celebration of American air power and its stunning defeat of the Iraqis in the Gulf conflict. F. G. Ludwig, captain USN and president of the Association, declared that the convention would prove to be the "Mother of all Hooks."[84] Yet incidents of sexual harassment and abuse reported at the convention sullied the reputation of the fliers and quelled the euphoria of victory in the Gulf.

Although only two thousand registered for the convention, over five thousand participated in a gathering supposedly devoted to discussions of strategy and tactics of air combat and the development of new weaponry. But, although the organization officially serves as a liaison among fliers, their commanders, and defense contractors to improve the morale and battle readiness of American air forces, the annual conventions had the reputation for three days of drinking, partying, and general rowdiness. Captain Ludwig warned all members before the convention of "certain problems we've had in past year's [*sic*],"[85] including underage drinking, drunkenness (particularly from "quick hit" drinks), abuse of long-distance phone lines, extensive damage to rooms and hotel common areas, and "LEWD AND LASCIVIOUS BEHAVIOR." The captain urged Tailhook representatives to ensure that all duty officers remain sober.

The rank-and-file, however, chose to ignore the warning. Over $23,000 in damage to the hotel was reported, but worse than the damage was what Ludwig called the participants' "'unprofessionalism' and I mean *unprofessionalism* underlined [*sic*]."[86] The actions ranged from juvenile to vulgar, even criminal, behavior. In one incident reminiscent of a fraternity prank, a "pressed ham" (naked buttocks pressed against a window pane) pushed out an eighth floor hotel window. Fortunately neither the perpetrator nor passersby below were injured. Parties were held in twenty-six hotel suites, at least half of which had performances by strippers and showings of pornographic videos. The first part of the report issued by the Defense Department's Office of the Inspector General, published in September 1992, noted that "investigative activity to date has confirmed more than isolated instances of men exposing themselves, women baring their breasts, shaving of women's legs and pubic areas, and women drinking from dildos that dispensed alcoholic beverages."[87] The second part of the report, released in April 1993, noted that Tailhook had an evolving lexicon of these offensive practices, including "ballwalking" (the public display of men's testicles to women), "sharking" (the biting of women's buttocks), and "zapping" (slapping squadron stickers on the buttocks and breasts of female personnel). As tasteless as these activities were, both the president of the Tailhook Association and the secretary of the Navy were most upset by reports of physical assaults on women, both military officers and civilians.

Every night a sizeable group of male officers of the Navy, Marine Corps, and Air Force—estimated to be as large as two hundred—lined the hallways outside a bank of hotel elevators. Women who made the unfortunate mistake of stepping off on that floor were forced to "run the gauntlet" and subjected to fondling of the breasts and buttocks, obscene suggestions, and in some cases more violent assault. In one instance, a teenage girl was stripped naked by the aviators. Such behavior by military personnel was found to be particularly dishonorable in light of the Navy's own "zero-tolerance" of sexual harassment policy, established just the year before. But perhaps even more shocking was the attitude of the fliers, including officers, revealed during the course of the investigation.

As the Naval inspector general concluded, "A common thread running through the overwhelming majority of [Naval Investigative Services] interviews concerning Tailhook '91 was—'what's the big deal?'"[88] Most of the midlevel officers, as well as some of their senior commanders, seemed to think that such behavior was either innocuous and all in good fun or expected by the women who attended the convention. It was implied that they simply could not be ignorant of Tailhook's reputation. The original investigation itself was compromised by the commander of the Naval Investigative Service, who allegedly stated that "a lot of female Navy pilots are go-go dancers, topless dancers, or hookers."[89] In retrospect, the admiral claimed that the gauntlet "appeared to be in fun, rather than molestation" and that women "would not have gone down that hall if they didn't like it."[90] In response to an admiral's aide, Lt. Paula Couglin, who vehemently lodged the original complaint about the Tailhook gauntlet, the NIS commander reportedly stated to an NIS agent that "[a]ny woman that would use the F word on a regular basis would welcome this type of activity."[91]

Although the original Naval inspector general's inquiries concluded that twenty-five women were attacked, among them, fourteen naval officers, the final report determined that some eighty-three women and seven men were victims of assault. The inspector general concluded that "misconduct at the 1991 Tailhook Symposium was more widespread than previously reported by the Navy." One hundred seventeen officers were implicated in this misconduct, and fifty-seven were believed to have committed perjury in an attempt to cover up their misdeeds. Of course these were the most egregious cases. Viewing porno films, strip shows, and public acts of consensual sex—conduct that might be deemed "unbecoming an officer"—were largely ignored, in part because they were so widespread and in part because it was not assaultive behavior. The final report was accompanied by photographs taken at the event—one depicting a stripper standing astride a prone officer in one of the suites, the other an image of a participant wearing a T-shirt emblazoned "Women Are Property." Although President Clinton was appalled by what he read in the reports, he concluded that "[i]t should not be taken as a general indictment of the United States Navy."[92] The report itself implied otherwise.

The Naval inspector general posed the question of whether these abuses were a result of a "cultural problem" and concluded his investigation with an answer in the affirmative. The commander of the Naval Investigative Service voiced to the undersecretary and the special assistant to the secretary of the Navy what appeared to other investigators to be a commonly held belief in the service. "[M]en simply do not want women in the military."[93] Since the Naval inspector general found the abuses at Tailhook '91 to be evidence of a "cultural problem" in the military, he believed that in effect the military itself had allowed these events to take place and must ultimately assume responsibility. Admiral Frank Kelso, chief of Naval Operations and the officer responsible for the Naval Investigation, admitted that "we had an institutional problem in how we treated women."[94]

Although the Tailhook scandal resulted in the disassociation of the military from the organization and even compelled the resignation of the secretary of the Navy, it must be asked whether these abuses, as manifestations of the military's "cultural problem," were an aberration from the true identity of the armed forces. The discursive construction of the Gulf War suggests that, while the conflict allegedly may be justified for political and economic reasons, it functioned as a collective ritual to reassert the masculine identity of the American social order. From the man on the street to the politicians in the White House, from the battlefields of the Middle East to the reporters on national television, the rhetoric of war sought to depict the enemy through images of sexual emasculation and phallic penetration. If that is the case, then perhaps the "cultural problem" surmised by investigators in the male-dominated military services, indeed in society-at-large, has to do with the construction of the enemy as "woman." Perhaps the resistance to admission of women into combat roles and to the recognition of homosexual men in the armed services is no accident but rather a part of a larger schema in which male identity, as presently conceived in American culture, is predicated on the domination and abuse of "women."

Ironically the only way that Naval officers in command could understand how offensive Tailhook was to women was by its comparison to homosexual rape. Barbara Spyridon Pope, the Navy's assistant secretary for manpower and reserve affairs, found that many flag officers saw nothing wrong with the debauchery. She even threatened to resign because of what she perceived as the service's stonewalling; however, when she likened the experience of women at Tailhook to what these heterosexual male officers would experience if assaulted by "homosexual" men, "[t]hey understood that personal violation."[95] As the turning point in the investigation, this comparison reveals the masculinist mentality that is present in all of the armed services, not only the Navy. The ominous character of Tailhook's sexual "fun" becomes evident only when men put themselves in women's places, when they have done to them what they do to women. But rather than see the injustice of the gendered construction of power, these male officers see Tailhook egocentrically. As men they would not want to be in a woman's place. Instead of Tailhook becoming a breakthrough in the reconfiguration of gender power—a genuine transfiguration of military consciousness, it had regressive results. The abuse of women was condemned largely because it carried out in public what in the minds of many men should remain private. Unrestrained public debauchery was deemed "unmilitary" behavior, not so much because it was unseemly or even criminal, but because, as Barbara Spyridon Pope emphasized, it impinged upon the military's combat "readiness." Senior Pentagon officials did not regard these "Animal House" antics harmless because they undermined the discipline necessary for effective military operations and jeopardized public support normally granted the armed forces. In terms of the Pentagon's agenda, the question of the abuse of women *per se* seemed to be a secondary issue. Moreover most military officers declined to take this opportunity to reassess the psychosexual ideology of the armed forces. Rather than recognizing both women and gay men as victims of a masculinist ideology of power, they offered little sympathy either to women or openly gay men serving in the armed forces. Defined in the masculinist imagination as the submissive partner in sexually coercive relationships, gay men embody the castration anxiety of heterosexist males who invest their masculinity in the domination of women, whether their submission occurs in public or private spheres. Thus, although in the aftermath of Tailhook '91 the Navy directed Vice Admiral Jack Fetterman, chief of Naval Education, to develop a "core values" officer training program which would focus on racism, sexual harassment, and domestic violence, he was fired just a few short months after the investigation had been undertaken because he had sought to protect a staff member accused of being a homosexual. The "lesson" of Tailhook was limited to public relations and did little to address the "cultural problem" of the military.

Former Lieutenant General Bernard E. Trainor, director of the National Security Program at Harvard University, openly stressed that the American armed forces ground military effectiveness in an "ethos" of masculinity. It is deemed that the admission of openly homosexual men to the services threatens to undermine that masculinity and, with it, military preparedness. Trainor voices an attitude that is pervasive in the officer corps of the major services. The Pentagon reported dismissals from the military for homosexuality numbering from a high of some one thousand eight hundred in 1982 to seven hundred in 1992. The *New York Times* has noted Department of Defense statistics that indicate that the Navy discharges gay men and women at a rate twice that of Marines and three times that of the Air Force and Army. Defenders of this discriminatory policy, like Senator Sam Nunn, chair of the Senate's Armed Services Committee, frequently allude to the need to balance civil rights claims against "the basic need of the military"—combat readiness based on a masculinist psychosocial model of power. Because homosexuality is read as effeminate, the presence of openly homosexual men shatters the homosocial unity ("morale and discipline") needed to successfully carry out aggression against the enemy conceived as less than a man, that is, a woman. In his testimony before the Congress, General Norman Schwartzkopf, the victor in the Gulf and therefore a "man's man," warned against tolerating avowed homosexuals in the service. To do so, he reasoned, would demoralize the troops to such an extent that they would be no more soldierly than the Iraqis who surrendered en masse to Coalition forces in February 1991. Gay men are therefore regarded as the enemy within. Although AIDS is a communicative—not a contagious—disease, it serves as a metaphor in the homophobic imagination for the "spread" of homosexuality that would corrupt not only the military but also the entire body politic.

First established in boot camp by drill instructors, this ethos is continually reinforced through misogynist and homophobic attitudes that probe for weaknesses in the consciousness of military units. Coming out at the National Gay March on Washington in May 1993, Jose M. Zuniga, the Sixth Army's "Soldier of the Year" serving in the Persian Gulf, painfully recounted his experience of a military climate that coerced individuals to prove their "masculinity." "In my three years of military service, I have lived the life of a heterosexual soldier. I have told jokes about homosexuals. I have witnessed their harassment and not said a word."[96] This attitude, which claims that military service is "a man's job in a man's world," is tacitly understood. In the words of former Lieutenant General Trainor, the openly declared homosexual "threatens the strong, conservative moralistic tradition of the troops."[97] Trainor's claim seems patently hypocritical in light of both Tailhook and the brothels surrounding American bases in Third World countries, encouraged as a means to satisfy the "basic need of the military."[98] But it has everything to do with the maintenance of a particular consciousness in the military which sees itself not only as the defender of the country but the symbol of the country's heterosexist values. Homosexuals may exist in the military, but masculinist personnel don't want to know about it. In other words, they are acceptable as long as they live the lie that Sergeant Zuniga found so uncomfortable. According to this twisted logic of Department of Defense regulations, a member of the armed forces may be excused for an isolated homosexual encounter, if the accused avows his heterosexuality and rationalizes it as a lapse due to extraordinary circumstances. Hence, whereas a homosexual act does not necessarily entail discharge from the military, an unrepentant affirmation of homosexuality does, even if no act is committed. The so-called compromise of the Clinton administration with its critics on the Hill—"don't ask, don't tell"—therefore fits the prejudice of homophobes in the military. The military as a symbol of masculinist sexuality remains as long as it is not confronted with recognizing the legitimacy of sexual alterities in its own ranks.

Although, as Alisa Solomon has pointed out, the focus of the controversy seems to be on gay men,[99] the presence of lesbians in the military also disrupts this psychosocial model of masculinist power. For if, according to this model, gay men don't act like "real" men, lesbians don't act like "real" women. In this masculinist consciousness, gay men are read as a direct threat because they conjure up the heterosexist fear of isomorphic identification with the penetrated subject. Although lesbians don't directly threaten the heterosexist self-image, they do embody the rejection of women's subjugation by men—a necessary prop to masculinist consciousness. What is particularly Machiavellian about the persecution of lesbians is that heterosexist men can use the proscription against lesbianism in the military to coerce women into having unwanted sexual relations with them. Rejection of male advances is read as proof of lesbian orientation. Thus lesbians are discharged from the armed forces at over twice the rate of gay men (8.1 per 10,000 as opposed to 3.4 per 10,000).

Although in April 1993 the Department of Defense lifted the ban on women assigned to combat positions in the Air Force and Navy (while still excluding service in frontline ground combat units), many in the Pentagon still oppose women in combat. Women in combat units strike them as anomalous to the very purpose of "this man's army." Opposition was largely justified in the past by the military's ideological plaint of "upper body strength." Women were not as physically strong as men, *ergo* they could not serve in traditionally masculine roles. Although clearly the gendered segregation by sex disregards the overlap between individual men and women in physical size and strength, the technological revolution in weapons development has minimized the effect that physical differences between men and women have on job performance. But while many male officers admit that women may be able to fly a plane or fire a missile as well as any man, it is the *idea* of women in combat that disturbs them so. Like lesbians women in combat don't seem to act like the women of the masculinist imagination. They therefore undermine the ethos of the military, so fragile and so in constant need of reinforcement. A woman, like a "known" male homosexual, allegedly shatters the monolithic identity of heterosexual bonding so precariously won through basic training, "war games," and actual combat. How can the enemy be emasculated, penetrated, and destroyed when heterosexual women, gay men, and lesbians are your comrades in arms. It is deemed simply incongruous.

Unless that ethos is vigilantly protected, it is argued, the military, as we know it, a male society dedicated to the maintenance of masculinist domination, would come to an end. Some Americans would welcome such an end, but for many others, the struggle for equal treatment of women and gay people in the military threatens the very existence of America. And it is not because of a lack of military preparedness against foreign enemies but because of the fear that it will unwrite the masculinist psychic economy of the social order itself. From this point of view, the presence of women in general as well as homosexuals in the military is perceived as potentially a greater threat than Saddam Hussein. Homophobes and sexist males see the latter as an enemy who can be beaten, but male heterosexual solidarity can only lose if restrictions are dropped against gay men and women in combat.

This sentiment can be found not only on the battlefield, but on the homefront as well, and not just among male military personnel but also among civilian males. To many men it is imperative to keep the psychosexual ideology of male territorial games intact. Not surprisingly the most popular domestic male territorial game, football, reinforces these attitudes. One rather notorious incident that occurred during the very beginnings of the Gulf War buildup provides a perfect illustration. On September 17, 1990, a news reporter, Lisa Olsen, was interviewing a New England Patriots player in the team's locker room. At that moment another player, completely naked, chose to walk toward the reporter, fully exposing himself to her. A number of Patriots urged him to "make her look!" and the player allegedly challenged the female reporter by stating, "Here's what you want. Do you want to take a bite out of this?" Reports of this sexual harassment and assaultive behavior were met in some circles within the NFL and in many bars around the country by responses that presaged the Tailhook scandal: "What's the big deal?" Indeed Victor Kiam, the owner of the New England franchise, made a joke of the entire incident, asking, "What do Iraqis have in common with Lisa Olsen? They've both seen Patriot missiles up close." Women, like Iraqis, are regarded as fair game, both of which are to be taught to fear the sexual potency of "real" American men. Led in part by the syndicated columnist Ellen Goodman, the protest across the country by women, scandalized by these events, caused the National Football League to reprimand both the owner of the Patriots and his players. Nonetheless the incident suggests that beneath the veneer of civility there exists this disturbing attitude toward women, and not just those who are deemed as such on foreign battlegrounds but also those in the very living rooms of America.

NOTES

1. Saddam Hussein, Taha Yasin Ramadan, Tariq 'Aziz, Dr. Sa'dun Hammadi, Latif Jasim, Saadi Mahdi Salih, *Iraq Speaks: Documents on the Gulf Crisis,* trans. Fred Moore (Palo Alto, CA: privately published 1991), 3.
2. *Energy Statistics Sourcebook* 7th ed. (Tulsa, OK: PennWell, 1992), 339.
3. Hussein et al., *Iraq Speaks,* 7.
4. Ibid., 3.
5. *War Crimes: A Report on United States War Crimes Against Iraq. Ramsey Clark and Others Report to the Commission of Inquiry for the International War Crimes Tribunal* (Washington, DC: Maisonneuve, 1992), 14.
6. 1923 Hague Rules, Article 24, ¶ 1, ¶ 2, ¶ 3; 1977 Geneva Protocol I, Chapter II, Article 51, 5 ¶ b and Chapter IV, Article 57, 2 ¶ a (i).
7. United Nations, *The Impact of War on Iraq: Report to the Secretary-General*

*on Humanitarian Needs in Iraq in the Immediate Post-Crisis Environment by a
Mission to the Area Led By Mr. Martti Ahtisaari, Under-Secretary-General for
Administration and Management, Dated 20 March 1991* (Westfield, NJ: Open
Magazine), 1991, 5.

8. George Bush, "Toward a New World Order," Address before a Joint Session
of Congress, Washington, DC, September 11, 1990, *US Department of State
Dispatch,* September 17, 1991, 91.

9. On January 18, 1985, the U.S. government informed the International Court of
Justice that it would not recognize the World Court's jurisdiction in the case
of *Nicaragua* v. *United States,* filed by the Sandinista government on April 9,
1984. Established by the U.N. Charter, only the court itself was specifically
authorized under Article 36 to determine whether it exercised jurisdiction. The
decisions of the court were held to be final and its directives obligatory. Although the U.S. government accepted the authority of the court in principle,
the Reagan administration made specific an exception for all disputes involving Central America, including the court's finding in favor of the Nicaraguan
government. The United States refused to pay the over \$12 billion in compen-
sation demanded by Nicaragua. 1986 I.C.J. 1 (June 27, 1986).

10. As early as March of 1991, the *New York Times* reported that the U.S. Commerce Department issued export licenses for American high-tech products
to Iraq, many of which could be used for military purposes. "U.S. Tells
of Prewar Technology Sales to Iraq Worth \$500 Million," *New York Times,*
March 12, 1991, A13. Despite a congressional investigation which cleared
Ambassador Glaspie, independent presidential candidate H. Ross Perot argued that the U.S. ambassador had signaled American acquiescence to Saddam's
plans for the invasion. Such speculations were fueled by the ambassador's
alleged statement in a private meeting with Saddam Hussein on July 25,
1990 that "we hold no opinion about inter-Arab disputes, like your border
disagreement with Kuwait." "The Glaspie Transcript: Saddam Meets the U.S.
Ambassador (July 25, 1990)," *The Gulf War Reader: History, Documents
Opinions,* ed. Micah L. Sifry and Christopher Cerf (New York: Random House,
1991), 130.

11. George Bush, "State of the Union Message," *New York Times,* January 30,
1991, A12.

12. Quoted in Maureen Dowd, "War Introduces a Tougher Bush to Nation," *New
York Times,* March 1, 1991.

13. Quoted in Rick Atkinson and Ann Devroy, "Bush: Iraq Won't Decide Timing
of Ground War," *Washington Post,* February 2, 1991, 1.

14. George Bush, "Toward a New World Order," 91.

15. George Bush, "Operation Desert Storm Launched," Address to the Nation Broadcast from the White House, 9:00 P.M., January 16, 1991, U.S. *Department of
State Dispatch,* January 21, 1991, 37.

16. Quoted in *New York Newsday,* January 17, 1991, 8.

17. George Bush, "State of the Union," A12.

18. John Kifner, "Mud Is the Strongest Enemy as the 101st Takes Central Iraq,"
New York Times, February 28, 1991, A7.

19. George Bush, "Toward a New World Order," 93.

20. George Bush, "Operation Desert Storm Launched," 37.

21. Andrew Rosenthal, "Pentagon Is Confident on War but Says Iraqis Remain
Potent [*sic*]," *New York Times,* January 24, 1991, 1.

22. Rosenthal, "Pentagon," 1.
23. Philip Shenon, "To Saddam," *New York Times,* February 9, 1991.
24. "Excerpts from Schwartzkopf News Conference on Gulf War," *New York Times,* February 28, 1991, A8.
25. Sigmund Freud, *An Outline of Psychoanalysis, The Standard Edition of the Complete Psychological Works of Sigmund Freud,* ed. & trans. James Strachey (London: Hogarth, 1974), XXIII: 190, n.1.
26. "Excerpts from Schwartzkopf News Conference," A8.
27. *This Week with David Brinkley,* January 20, 1991.
28. Richard Nixon, *60 Minutes,* CBS News, Vol. XXIII, Number 30, Transcript #2331, 7, and R. W. Apple, Jr., "Allies Destroy Iraqi's Main Force; Kuwait Is Retaken After 7 Months," *New York Times,* February 28, 1991, 1.
29. Norma Pecora, "Superman/Superboys/Supermen: The Comic Book Hero as Socializing Agent," *in Men, Masculinity and the Media,* ed. Steve Craig (Newbury Park, CA: Sage, 1992), 61–77.
30. Sigmund Freud, "Medusa's Head," *Standard Edition,* XVIII: 274.
31. "Caught in a Desert Storm," *The Punisher,* Marvel Comics, April 1991, 14.
32. "Next Stop: Baghdad," *The Punisher,* Marvel Comics, May 1991, 1.
33. "Next Stop: Baghdad," 25–26.
34. Ibid., n.p.
35. George Bush, "The Arabian Peninsula: U.S. Principles," Address to the Nation Broadcast from the White House, August 8, 1990, *U.S. Department of State Dispatch,* September 3, 1990, 53.
36. Quoted in *Washington Report on Middle East Affairs,* January 1991, 18.
37. Quoted in *U.S. News & World Report,* May 6, 1991, 19. Cf. Charles Krauthammer, "Nightmare From the Thirties," *Washington Post,* July 27, 1990, and William Safire, "The Hitler Analogy," *"New York Times,* August 24, 1990.
38. Vide, Murray Waas, "Who Lost Kuwait? How the Bush Administration Bungled Its Way into War in the Gulf," *Village Voice,* January 22, 1991, 31, and Jeff Cohen, Executive Director, FAIR, *Operation Dissidence* (video), *The Gulf Crisis TV Project,* Paper Tiger Television, 1991. Charging "media demonization" Cohen argued that the *New Republic* photo of Saddam Hussein first appeared as the August 13, 1990 cover of *Time* magazine with his moustache uncropped. The apparently orchestrated similarity in appearance between Hitler and Saddam was unmistakeable even to contributors to this very issue of the *New Republic.* Edward Luttwak, an advocate of an armed response to the Iraqi invasion, commented in his article "Kuwaiting Game" that "[c]artoonists all over the world have happily embraced the Hitler/Hussein analogy (see cover)," 25.
39. William L. Shirer, *The Rise and Fall of the Third Reich* (New York: Fawcett, 1960), 20–21.
40. Vide, Sigmund Freud, *Group Psychology and the Analysis of the Ego, Standard Edition,* XVIII, 67–143.
41. Albert Speer, *Inside the Third Reich,* trans. Richard and Clara Winston (New York: MacMillan, 1970), 46.
42. Ernst Hanfstaegl, *Unheard Witness* (New York: Lippincott, 1957), 72.
43. Adolf Hitler, *Mein Kampf,* trans. Ralph Mannheim (Boston: Houghton Mifflin, 1971), 42.
44. *OSS Source Book* (OSS documents collected in 1942–43), National Archives, #58, 627.
45. Speer, *Inside the Third Reich,* 138.

46. Neville Henderson, *Failure of a Mission* (New York: G. P. Putnam's Sons, 1940), 42.
47. Klaus Theweleit, *Male Fantasies, Volume 1: Women, Floods, Bodies, History*, trans. Stephen Conway, in collaboration with Erica Carter and Chris Turner (Minneapolis: University of Minnesota, 1987), 435.
48. *OSS Source Book*, 22.
49. Walter C. Langer, *The Mind of Adolf Hitler* (New York: Basic Books, 1972), 134.
50. Norbert Bromberg, "Hitler's Character and Its Development: Further Observations," *American Imago* 28, no. 4 (1971): 300, n. 4. For a full discussion of the various psychological interpretations of Hitler, see Helm Stierlin, *Adolf Hitler: A Family Perspective* (New York: Psychohistory, 1976).
51. Lev Bezymenski, *"The Death of Adolf Hitler": Unknown Documents from Soviet Archives* (New York: Harcourt, Brace & World, 1968).
52. Leonard L. Heston and Renate Heston, *The Medical Casebook of Adolf Hitler*, introd. Albert Speer (New York: Stein and Day, 1982), 113 and 71.
53. Cf. George G. L. Waite, *The Psychopathic God: Adolf Hitler* (New York: Basic Books, 1977), 150–62.
54. Cf. George Bush, "Toward a New World Order," 91, and George Bush, "Operation Desert Storm Launched," 38.
55. *Washington Report on Middle East Affairs*, September, 1990, 11.
56. Erwin R. Parson, "The Psychology of the Persian Gulf War: I. Gulf-Nam and Saddam Hussein's Nebuchadnezzar Imperial Complex: A Political Psychological Analysis," *Journal of Contemporary Psychotherapy*, 21, no. 1 (Spring 1991): 25–52.
57. Michel Foucault, *Madness & Civilization. A History of Insanity in the Age of Reason*, trans. Richard Howard (New York: Random House, 1965), 46. Vide President George Bush, "Transcript of George Bush Accepting the Nomination for Another Four More Years," *New York Times*, August 21, 1992, A14: "We destroyed a threat, freed a people and locked a tyrant in the prison of his own country."
58. "Air Force Chief of Staff Dismissed for His Comments on Gulf Plans," *New York Times*, September 18, 1990, A12.
59. Patrick J. Sloyan, "Missiles Hit Saddam's Command HQs," *New York Newsday*, January 17, 1991; Barton Gellman, "Strike on Saddam Foiled by Storm: Iraqi Leader Is Part of Command-and-Control Structure Allies Seek to Decapitate," *Washington Post*, January 25, 1991, A1.
60. George Bush, "Toward a New World Order," 92.
61. "The normal prototype of all fetishes is the penis of the man." Sigmund Freud, *Fetishism, Standard Edition*, XXI.
62. Dr. Helen Caldicott, *Missile Envy. The Arms Race & Nuclear War* (New York: Bantam, 1985), 308–49.
63. Carol Cohn, "'Clean Bombs' and Clean Language," *Women, Militarism, & War. Essays in History, Politics, and Social Theory* (Savage, MD: Rowman & Littlefield, 1990), ed. Jean Bethke Elshetain & Sheila Tobias, 35.
64. Brian Easlea, *Fathering the Unthinkable. Masculinity, Scientists and the Nuclear Arms Race* (London: Pluto, 1983), 10–39.
65. William Raspberry, "Support Not Protest," *Washington Post*, January 23, 1991, A17.
66. Chris Hedges, "Finding Life's Meaning in Winds and Rains of War," *New York Times*, January 24, 1991, A13.

67. Allan Farnham, "What to Use When War Gets Personal," *Fortune,* 123, no. 4, February 27, 1991, 50.
68. Cf. Sigmund Freud, *Female Sexuality, Standard Edition,* XXI: 229. "One thing that is left over in men from the influence of the Oedipal complex is a certain amount of disparagement in their attitude toward women, whom they regard as being castrated."
69. Cf. Sigmund Freud, *Three Essays on the Theory of Sexuality, Standard Edition* VII: 195: "The assumption of the same (male) genital in all persons is the first of the remarkable and consequential infantile sexual theories." And see also, *The Infantile Genital Organization (An Interpolation into the Theory of Sexuality), Standard Edition,* XIX: 144–45: "the child believes that it is only unworthy female persons that have lost their genitals. . . . Women whom he respects, like his mother, retain a penis for a long time. . . . It is not till later, when the child takes up the problems of the origin and birth of babies, and when he guesses that only women can give birth to them—it is only then that the mother, too, loses her penis."
70. Sigmund Freud, *Fetishism, Standard Edition,* XXI: 154.
71. "'In a broadcast over Baghdad radio monitored in Nicosia, Cyprus, Mr. Hussein said 'the mother of all battles' has started after the 'Satan Bush' committed his crime,' Reuters reported." "U.S. and Allies Open Air War on Iraq," *New York Times,* January 19, 1991, 1.
72. "What Do Sexual Politics Have to Do with the War? Quite a Lot," *Ms.* 1, 4 (March/April 1991): 87.
73. Jack Anderson and Dale Van Atta, *Stormin' Norman, An American Hero* (New York: Kensington, 1991), 113.
74. Molly Moore, "U.S. Hunt for Missile Launcher Like 'Needle in Haystack' Search," *Washington Post,* January 19, 1991, A18.
75. From the Freudian perspective of the masculinist psychic economy, "*paedicatio* with a male owes its origins to an analogy with a similar act performed with a woman." Sigmund Freud, *Three Essays on the Theory of Sexuality, Standard Edition,* VII: 152.
76. It might be argued that the reference is to the actual wife of the Iraqi leader, rather than a castrated Saddam, and therefore was an attempt to humiliate him through cuckolding. In either case, the result is that Saddam is made to look as less than a "real man."
77. Tony Engelhart and Pat Foran, *Sword in the Sand: U.S. Marines in the Gulf War* (Hong Kong: Concord Publications, 1992), n.p.
78. Bill Carter, "Giant TV Audience for Bush's Speech," *New York Times,* January 18, 1991, A14.
79. Paul Virilio and Sylvère Lotringer, *Pure War* (New York: Semiotext(e), 1983), 18.
80. Vide, Beverle Houston, "Viewing Television: The Metapsychology of Endless Consumption," *Quarterly Review of Film Studies* (Summer 1984): 183–95.
81. The advertising blurb for the "Desert Shield Condom" seems particularly tasteless: "From its big muzzle to its tapered smooth bore, each Desert Shield Condom is designed to stand up to the heat of intense surface-to-surface contact. Perfectly aerodynamic, this heat-seeking missile finds its mark every time—and with no pre-mature blow-ups." Vide, Richard Goldstein, "Season of the Kitsch: Watching and Shopping the War," *Village Voice* March 5, 1991, 30.
82. Susan Sachaws, "First Sorties Hit Hard and Return Safely," *New York Newsday,* January 17, 1991.

83. "The Tailhook Association is a private organization composed of active duty, Reserve and retired Navy and Marine Corps aviators, Defense contractors, and others." Office of the Inspector General, Department of Defense, *Tailhook '91: Part 1—Review of the Navy Investigations,* 1992, 1.
84. Letter to membership, October 11, 1991.
85. Letter to membership, August 15, 1991.
86. Letter to membership, October 11, 1991.
87. *Tailhook '91,* 4.
88. Ibid., 10.
89. Ibid., 15.
90. Michael Gordon, "Pentagon Report Tells of Aviators' Debauchery," *New York Times,* April 24, 1993, 9.
91. *Tailhook '91,* 16.
92. Gordon, "Pentagon Report," 1.
93. *Tailhook '91,* 15.
94. Gordon, "Pentagon Report," 9.
95. Ruth M. Bond, "The Civilian Old Salt Who Took On the Navy's Cover-up of Tailhook," *New York Times,* May 14, 1993, E7.
96. Jose M. Zuniga, "Good Soldier, Gay Soldier," *New York Times,* April 25, 1993, E17.
97. Catherine S. Manegold, "The Odd Place of Homosexuality in the Military," *New York Times,* April 18, 1993, E1.
98. Vide, Cynthia Enroe's work on the "militarization of prostitution" in *Does Khaki Become You? The Militarization of Women's Lives* (Boston: Pandora, 1988), 18–45.
99. "After all, no one is whimpering about dykes in the women's showers. What's at stake is America's manhood." Alisa Solomon, "An Army of Others. Why the Gay Ban Makes the Man," *Village Voice,* February 9, 1993, 25.

T h r e e

FROM BATTLE FRONT TO HOME FRONT:
FOOTBALL METAPHORS AND AMERICA'S "SUPERBOWL"

This ain't a game for pussies.

—"Mean" Joe Greene, Former Defensive Tackle, Pittsburgh Steelers

THE COMPARISON OF FOOTBALL players' genitals with weapons of war seemed an absurd piece of male bravado, albeit with the disturbing consequence that women and Iraqis were placed in the same position. Of course the controversy was dismissed in some quarters as adolescent humor; nonetheless it should be asked why many men across America—and not just some in professional athletics—found the joke funny. As Freud suggested in *Jokes and Their Relation to the Unconscious* (1905),[1] the punchline brings to the surface in one cathetic release associations that are hitherto repressed. The explosion of laughter may be attributed to the explicit sexual display of male genitalia in a woman's face, but the image of oral copulation alone is not sufficient to account for the analogy to war that provides the substance of the joke. It is the warlike potency of the "missile" in the face of the enemy that provides the force behind the joke. The implication is clear: "shooting the missile" will be the undoing of the "enemy," who, overwhelmed by its power, will be compelled to submit to her/his own destruction. War is savored through the lens of oral rape. Sexuality is distorted through the lens of coercive power. The joke suggests that there is an intimate relationship between sexual violence, on the one hand, and war and football, on the other. Some sportscasters felt that, as distasteful as the joke was, too much had been made of it in the press. But in the eyes of others, the scandal in the New England Patriots' locker room and Victor Kiam's coarse attempt at humor demeaned both the world of sports and the war effort itself. Professional sportsmen presumably are imbued with a certain dignity of purpose, foremost among which is to serve as role models for the youth of America, and so the sexual harassment of Lisa Olsen did not help to improve the image of football. Nor did Kiam's phallic interpretation of Raytheon's Patriot missile, deployed to knock down incoming SCUD missiles over Israeli territory, reflect the seriousness with which the war was fought. Yet Kiam's joke, at Olsen's expense, was not the only rhetorical gesture to allegedly trivialize the conflict.

On *This Week with David Brinkley*, General Schwartzkopf himself upbraided Cokie Roberts for asking a question about the similarity between the war footage of strategic bombing and the Nintendo video game. *"You don't see me treating this like a game,"* he remarked indignantly. "And you don't see me laughing and joking about it going on. There are human beings being killed when that happens." Despite the general's condemnation, in one breath, of the game metaphor, in the very next breath he employed what might be regarded as an unconscious slip of the tongue. *"And at this stage of the game,"* he angrily emphasized, "it is not a time for frivolity on the part of anybody."

The parapraxis in the general's statement indicates that, despite the fear of trivialization, the rhetoric of games does not seem foreign to the art of war. Nor are such "games" harmless. They are a serious business which, as men play them, threaten those deemed the enemy with humiliation and, in some cases, even death. Although social scientists have noted the recent inclusion of sport metaphors in politics,[2] the use of such metaphors has long been evident in the American military, for example, the application of game theory to military strategy and its practical application in "war games." As Colonel Dennis Long, a planner for U.S. armored strategies at Fort Knox, asserted after the fall of the Soviet Union,

> For 50 years we equipped our football team, practiced five days a week and never played a game. . . . We had a clear enemy with demonstrable qualities, and we had scouted them out. . . . [Now] we will have to practice day in and day out without knowing anything about the other team. We won't have his playbook, we won't know where the stadium is, or how many guys he will have on the field. This is very distressing to the military establishment, especially when you are trying to justify the existence of your organization and your systems.[3]

The appearance of sport metaphors, especially those of America's most popular game, football, was therefore to be expected in the rhetoric of the Gulf War. One chief warrant officer for the 82nd Airborne enthusiastically welcomed the advent of hostilities with the quip, "It's time to quit the pregame show."[4] Reporters noted one sign in a Saudi Arabian hotel that facetiously compared the opening phase of the aerial war to a football kickoff. "Iraq has won the toss and elected to receive."[5]

Brought up in a culture that cherishes the competitive spirit of football, U.S. military personnel frequently gave voice to feelings about their opponents in a language that comes almost as second nature to Americans. Pilots compared their air strikes to the thrill of scoring. One aviator exclaimed after returning from his first mission over Baghdad, "We've scored a touchdown and no one was home!"[6] But another Air Force officer reportedly attempted to quell over-optimism by adding, "We had one good morning. You sting 'em quick, you're winning 7–0, but it's not over."[7] The anticipation experienced by American GIs was sometimes articulated in terms familiar to male adolescents. "Tomorrow we cross [the border]," confessed one tank gunnery sergeant. "We feel like a football team prior to the big game."[8] Even when GIs wanted to express the seriousness of the impending battle, many, like General Schwartzkopf, could not restrain themselves from using similar football metaphors. "It's like the Dallas Cowboy football team," claimed one officer. "They weren't a real emotional team. That's exactly what it's like with these pilots out here. They know exactly what they've got to do."[9] Another Marine officer compared his experience of the war to that of the viewers at home in the living rooms of America; they only watched "highlights on CNN," whereas he "got to see the whole season."[10]

Even news reporters were not immune from invoking "footballspeak" as a way to communicate the excitement and significance of the conflict. The *Los Angeles Times* compared the size of bomb craters, caused by the raids of coalition air assaults, to that of football fields.[11] And in his piece that detailed the horrors of the "Road to Hell" from Kuwait to Basra at the close of the war, John Balzar, a reporter for the *New York Times,* described the appearance of enemy troops, fleeing before the onslaught of Apache helicopters, in terms comprehensible to the American sports fan: "Iraqi soldiers, as big as football players on the television screen, run with nowhere to hide. These are not bridges exploding or airplane hangers. These are men."[12] Although Balzar's remarks were intended to dispel the implications of innocence derived from the use of the Nintendo simile, it is curious that he chose to describe the Iraqi soldiers' humanity in terms of American football players. The comparison suggests that in American culture the game of football, like war, while alien to everyday life, reveals something that is quintessentially human. These gladiators who appear so threatening in their full regalia, be it football or military uniforms, are vulnerable to grievous physical injury and, in some way, are to be pitied.

Like football players, the fate of soldiers lies preeminently in the hands of their superiors, be they generals or coaches. That relationship lends itself to the interchangeability of terms in these two kinds of male territorial games. In light of the brilliant strategy that secured victory for the coalition forces, Schwartzkopf was hailed by *Newsweek* as a "Vince Lombardi in Army Greens."[13] As the coach of the Green Bay Packers during their heyday as the dominant team in the National Football League during the late 1950s and early 1960s, Lombardi achieved nearly legendary stature as a strict disciplinarian and a tactical genius on the football field. It is difficult to overstate the respect that his name commands among football fans and professionals. Indeed his fame is such that the trophy that symbolizes the ultimate victory in this sport, a Superbowl championship, is named after him. And for those whose understanding of the war was shaped by the semiotics of football, the appellation given to Schwartzkopf seemed appropriate.

But it was not only the foot soldiers and reporters who expressed themselves about the Gulf War in sports metaphors; it was the general staff itself. General Colin Powell, chairman of the Joint Chiefs of Staff, warned the president before the commencement of hostilities that he would have to be prepared for the ultimate test. He chose to convey the seriousness with which he regarded Operation Desert Storm by warning the president that "[t]his is the Super Bowl. Don't count on the easy ways."[14] Although the commander in the field originally had but a rudimentary sketch of war games exercises for armed intervention in the Kuwaiti theater, General Schwartzkopf eventually devised a strategy designed to outflank the Iraqi forces in Kuwait by moving armored and air mobile divisions to the far west, penetrating Iraqi territory, cutting off supplies, and rolling up the enemy's front line defenses. Although Schwartzkopf expressed his distaste for game metaphors to Cokie Roberts, he did not hesitate to see himself as a quarterback who, in football jargon, is dubbed the "field general." "Once we had taken out [Saddam Hussein's] eyes," he declared to reporters in his February 28, 1992 news conference which marked the official announcement of impending victory,

we did what could best be described as the "Hail Mary" play in football. I think you recall, when the quarterback is desperate for a touchdown at the very end, what he does is, he steps up behind the center, and all of a sudden every single one of his receivers goes way out to one flank, and they all run down the field as fast as they can and into the end zone, and he lobs the ball. In essence, that's what we did.[15]

The apparent ease with which this imagery came to the field commander amid a predominantly male audience of reporters suggests that Schwartzkopf's discomfort with Cokie Robert's question had everything to do with gender politics. Perhaps the underlying fear was the belief that women do not take these metaphors as seriously as men. Or perhaps that Nintendo was not as serious a game as football. In either case women reporters seemed particularly disturbed by the language of sport employed by their male counterparts as well as male officers and enlisted men. "Do these pilots really think that bombs are as harmless as footballs," asked one female commentator. "[T]hat wars are like games, with scoreboards, time limits, and cheering fans?"[16] On its face it seems absurd to believe that men would assume war to be as "harmless" as football. War is not a game played for the sake of sheer enjoyment, but then again neither is football.

WITHOUT ANY WINNERS, WE WOULDN'T HAVE ANY GODDAMN CIVILIZATION

As the author of *From Ritual to Record: The Nature of Modern Sports* and *Sports Spectators,* Allen Guttmann has written on the history and sociology of sport and its role in American culture. Although individual players may have economic motivations in playing the game, Guttmann argues that football is an autotelic contest. It is played for its own, self-defined purposes: to win according to its own rules. Arguments may be advanced that suggest that football might be an outlet for aggressive feelings, but that is not its purpose. Its purpose lies in the pleasure derived from participation, either immediate or vicarious, in an athletic contest.

The ritualistic aspect of the game belies an interpretation of football for its own sake. Its elaborate rules, its uniforms, its boundaries of time and space, its ceremonies and public standing, indeed, the very seriousness with which the game is undertaken, all indicate that football serves as a means to move the spectator and the participant from one way of being into another, from the world of everyday life into the world of the male territorial game. This reality is one that remains relatively unknown to millions of women in the United States, but it seems to have tremendous significance for what it means to be male in American culture. And while there may be a relationship between football and the "pleasures of the game," the enjoyment seems to be derived from a socially constructed pleasure based on an initiation into and reiteration of a masculinist psychic reality.

In this respect Guttmann has speculated that the origin of sports seems to lie in the irrational dimension of the human psyche from which emerges a powerful desire toward physical expression. Like war it draws on the release of what Guttmann regarded as instinctual, primal energies that may be harnessed for some rational purpose, usually the domination of one's opponent. The release of this energy also entails a certain danger—that of uncontrollable violence. As in war, football is a liminal experience which, in a sense, steals this vital energy at great risk. "Football," Vince Lombardi once claimed, "is a game for madmen. In football we're all mad." Lombardi's warning hints at the dynamic of both football and war: its power to transform both men and their cultures.

It is for that reason that the "blood sport" of football becomes a semiotics that mediates between the unreason of desire and the order of civilized society. It is a Janus-faced *agon* in which aggression is unleashed within the constraints of rules, and it is precisely this experience that serves to instruct the young in the substance of what it means to be male. In examining references to the sport, I have noted how often football is lauded for its pedagogical significance. Its presumed standards of excellence, in both physical and academic prowess, allegedly bring out what is best in young men. As a form of character ethics, football inculcates a virile asceticism of fortitude and discipline that will serve men well in the society-at-large in much the same way as does the military. "For youth, as it crosses the threshold of manhood," argued Douglas MacArthur, "football has become a rallying point to build courage when courage seems to die, to restore faith where there seems little cause for faith, to create hope as hope becomes forlorn."[17]

For its advocates football effects a metamorphosis in young men by mediating between a transcendent ethos and masculine violence. Or, as one psychiatrist who served as a consultant to the San Diego Chargers noted, success lies "[s]omewhere between the astronaut's cool and a male dog's fight for a mate."[18] The *agon* of the football athlete is therefore not merely a battle with the other team but a struggle with himself in order to give birth to a socially recognized and esteemed masculine identity. Thus, descriptions of football as a game of either "good, clean violence" (Bob Timberlake, former University of Michigan quarterback) or "clean hatred" (Ronald Reagan) are not as oxymoronic as they first appear.[19] Violence and hatred are stimulated by the game itself for a higher purpose, not merely for their own sake. They are the means by which the individual male can redeem himself and recognize himself as a man in his own eyes and under the male gaze of his peers. The war for the culturally fabricated male ego is therefore played out within the socially constructed world of football—a game separated from everyday life by artifice and ritual.

It would seem then that a space had to be created within the culture for football—a space that would otherwise not exist within that culture. Although armed conflict may have provided an outlet for the masculine ego and the test of one's manhood outside the borders of the nation, it was neither always available nor desirable for the society-at-large. War had to be domesticated in order to preserve its psychological function and limit its physically destructive consequences. Nonetheless the violence that the sport releases is so dangerous that it necessitates well-defined boundaries, separated from everyday walks of life by an arbitrary construct of time and space and a complex set of rules.

Although a cursory examination of football and its history might give the illusion of a "natural" competition, undertaken out-of-doors the time-space continuum of the game is anything but natural. The temporal dimension of the game is chronological, not biological time—arbitrarily divided into four 15-minute quarters. As the chronological template superimposed on the spatial dimension of the contest, the game clock is subject to rational control. The rules of the game allow for its interruption or suspension through a series of alternatives available to the teams, for example, incomplete passes, moving the ball out-of-bounds, and the three "time-outs" granted each team per "half" (the first and second two quarters). The halves of the game are separated by a "half-time," a fifteen-minute period during which teams rest and regroup and spectators usually witness a ritual celebration, characterized most often by marching bands and cheerleaders. To ensure the flow of the game, the play clock creates the temporal buffer between each discrete team action or play, and its maximum allowance of forty seconds produces an ersatz sense of the passage of time. In the parlance of football, it is therefore imperative for a team to "control the clock." Like Chronos, the god who ate his children, the chronological time of the game and play clocks hold sway over the teams and may ensure either their victory or defeat. This "control of the clock," however, is really a mark of internal control by which an offensive team, under the direction of its coach and quarterback, can organize and execute a rational plan through effective plays which advance the ball through the space-time continuum of the football field.

Although the artifice of football has become more evident through the proliferation of in-door stadiums and artificial grass playing fields (referred to as "Astro-turf" or increasingly as the "carpet"), the game has always been played within the dimensions of a fabricated rather than natural space. The field in professional American football is 100 yards long from goalline-to-goalline, 53 1/3 yards wide, and 6,400 square yards in total, including the end zones in which stand the respective goal posts. The field itself is drawn in one- and five-yard increments, that are used to mark the advance of the offensive against the defensive team. Although no formal designation exists, the field is also divided along the fifty-yard line by an imaginary boundary that marks the territories of the respective teams. The temporal dimension is distinguished by internal control, that is, control of the clock, and the spatial dimension is expressed through external control, that is, control of the ground. Football is thus a male territorial game in which the teams attempt to wrest domination of the field from their opponents.

This battle of the players for control of both the field and themselves is mediated by the football itself. The football and its history within the space-time continuum of each game signifies the extent to which one team has demonstrated its superiority over the other. "Time of possession" and average yard line indicating "start of possession" evidence the role of the ball as the preeminent signifier in the balance of power between the two teams.

In repetitive fashion, the offensive team in possession of the ball is assigned the task to move it "downfield" at least a minimal distance of ten yards in up to four discrete "plays" or "downs." When that minimal distance is achieved, the team is granted another cycle of plays.

The defensive team attempts to stop both the offensive team's "running" and "passing" game by tackling ball-carriers or knocking down the ball usually thrown by the offensive team's quarterback to eligible offensive "receivers," so designated by the rules. The purpose of the offense is to advance the ball not just through a field of physical obstacles (opposing players' bodies) but to negotiate a passage through a complex set of rules in order to move the ball into the opponent's end zone, that area beyond the goal line that signifies the opposing team's most guarded and valuable territory. Because failure to achieve the necessary ten yards ensures the surrender of the ball to one's opponents, the offensive team usually attempts to attain the requisite ten yards in three "downs." If it does not, the coach of the offensive team most often feels compelled by the logic of the rules to anticipate the upcoming change of possession by kicking or "punting" the ball downfield as far away as possible from his own end zone. On receipt of the punted ball, the game undergoes an inversion in that the offense becomes the defense and the defense becomes the offense, awarded the next cycle of four plays to advance the ball ten yards.

By either passing the ball to one's own eligible receiver or carrying the ball into the opponent's end zone, a team scores a touchdown—a penultimate sign of successful domination, quantified according to the rules as six points. Kicking the ball through the uprights of the goalpost located in the opponent's endzone yields a similar, if less valued, result, called a field goal, worthy of three points. After a touchdown the offensive team is also granted the additional opportunity of kicking the ball in a fashion similar to the field goal but valued at only one point. The defensive team is eligible to score a touchdown only if it wrests control of the ball from the offensive team through the interception of a pass or a fumble recovery (dubbed a "turnover") and if it carries the ball into the offensive team's end zone. Alternatively the defensive team is awarded two points if it tackles an offensive ball-carrier in his own end zone, an act awarded two points. The team that scores the most points at the end of four 15-minute quarters is the victor.

The complicated rules of the game, that are reviewed each year, seem to reflect the cool rationality of a technocratic culture; yet, although football teams belong to a professional sports industry in a modern social order, they employ totemic emblems, suggestive of the Durkheimian model of aboriginal cultures. Football therefore mediates the rupture of the modernist project. The cool rationality that characterizes the logic of dominion over the world men survey is flawed. It cannot bend the world to its order, and in that moment of impending chaos, when the world threatens to slip out of their grasp, men attempt to impose their will through the outburst of male solidarity, albeit in the form of ritual participation. While the names of the teams are a transparent cultural fiction, both the players and their fans, that is, the abbreviation for "fanatics," suspend disbelief in order to act as if the emblem signified the mechanical solidarity of the whole. With something akin to religious devotion appropriate to a sacred space, that is, *fanum,* they participate in a sort of planned "collective effervescence," evident in the chanting of slogans, the display of signs, and the waving of emblematic banners throughout the stadium. Among the totemic emblems so chosen for these teams are the names of animals and birds (Bears, Lions, Broncos, Rams, Seahawks, Eagles, Falcons, etc.) as well as classes of beings, both human and nonhuman, mythologized in the imagination of contemporary Americans (Redskins, Chiefs, Cowboys, 49ers, Vikings, Saints, Giants). "Football is very tribal in that way," reasoned one sports writer. "You paint your face and you put on your colors and you square off against a tribe from another part of the country with different colors. And sometimes it gets a little ugly."[20]

The game therefore is not simply a competition between two groups of individuals who have the opportunity to exhibit their athletic prowess and skills but a simulation of war between two collectives in which the wholes are greater than the sum of their parts. Within the sixty minutes and sixty-four hundred square yards of football's space-time continuum, players, coaches, and fans alike live in and through the fortunes of their teams. As in war their identity is invested in the success or failure of those to whom they owe allegiance. Football fans in particular experience the uncertainty implicit in being a partisan observer and yet, at the same time, thrill to the moves of players with whom they identify. The experience is not only eudaemonistic; it is also didactic. For football embodies those manly virtues, that is, *vir,* which give meaning to the self in a society dominated by males—fortitude, courage, discipline, desire, and, above all, domination. The philosophy of the male territorial game is sometimes summarized in American popular culture by the statement often ascribed to Vince Lombardi, the man who epitomized the American football coach. "Winning isn't everything. It's the only thing."[21]

Although Lombardi cannot be legitimately credited for the remark, he did claim that "defeat is worse than death."[22] Death betokens the cessation of suffering, but defeat for the survivors must be suffered as a badge of shame and humiliation, at least for the week intervening between football games. Fans, players, and coaches experience depression following a loss and euphoria in the wake of victory. Victory therefore appears as a necessary constituent in the psychic economy of the football enthusiast. "Without any winners," asserted Woody Hayes, legendary coach of the Ohio State football team, "we wouldn't have any goddamn civilization."[23] (Critics may be reminded of Walter Benjamin's comment that civilization was written by barbarians.[24]) In an era of sophisticated and complex game plans, it might be unfair to stereotype the football player, yet the game of football reinscribes war and the concomitant values of the warrior as a template for the identity of football enthusiasts—the vast majority of men in America.

FOOTBALL IS HELL

The seriousness with which football is undertaken suggests that it is conceived not merely as play but rather as work. Many football coaches invoke the work ethic to urge their players to become more disciplined, to use the weight room, to put extra effort into scrimmages held at least four days per week during the regular season. As conceived by Max Weber in his classic work on the subject, the Protestant work ethic promised the believer the knowledge of her/his own salvation. But what does the work ethic in football promise the athlete? Certainly material success. Many professional football players now receive over $1 million per year, and for those who have achieved star status, product endorsements assure even further financial enhancement. But football players will tell you that the work ethic means more than money. It breeds a deep sense of pride in oneself as an athlete and as a man.

Yet, because football is a game repeated by professional teams perhaps as many as eighteen times during a "season," masculinity becomes an identity constantly deferred, for there is always yet another test. "You have to prove your manhood more times in one season than most men do in a lifetime," lamented Dan Goich of the New York Giants. "When you don't make it, when you can't perform or you get beat or get cut, you're cut as a man."[25] As a ritual of American masculinity, football is a gender performance in which athletes attempt to demonstrate by their practice that they are men, that is to say, not women. This understanding of the gendered character of the exercise implies that only men really enjoy football, and anyone who does not is therefore not a man. As Dan Dierdorf, a commentator for ABC's *Monday Night Football* and former offensive lineman, commented on a run by a Buffalo Bills halfback during Superbowl XXV, "If you don't like Thurman Thomas, you don't like anything about this game. You ought to be home watching soap operas." "Real" men are assumed to have little interest in or patience for the romantic relationships and domestic crises of soap operas that draw a predominantly female audience. Neither is considered as important as football. Although admittedly some women do watch football, the game itself focuses on that which concerns and pleases men in an androcentric and competitive society—violence and power.

"From the sideline of a football game," wrote a sportswriter for the *New York Times,* "a viewer can tell the sport is warfare, confined to 100 yards. It's amazing that more don't get maimed. The huge bodies in shoulder pads crashing resoundingly into each other, the groans and screams, the mangled bone, the spurt of blood and the boom of a punt are reminiscent of combat."[26] As a matter of fact, injuries are so common in the game that one commentator, a former professional football player and current philosophy professor, suggested that "body shattering is the very *point* of football, as killing and maiming are of war."[27] Defenders of the game, however, are concerned that this exclusive focus on violence distorts the meaning of football. The sport may be incidentally violent, they argue, but its image is tarnished not by football, as it is supposed to be played, but by a so-called "criminal element" whose use of excessive force has resulted in highly publicized injuries.

In this respect, the ethos of football parallels the internationally recognized code of conduct governing war which is articulated in various legally binding conventions and in the Western custom of "just war" theory. Under this tradition combatants are restrained from directly attacking noncombatants; however, in some cases noncombatants may suffer physical injury or even death in the course of battle among combatants. In these instances both law and custom recognize the principles embodied in the "law of double effect." Where armed military conflict indirectly results in civilian casualties, combatants are not responsible for consequences that are foreseen but not intended. The operative normative criterion is intent. As long as the violation of "civilized standards" governing the use of force is not intended, combatants are not guilty of any transgression. And just as this principle governs the conduct of war, so, too, does it reign in the world of professional football.

Although football players, like the ex-Detroit Lions' star and actor Alex Karras may well believe that they were given a "license to kill" on the field, violence is acceptable as long as it is expressed within the rules of the game. Yet both players and fans alike have been stunned by some of the more traumatic injuries over the years, many of which seem to have been intentionally caused. Perhaps the most notable was the literally crippling tackle of the New England Patriot receiver Darrell Stingley in 1978 by Jack Tatum, an Oakland Raider defensive back who authored an autobiography entitled *They Call Me Assassin.* As Stingley recalled the moment, Tatum seemed to have the intent not just to knock him down but, like a man possessed, to do him permanent bodily harm. Harvard psychiatrist Chester Price has commented that the philosophy that undergirds the pep talk of every coach is kill or be killed. To many in the National Football League, Tatum did not seem to take that idea as hyperbole. As he was to confess in his autobiography, "it all becomes war, and I am simply a warrior in every respect." But like the *hashshashin* of Arabic lore, Tatum appeared to some as intoxicated with a madness that obviates the code of rationality that governs acceptable behavior in male territorial games.

Joe Kapp, the former quarterback for the Minnesota Vikings, has suggested that the canon of rules is an illusory civilized veneer to the sport. "Is it normal to wake up in the morning in a sweat because you can't wait to beat another human's guts out?"[28] The world of football was jolted again when in November of 1991 Mike Utley, an offensive guard for the Detroit Lions, was paralyzed from a spinal cord injury in a similar incident. And although regrettable, such injuries are sometimes deemed almost inevitable given the violent character of the game. As Bob Golic, a defensive tackle with the now-Los Angeles Raiders, concluded in one recent interview with *Sport* magazine, "No morals, no ethics. We're defensive guys. We're not allowed to have them."[29] When two hundred fifty to three hundred pound men go all out to intimidate and dominate their opponents, rules governing proper behavior recede into forgetfulness. Michigan's celebrated coach Duffy Dougherty seemed to capture this reality with the remark that football was more of a "collision" than contact sport.

That is all the more reason why critics both outside and inside the game protest the "cheap shot" in football—those bone-crushing tackles made against players at their most vulnerable moment. They may be "speared" while lying on the ground out-of-bounds or after the play has been "whistled dead," or they may even be "blindsided" when their backs are turned. Some players restrain themselves through the invocation of an informal rule: don't go for the knees. In one sense, it is reminiscent of the story told by George Orwell that Michael Walzer recounted in his classic work *Just and Unjust Wars*. Orwell recalled that during the Spanish Civil War, as an international volunteer for the Republic, he had the opportunity to shoot a fascist soldier running atop the opposing trenches. Half-undressed and pulling up his pants, the soldier looked less like the enemy and more like a vulnerable human being. Orwell desisted from killing him.[30] In the unwritten code of male society, such an act of killing might be regarded as unmanly. However, such compassion is rarely observed in war. Al Davis, the controversial owner of the Los Angeles Raiders, has admitted that football, like war, is hell. And so just as Sherman violated the *jus in bello* code of conduct in his scorched earth policy through Georgia, onlookers should not be surprised by the "take no prisoners" attitude evinced by many players and coaches on the modern field of battle.

Within the world of football itself, the objections against this attitude are not criticisms against violence *per se* but rather the use of *excessive* force. Sufficient force, that is, violence governed by rational purpose and normative bounds, is considered essential to the game. To Gene Klein, former owner of the San Diego Chargers, football is a sport of "refined violence." Hence, there is nothing "incidental" about violence in football. The distinction between sanctioned and "criminal" violence is one that functions ideologically to shroud the sport in an air of respectability, but very few players accept this distinction that seeks to sanitize the game. They pay the price each week with their own bodies. And if the sport is preeminently a "physical game," as commentators on televised football broadcasts incessantly remind viewers, their bodies are inscribed as a weapon of war.

Although the equipment that shrouds the player's frame ostensibly is designed to protect the body from injury, it serves as armor reminiscent of the medieval knight or ancient gladiator whose form stood as an icon of masculinity. Suiting up for the game betokens a ritual transfiguration of the individual from a fellow member of civil society into a warrior. The augmented physique that accentuates masculine attributes also elevates the athletic event in the spectator's eye to the battle of mythic heroes. In this "larger than life" environ, players use their bodies as the sign of dominion, cutting their opponents down, running through and diving over their rivals. As Red Hickey, former coach of the San Francisco 49ers once said, "All I want is 100 percent and a willing disregard for the consequences."[31] Like soldiers, they bear the marks of battle on their bodies, suffering the agony of pulled hamstrings, torn ligaments, concussions, cracked ribs, and broken bones. In the same way as grizzled war veterans, they sometimes carry these scars for life.

The field serves as a map of friendly and enemy territory across which are thrown ground and aerial assaults (the running and passing "games"). The focus of the battle lies along the front line, the so-called line of scrimmage, where hand-to-hand combat takes place among the huge linemen. Offensive and defensive lines alike must exhibit both the aggressiveness and the will needed to ensure the hegemony of one team over the other. Like the war room of a military headquarters, the locker room of a football team shelters the staff who plot a strategy of conquest in the most minute detail. Chalkboards are filled with complex diagrams of offensive and defensive formations. To the players who have memorized the pages of the team's playbook are given those final alterations tailored to the latest changes in personnel. Quarterbacks are rehearsed in the desired sequence of offensive thrusts. But while the coaching staff and the quarterbacks may provide the method to this madness, those "in the trenches" need provide the requisite "mental toughness" so aptly summarized in the ads of one of football's favorite sponsors: Nike's™ "Just Do It."

Announcers talk about the drives of football teams in much the same way as do books about the military conflict in World War II. The operation is conducted under the immediate direction of the quarterback, dubbed the "field general," who issues his commands to his teammates huddled together behind the line. Prior to the commencement of each play, he "reads" the defense and, like a Marine drill instructor, barks out his orders at the line of scrimmage. Quarterbacks must choose the appropriate "point of attack" and direct their blockers to "open a hole" in the opposing line so that ball-carriers can "knife" inside or trick the defense with feigned attacks so that receivers can outflank their opponents. As the pivotal player of the game, the quarterback embodies football's war rhetoric. Colloquially, his arm is a "gun," a "rifle," or "cannon" that "fires the ball" down-field out of a variety of offensive formations, including such novelties as the "shotgun" or the "run and shoot." By "gunning" the ball and throwing the "perfect strike," by completing a "long bomb," the quarterback can almost instantaneously create the momentum needed to win the game. And if he is successful, one can expect to see the receiver do some variation of a war dance in the end zone, a ritual that has become almost *de rigueur* in the National Football League.

The defense, on the other hand, must anticipate the offensive attack in order to swarm into the breech created by the offensive front line or halt an attempted sweep around its flank. It might even attempt to thwart the offense's aerial attack by overwhelming the offensive lineman in a lightning attack, a blitzkrieg, abbreviated in the language of the game to a "blitz." Blitzing an opponent may even yield the penultimate victory in the war plan of any defense: the "sack" of the quarterback. By eluding those offensive players assigned to stop forays beyond the front line, defensive players get the opportunity to tackle a quarterback behind the line of scrimmage. "Sacking" the quarterback, like the sack of a city, involves an enemy's significant loss of territory—a loss from which the enemy may not recover. The opposing team may be compelled to give up possession of the ball, and therefore the tide of battle itself may shift. Invoking yet another expression popularized in war, one defensive "linebacker" described his basic assignment as a "seek and destroy" mission. The football field, recalled former Oakland Raiders defensive back Lester Hayes, is "like Vietnam on Sundays."[32]

THE BUCKS ARE STARTING TO RUT

In this "man's war" it is clear that there is little room for women. In the opinions of many men, shared in the barrooms of America, women have very little grasp of either the rules of the game or its existential meaning to men. And yet women are well aware of the gender boundary that protects this weekend ritual from defilement. Football is largely ignored by women and is very rarely criticized in a serious fashion by them. They recognize football's power in the male imaginary, and although its hypnotic effect remains something of a mystery to them, football, noted the writer John Fowles, "keeps women from laughing." They seem to intuit that the game is more than an idiosyncratic male pleasure and that its violence, albeit restrained by the bounds of convention, represents in some sense a thinly veiled threat. In one of the few books by women that has commented on the effect of football on American culture, Elayne Rapping concluded that football

> embodies an image of masculinity that is physical but not sexual. . . . Women have no part in male activities of this kind. In the realms of power, whether symbolic or real, women and sex are dispensable. Team spirit, male bonding, the will to win, the need for mass adulation and reward for destroying an enemy and achieving dominance and glory are all part of football. So, increasingly, is violence. That football has replaced baseball as the national pasttime is surely—as so many have observed— related to its glorification of violence. As a metaphor for American military values, football reveals an increasing brutality in the national soul.[33]

Rapping's opinion reflects the view long held by one of the earliest critics of football machismo, Eugene Bianchi, who believed that the game resulted from the inability of men in this culture to express tenderness. Although he concluded that the sexist attitudes encouraged by football contributed to violence against women off the field, he, too, held that the game itself had little to do with women. "They can shout and squeal from afar, but their roles are accessory to the male event."[34]

Yet, despite the conspicuous absence of the "opposite sex" in the flesh, the discourse of football, like the discourse of war, seems to be infused with sexual language. Although the "man-made" schedule of games in the N.F.L. stretches from the end of summer to the beginning of winter, the descriptor employed to signify this arbitrary temporal framework is derived from the discourse of nature: the football "season." Football enthusiasts will even wax rhapsodically in the autumn about the smell of the falling leaves, the cold wind, and the lure of the gridiron—associations that hardly fit the reality of football training camps in June and July. Nonetheless, the discursive naturalization of football is expressed in some rather surprising ways. Looking for a simile that would capture the anticipation that players experience, Joe Fields, the former All-Pro center for the New York Jets, hypothesized that "[i]t's like when they're getting ready for breeding season and the bucks are starting to rut. When spring comes, it's time to get ready to play football."[35]

In Field's view the banging of helmets and the pop of shoulder pads bears a similarity to the clash of horns between stags or rams who vie for supremacy in the pecking order of males. For linemen it is a contest of physical prowess, encoded in the language of football, as in war, as "upper body strength." Although the military has attempted to exclude women from combat duty by virtue of their lack of upper body strength, women clearly have the capacity to master the technical skills of advanced weaponry. However, in a game where upper body strength seems to be the prerequisite for participation, women are excluded from the outset. Football exceeds even the military in the preservation of its gendered boundaries; yet its macho character does not leave all reference to women behind. Indeed, women make their presence felt in the obsessive compulsive regimen of football that compels men to prove they are not women.

Faced by men the size of giants, trained to unleash a violence that would put the average person in the hospital, coaches and their assistants frequently treat their charges as if they were adolescents. During training camp and throughout the season, the coaches regulate the lives of their players, overseeing their diet, supervising their workouts, and even enforcing a curfew. The infantilization of the players makes them dependent on their coaches as father figures and casts them in the role of rebellious sons. This process of regression is frequently eclipsed by the threat of emasculation that coaches use to both shame their players and drive them toward superhuman efforts in attempts to prove their manhood.

Like Marine drill instructors, many coaches belittle their athletes by invoking the player's castration anxiety. Dave Kopay, an N.F.L. veteran of nearly a half-dozen teams, recalled that "[f]rom grade school on, the curse words on the football field are about behaving like a girl. If you don't run fast enough or block or tackle hard enough you're a pussy, a cunt, a sissy."[36] It is reported that Jerry Glanville, the colorful coach for both the Houston Oilers and the Atlanta Falcons, used to taunt his players by asking them if they were going to wear skirts and high heels. Like Dan Dierdorf's question posed to viewers about soap operas and gender affiliation, the coach's badgering purportedly tests the depth of the players' commitment to football's culturally constructed model of masculinity. Some coaches might find such language vulgar, but many defend the practice because that model of masculinity is commonly regarded as the *sine qua non* to success on the field. Football is not just a war but rather a game of sexual encoding that employs both castration and phallic rape imagery to describe the domination of the enemy.

Excluding scantily clad cheerleaders, first introduced into the game some twenty years ago by the Dallas Cowboys, the public seems to be relatively oblivious to the sexual imagery of the game. Even feminist critics, with few notable exceptions,[37] have largely ignored the issue. Yet the discourse of football is replete with sexual allusions. Because the action within the game's space-time continuum is focused on the disposition of the ball, the observer should not be taken aback by the phallic associations conjured by the football itself. Each play commences with the "snap" of the football, colloquially referred to as the "pigskin"—the material from that the ball was originally made. An offensive lineman, appropriately designated the center, squats down over the line of scrimmage with the ball on the ground directly in front of him. Placing one hand on the ball itself, he swings the pigskin back between his legs at the command of the quarterback. Placing his hands between the legs and under the anus of the center, the quarterback receives its delivery—an act that renders the ball "alive." The act's isomorphic reiteration of birth suggests that the ball itself bears the markings of a fetus.[38] It is precisely this conclusion that is borne out by a psychoanalytic reading of the "snap." The snap of the ball marks not only the birth of the play but the reanimation of chronological time through the restarting of the play clock. Plunging the teams into the space-time continuum after the brief hiatus between plays, the hike of the ball brings participants and spectators together in a heightened intensity that lives out the fate of the ball and the men who play the game.

The game of football is therefore not merely a weekend pasttime for American men; it is ritualized reiteration of life with its associated moments of birth trauma and anxious expectations. In a sense the spectator who identifies himself with the practice is both father and son. On the one hand, at the moment of the ball's delivery the viewer can stand in the shoes of the quarterback, contemplating the action of this living entity as the play develops. On the other hand, the ball is the viewer himself, the son, whose fate awaits him. However, whereas in the game of life the American male may well feel that his future is beyond his control, the doubled identity of the spectator allows him to take his life as fetus/ball into his own hands, that is, the hands of the quarterback. This propitious conjunction produces an euphoria that thrills both fans and players alike. "There ain't nothing like it," Joe Klecko, a defensive star of the New York Jets, fondly remembered. "People talk about their kid being born as a rush. Well, this happens every Sunday. That's what makes it great. It's an unbelievable feeling."[39]

The identification of the male football enthusiast with the fate of the ball itself reinforces the claim that the pigskin is a fetish that functions as a surrogate phallus. Freud's theory of human sexuality hypothesizes that to the male child even the mother is the possessor of a phallus. It is only in the phallic stage that he discovers to his alarm that the mother is lacking this physical attribute. The shock of the sight of the female genitals produces castration anxiety but not a fundamental revolution in the male imaginary. As both child and man, the male assumes that possession of the phallus is a normative sign of being human. Freud himself shared this view with the conclusion that women universally validate this masculinist presupposition through their penis-envy and their "natural" drive to acquire the phallus through marriage and through giving birth to the normatively male child. Although the Freudian claim to have uncovered the "true nature" of human sexuality is problematic, nonetheless it may serve to describe the presuppositions of a culturally constructed masculinist psychic economy in Western societies. Whereas the sexual references sprinkled throughout the discourse of football may be regarded as coincidental and of no significance, there seems to be too many of them to be of no consequence.

The Freudian description of the masculinist psychic economy permits a reading of football that unites the apparently disparate references in the game's primary signifier—the ball as both fetus and phallus. Given this assumption, both the attitudes and emotions of players and fans are far more comprehensible. Those athletes who are the chief ball-handlers—the center, the quarterback, the running-backs, and the receivers—are expected to have great hands. Commentators on the game emphasize that these positions require a great sensitivity to touch lest the ball be dropped. Coaches particularly seek receivers with "soft hands"—who can gather the pigskin into their arms no matter how hard the ball is thrown to them. In one practice, no longer permitted in the National Football League, receivers attempted to enhance their pass-catching ability by applying an adhesive, nicknamed "stick 'um," not only all over their hands and arms but sometimes even on their uniforms.

Such qualities and practices help to ensure that the ball will not be fumbled and recovered by the defense—an act that humiliates the player who drops the ball and dishonors the team as a whole. To be stripped of the ball is to be stripped of one's manhood—a condition readily apparent by the cries of anguish and sometimes even boos that emanate from the stands and the team's bench. When the offense loses the ball, the team and its fans lose the opportunity to control their own fate. They frequently experience disappointment, frustration, disarray, and a sense of powerlessness. Forced to go on the defensive, the now ball-less team must be subjected to a series of offensive assaults by its more aggressive opponent. As the loss of the primary signifier, the fumble, in some sense, represents a loss of themselves, and commentators talk about the need to regroup and concentrate on getting the ball back.

As the primary ball-handler, the quarterback plays a key role in both the action of the game and the collective psyche of the team. On most teams, the quarterback is regarded as the natural leader. Frequently chosen for his tall stature so that he can see over the outstretched hands of defensive linemen, the athlete selected to play quarterback is also expected to be intelligent, for as the team's field general he must direct the offense's attack. In order to do so, he must be able to "read" the defensive formations at the line of scrimmage quickly and, if need be, change the command agreed upon in the huddle by calling an "audible."

As if by an act of contagious magic, the quarterback also is identified with the ball itself. The fate of the ball/team lies in his hands. Thus, the phallic imagery of the ball is also associated with the person of the quarterback. The quarterback frequently functions as the ego ideal for the rest of the players. From his undergraduate days when he was lauded as the "Big Man on Campus," the professional quarterback becomes accustomed to his idolization, particularly by women. The stereotypic image of the quarterback conjures up the figure of a tall, lean, and handsome man whose reputation for his skills with a football translate into an assumed heterosexual prowess off the field. Surrounded by adoring, beautiful women, the quarterback embodies the promise of "supermasculinity" that football holds forth.

As the icon of manhood, the quarterback evinces both courage and discipline by waiting until his receivers downfield are "open" for the pass of the football. Scanning his field of vision with piercing eyes, the quarterback uses his male gaze to penetrate the defensive formation. He is particularly vulnerable to attack at this moment and therefore his offensive front line forms a womblike "pocket" in that he seeks shelter during the course of the play. The collapse of the pocket by an aggressive defense, which breeches the front line, may force the quarterback to run undefended, thereby risking both possession of the ball and injury to the primary ball-handler.

His role is so pivotal both to the action and the meaning of the game that the National Football League has established special rules to extend extraordinary protection to the play-caller. Tackling a quarterback after he has already thrown the ball is termed "roughing the passer," subject to a loss of ground penalty assessed the defense. And at their discretion officials on the field may stop a play when the quarterback is "in the grasp" of a defensive player in order to prevent the possibility of injury. However many defensive players suggest that these special rules to protect the offensive team's most exposed point, its primary ball-handler, is not indicative of manliness. Jack Lambert, one of the N.F.L's premier defensive linebackers, complained that you "[m]ight as well put them in skirts."[40] The quarterback can enhance his own defense through sleight-of-hand; he can successively hide and reveal the ball, by feigning the "hand-off" to a running back and either "bootlegging" the hidden ball behind his leg or passing the ball downfield. Frequently he fakes the hand-off to one running back and gives it to another. The runningback, like the quarterback, seeks to exploit "holes" through the defense—spaces between players in the opposing team's defense. The offensive line attempts to breech the defensive wall and provide openings through which the ball is carried. The penetration of the defense by the ball/phallus therefore has connotations of sexual violence.

Most often this sexual content becomes evident in the act of "banging" it into the end zone, "going all the way" or "scoring a touchdown"—expressions used euphemistically in American popular discourse for sexual intercourse. "Broadway" Joe Namath, the former New York Jets quarterback whose exploits were renowned both on and off the field, made the association explicit. "It's an incredible feeling. It's like your whole body is bursting with happiness. I guess there's only one thing in the world that compares with it." The celebration that follows a score serves as an opportunity to express heterosexual excitement. Dave Kopay, whose announcement of his homosexuality sent shockwaves through the world of football, recalled that "[a]fter a touchdown you will see men embracing on the field like heterosexual lovers in the movies." This investment in scoring and winning as a performance of masculinity shapes the team's sense of social solidarity, expressed in such signs of homosocial and homoerotic bonding as "patting each other on the ass."[41]

The purpose of the defensive team is to stop the offense from scoring. Most often the defensive strategy centers around stopping the run by "plugging" up holes in its line and disrupting the passing game. Fred Smerlas, one of the National Football League's preeminent "nose tackles" and a veteran of over a decade in the football wars, recounted suggestions from Buffalo Bill fans on what to call their defensive squad. One suggestion was "the Virgins" since "you can't score on them."[42] That suggestion was rejected, in part because of the sexual politics of football's discursive construction. Although the offense genders itself as male and the defense female, the defense refuses to accept this designation. Indeed the purpose of the defense is to invert this construction of the game. Aggressive defenses are not simply satisfied with standing their ground, defending their "virginity"; instead, they use images of emasculation and rape to describe what they would like to do to the offense. As Smerlas concludes, "we sure as hell don't need to be told what to do when we get to the man with the football. We want to search and destroy, splatter and trample, rape and pillage. After that, we *really* get nasty."[43] Invoking this rhetorical castration of the offense, defensive players focus on the primary ball-handler, tackling him before he passes or stripping him of the ball. Faced by an aggressive defense, which finds it difficult to stop even after the whistle has signaled the end of the play, quarterbacks themselves realize the danger. Using explicit images of violence, John Elway, Denver's star quarterback, has complained that defensive players have "cold-cocked" him, that is, tackled him after the play was over.

Elway's response, however, is not unusual because the castration and rape imagery employed by football coaches and players is fairly common. During the fall of 1992, Jackie Sherrill, the coach of the Mississippi State football team, achieved notoriety in the press by having a bull castrated in front of his players in order to motivate them for the game. Although such literal acting-out of the castration theme is eccentric, to say the least, football has had a long tradition of the use of such language in the locker room, beyond the reach of the television camera. "We were told to go out and 'fuck those guys,'" reported Dave Kopay.

> ... to take that ball and "stick it up their asses" or "down their throats." The coaches would yell, "knock their dicks off," or more often than that, "knock their jocks off." They'd say, "Go out there and give it all you've got, a hundred and ten percent, shoot your wad." You controlled their line and knocked 'em into submission.
>
> Over the years I've seen many a coach get emotionally aroused while he was diagramming a particular play into an imaginary hole on the blackboard. His face red, his voice rising, he would show the ball carrier how he wanted him to "stick it in the hole."[44]

Oddly enough football has been defended by some of its advocates as being a wholesome way to channel the sexual energy of male adolescents and young adults and as a counter to allegedly deviant sexual development.[45] Yet its didactic message seems to inscribe an ideology of heterosexist violence against those who are construed as being castrated and therefore powerless. Because the opponents constitute another group of men, emasculation is regarded as the necessary first step in order to ultimately impose dominion. This rite of masculinity results in the denigration of those who are considered less than "real men": women and male homosexuals. Winning is the sign of true masculinity; there is no substitute for winning. Nothing less will do since nothing less confirms the masculinity of heterosexist males in American culture. "A tie," once lamented Duffy Dougherty, the legendary coach of the University of Michigan Wolverines, "is like kissing your sister."[46] In a world where exogamous sexuality is the rule and incest is tabooed, "kissing your sister" cannot be read as a "real" sexual conquest. It does not provide the release that the sexual domination of the Other provides. Thus, coaches, players, and fans all hunger for victory, because in victory they feel themselves to be "men."

SOMEONE ASKED IF THAT'S A FOOTBALL OR A SCUD

Although college championship games, like the Rose Bowl, Orange Bowl, and Sugar Bowl, have always had considerable followings in the country, no football game surpasses professional football's Superbowl for sheer mass appeal. Founded in 1967 as a championship game between professional teams of the National and American Football Leagues, the Superbowl has become more than a sports contest or even a secular holiday. It has evolved into something of a holy ritual—a reflection of what it means to be an American.[47] Dick Enberg, a longtime sportscaster of football, has even suggested that "it's almost anti-American not to be a viewer of the Superbowl."[48] Followed by over half the households in America and hundreds of thousands of American troops in Saudi Arabia, Superbowl XXV represented a modern-day spectacle that, in the eyes of many, would reiterate the values for which this country was fighting in the Gulf. The fear that the game would have to be postponed or even cancelled due to the threat of terrorism caused alarm both at home and abroad. To many sports fans it seemed a sacrilege far more serious than the invasion of Kuwait. "You wouldn't cancel Christmas?" asked one American GI in disbelief.[49] Other commentators have attempted to put the Superbowl into perspective by dismissing hyperbolic comparisons to religious holidays, but there seems to be no doubt that even here the Superbowl functions as a ritual of American social solidarity. "It isn't Christmas or Easter or Thanksgiving," admitted one sports writer, "but it is parades and fireworks and parties to be thought about all year, a national celebration. It unites all religions, all faiths, and all ethnic groups, without regard to race, creed or color—or time zones. At kick-off time, we are all one people, plus or minus seven points."[50] In this view, widely shared among the male populace-at-large, the Superbowl is a rite of bonding that transcends time and space (even if spectators are halfway around the world in Saudi Arabia) and embodies the American identity. In a society marked by plural socioeconomic and religious realities and an ideology of radical individualism, this rite lodges in the interstices of difference as a pseudo-ontological ground, providing an ersatz iconography of resemblance. It is easy for spectators to slip from the language of sociology to the rhetoric of theology. "He who has not drunk deep of the virtues of football," wrote the conservative Catholic critic Michael Novak in his paean to the sport, "has missed one of the closest brushes with transcendence that humans are allowed."[51] In the eyes of many men, football (and the Superbowl as its quintessential expression) is a protological event that revalidates the multiple meanings of what it means to be an American—normatively speaking, an American male.

In the mass culture of hyperreality, the Superbowl as televised simulation has become a mainstay in the pattern of American consumption and in the construction of American male consciousness. Previous to Superbowl XXV, Nielson Media Research reported that sixteen Superbowls ranked among the forty highest rated scheduled programs in television history, including eight of the top fourteen. Only the *M*A*S*H Special* (1983), *Dallas* (1980), and *Roots* (Part VIII) have drawn larger audiences. The Superbowls in 1982, 1983, and 1986 counted among its viewers about forty-nine percent of all American households. Advertising during the broadcast of the Superbowl is the most expensive in the business at $850,000 for thirty seconds of airtime. As a reflection of the weight given to the "reality" of each event, it is worth noting that the press corps at the Superbowl, some twenty-two hundreds, was three times the number covering the war in the Gulf. This disproportional representation of the print media only confirms what has long been recognized within mass media: the Superbowl is an indispensible part of American identity.

Because of its crucial importance to American male consciousness, it was deemed unthinkable to cancel the spectacle, even though the country was at war. Because the conflict in the Middle East was depicted largely as a conflict of wills between the forces of democracy and the ambitions of a bloodthirsty dictator, it became imperative in the popular imagination that the United States show no weakness. Although the potential security risk seemed to be enormous, Robert Smith, the Tampa Safety Director (dubbed the "most interviewed man in town"), finally gave the nod to go ahead with the world championship between the New York Giants and the Buffalo Bills. The metaphor of football as a "war game" was to collapse into a militarized reality. The stadium itself became a salient in the defense of American consciousness. A six-foot high wire fence and a concrete barrier were constructed around the site. The gates were outfitted with metal detectors, aided by police-trained, bomb-sniffing dogs. Security personnel, including police, numbered over fifteen hundred, twice the figure normally allotted to the Superbowl. And airspace over the stadium was restricted, lest the nightmare of the Hollywood movie *Black Sunday* be repeated. The suggestion that "real" events had eclipsed the frivolty of the Superbowl was somewhat disingenuous because the exercise in collective effervescence was as real for football as for the war rally. The Superbowl "show" itself integrated both into a solemn celebration of Americanist virtues.

Harangued by hawkers plying such wares as Giant and Bills pendants as well as "Fuck Iraq" and "Sack Iraq" T-Shirts, spectators at the stadium—many waving American flags—participated in a pep rally for Operation Desert Storm. In a moment now fetishized on compact disc as a saleable commodity, Whitney Houston initiated the ceremonies with her rendition of the national anthem, dedicated to the troops in the Persian Gulf. Normally devoted to generic male Americanism with majorettes twirling batons to the sound of John Philip Sousa marching bands, the half-time activities focused on the war itself. Organizers of the event brought together "Children of Desert Storm," festooned with yellow ribbons, shaping their love for their parents into an ideological celebration of the military adventure abroad. One child provided a stirring tribute to their fathers and mothers in arms by momentarily suspending belief in the football hero as the exclusive American icon of courage. "Tonight the real heroes are in the Middle East protecting peace for all of us kids."

Lest this unusual displacement of football undermine its primacy in American cultural reality, the organizers immediately reinscribed the sport in male consciousness by orchestrating a flash card demonstration in the stands, designed to form the image of a huge American flag with the Superbowl number "XXV" set amidst the standard's field of stars. Iconographically the canton in the flag's design represents a new constellation in the heavens which marked the birth of the American experiment. And just as those stars transcend the earthly realm, so, too, does this new nation transcend both past and future. In the minds of most Americans, the "Stars and Stripes" symbolizes a transcendent reality—the "essence" of America—which is both eternal and sacred. Waving the totemic emblem of the nation reaffirms the values of that social order. The initialing of that field with the Superbowl's anniversary number XXV identifies football not only with the enterprises carried out under the aegis of the flag but with the protological founding of the country. Although the latter-day arrival of football, particularly as the sport of mass culture, negates its historical role in the origins of the United States, its ontic significance in the existence of this country as America is largely unquestioned. To most American males America would be inconceivable without football. Hence the identification of the National Football League as a commercial enterprise with the enterprises of the nation-state seemed almost natural.

It was no surprise that the half-time activities culminated in a telecast from the White House featuring George and Barbara Bush. Tying together the politics of war, football, and Americanist values, the president and the first lady commended all the participants and spectators, at the stadium and in American living rooms, for their roles in this "wonderful game." To the strains of "America the Beautiful" in the background, the president congratulated the "Children of Desert Storm" and reiterated that their "mothers and fathers, brothers and sisters . . . are the true champions, the true heroes in our country." The first lady graciously thanked the audience for permitting them to "interrupt" the half-time ceremonies—quite consciously planned around the rhetorical interruption—and to bring together the Bush family with all American families. Although unarticulated, her affirmation of "family values"—present in her person as a mother—identified the fate of those values both with the consumption of football and the outcome of the war. The presence of the Bush family contrasted sharply with the absence of family, symbolized by the "Children of Desert Storm" standing alone in the center of the football field. In that moment, the president and the first lady functioned as surrogate parents, bringing together that which had been so "unnaturally" torn apart. Although his name was unmentioned, the spectre of Saddam Hussein loomed large in the background as that which undermined families and attacked "family values": love, respect, security, order. The White House message implied the children would be protected by their president—the father of "Desert Storm." Yet no one was naive enough to assume that this temporary configuration of children and the first family could eclipse the relationship of these children with their real fathers and mothers. It was a rhetorical gesture designed to suggest that, as stand-ins, the president and the first lady were committed to keeping the family together in a time of crisis. But rather than seeing the war as the cause of this crisis, the political implications of the message left no doubt that the war itself, that had torn families apart, was a consequence of an evil dictator. The restoration of family was therefore contingent on the successful outcome of violent confrontation in the Gulf. Invoking God's love for all the participants and spectators as well as all "freedom-loving peoples" (apparently excluding Iraqis), the president closed with his benediction. The solemnity of the occasion thereby fueled an enthusiasm for the game itself which was assumed to boost the morale of the troops and magically assist them in the war effort. Cheering for a commercial sports team was deemed patriotic.

In a news update that "interrupted" the telecast with "real" news from the front—a layering technique of the hyperreal, ABC News anchor Peter Jennings confirmed the existence of these mantic aspirations. "In answer to one of the more obvious questions of the day," he assured his audience, "yes, men and women in the war zone have been able to see the first half." Although it is estimated that only 10 percent to 15 percent actually saw the game on television beamed via satellite from Tampa, most Desert Storm personnel followed the action on radio. In the midst of a foreign land, far away from home, the game appeared surreal to many members of the armed forces; yet, just as the spectators in the United States managed to close the gap between image and reality, foreign and domestic, so, too, did the Americans of "Desert Storm." Like their field general who was planning to execute the Coalition forces' "Hail Mary" play, American soldiers listened and watched with interest as coaches Bill Parcells and Chuck Knox unfolded their strategies, designed to secure victory on the football field. Most feared was the "long bomb" of Bills' quarterback Jim Kelly whose capacity to score deep was compared to Iraqi missiles. One *Sports Illustrated* reporter on assignment with the troops in Riyadh captured this analogy by quoting the remarks of soldiers in the aftermath of Kelly's touchdown strike to James Lofton, propelling Buffalo into a 12–3 lead. "Someone asked if that was a football or a SCUD."

Appropriately enough the commercials used during Superbowl XXV reinforced the ideological message evidenced by the half-time show. Accompanying the red-white-and-blue of the National Football League insignia at commercial breaks were commercials for soft drinks, automobiles, and beer—each with a patriotic theme. Although the Coca-Cola Company suspended its "normal" advertising campaign to announce the grant of $1 million to the U.S.O., thereby redoubling the televised game's assistance to morale among the troops, the commercial for Anheuser-Busch Brewing Corporation emphasized the Americanist values of the Protestant Work Ethic, based on aggressive domination of the environment and self-sacrifice—certainly a perfect read of a nation on war-footing. As the images of an eagle, a stallion, American workers and baseball players—caps solemnly held over the heart in the flag salute—appeared successively before the viewer, the male voiceover articulated what is deemed to be uniquely American: pride, ambition, and success.

> If I thought that no one cared about the things I do in life, well I'd still care about working hard and making it turn out right. "Made in America": that means a lot to me. I believe in America and American quality. Here's to you America. My best I give to you.

Oddly enough the "best" the spectator can give here is to consume another Bud. But consumption, whether it be ideology or commercial products, is what American mass culture is all about. The viewing of the game, like the drinking of beer, circulates the ethos of power through an androcentric body politic.

It Is More Like an Ordeal, an Exercise, a Struggle Lived Through

In football male spectators participate vicariously in a ritual of male bonding that renews their spirit and enables them to return with confidence to the walks of everyday life, anxieties about their masculinity temporarily banished. As Michael Novak has confessed in his *Joy of Sports*, it is so cathartic that sometimes it doesn't even seem to be a game.

> During the game my palms sweat; impossible to gain my attention seriously. (I play act.) After the game, I am exhausted. Entertainment? It is more like an ordeal, an exercise, a struggle lived through. And not exactly vicariously.[52]

In part Novak's experience, like that of other men in barrooms and living rooms around the nation, is caused by the immediacy of television; but the feeling of both excitement and exhaustion may also be ascribed to the nature of the game. David Meggyesy, a former linebacker for the St. Louis (now Phoenix) Cardinals, noted that the players were not oblivious to the "millions of Americans who watch football every weekend in something approaching a sexual frenzy."[53] The game cannot be viewed dispassionately by most American men because it is seen as an *agon*—a test of the individual American male's masculinity.

As if the excitement of watching televised football were not enough, the newest interactive computer technology now allows viewers to second-guess the calls of offensive teams, as actual football games are being played, through the NTN Interactive Programming Lineup. This state-of-the-art computer game QB1 puts the ball into the hands of the viewer and allows him to test his expertise against the pros. The sense of participation is no longer merely an hypothesis—an image of identification once deferred. The viewer is now a coach/player; points are accumulated when the viewer at home success-fully guesses the plays chosen by the quarterbacks or coaches. One analyst who tracks the latest developments in sports computer games openly com-pared the skills obtained through these interactive breakthroughs to the tech-nologies of war evidenced in the Gulf.[54] But, of course, one need not use interactive technology to participate in the war on the football field. The open-ended structure of the game that makes its outcome contingent on the exhibition of masculinist virtues—physical strength, courage, tactical knowl-edge, and a "never say die" attitude—pulls men into the play-by-play drama that unfolds before their eyes. And even the conservative Novak is willing to admit that the visceral dimension of spectating is linked to the "images we derive from the male genitalia: balls, get it up, thrust, holding, driving onward and so forth."[55]

To Novak football is an orgy of violence that he ascribes to men's "rage"— a reaction that is allegedly rooted in the violent natures of human beings, particularly men. Football is seen as the living rebuttal to liberals who be-lieve that human nature is either essentially good or that it is capable of reform. Football is the mythic performance of an unredeemable and quin-tessentially human flaw within the constraints of the social order. Yet, as a former radical, now turned neoconservative, Novak argues from a neo-Weberian position that the game has become a vehicle by which both the football players and their fans are acting-out their unresolved aggression toward the "authorities." It is the "rage" of nature against culture. What seems remarkably absent from Novak's conclusion is that the relationship between the gender-specific imagery of football and the object of rage is marked by a conspicuous ellipsis. It is assumed that women are tangential to this exercise in the masculinist imagination. They apparently have noth-ing to do with the game itself nor do they even seem to understand their male partner's obsession. Novak notes the consternation of his wife in watching her husband becoming transformed by his watching of a game. There seems to be an abyss between the sexes in Novak's analysis, yet, if the rage of nature is arrayed against culture, and women are the culture-bearers of domesticity in Novak's upper-middle class world, then it begs the question to ignore the relationship between the exercise of male violence and women. But to accept Novak's cursory dismissal of cultural explanations for the origin of violence is to overlook the complex constructions of rules and rhetoric that surround the game as a performance of masculinist identity. As the domestic counterpart to foreign war, the Superbowl invents a particular image of manliness which has frightening consequences for women, both abstractly in what it means to be female in an androcentric social order and concretely in the violence against women associated with the game.

Although the reports of domestic violence on the configuration of battering, football, and war suggest the tangible effect of male territorial games on women, the links among these masculinist practices remain obscure. Are women scapegoats for male frustrations and inadequacies? Is violence against women and gay men a spillover from male territorial games? That is to say, are they the unintentional victims of "collateral damage" derived from the competition among heterosexual males for dominance? Or are the civilian casualties of male territorial games like football and war no accident? Perhaps they bear witness to something at the heart of the cultural constitution of masculinist identity in American society. And if so, are there alternatives available to transform this identity that has so pervaded American life as to seem to many to be "natural?" It might be argued that there have always been tests of masculinity in Western patriarchal cultures, from the loss of virginity to the exercise of war. Yet, in a country which is suffering from an epidemic of domestic violence, in a society still dominated by a military-industrial complex, and in a male culture virtually obsessed with a phallocentric sport, why have such tests reached a crescendo? Although football and war are held respectively to be harmless or unfortunately necessary, they are neither benign nor rational. The manifest life of these male pasttimes betrays a complex latent origin that men barely perceive and women avert, either out of fear or incomprehension. The remainder of this book explores different theoretical models that may offer some insights into this compulsive behavior.

NOTES

1. Sigmund Freud, *Jokes and Their Relation to the Unconscious, The Standard Edition of the Complete Psychological Works of Sigmund Freud*, ed. & trans. James Strachey (London: Hogarth, 1974), VIII.

2. Vide, Ike Balbus, "Politics as Sports: The Political Ascendency of the Sports Metaphor in America, " *Monthly Review* 26, no. 10 (March 1975): 26–39.

3. "Plans for Small Wars Replace Fear of Big One," *New York Times,* February 3, 1992, A8.

4. Guy Gugiotta and Caryle Murphy, "Warplanes Roar Off in Darkness in 'Desert Storm,'" *Washington Post,* January 17, 1991, A27.

5. Jack Anderson and Dale Van Atta, *Stormin' Norman* (New York: Kensington, 1991), 123.

6. Kari Points, "Reporting Conventions Mask Sexual Politics," *Media and Values* 56 (Fall 1991): 19.

7. Philip Shenon, "Allied Fliers Jubilantly Tell of Early Control of the Skies as Iraq Planes Fled," *New York Times,* January 18, 1991, A10.

8. Tony Engelhart and Pat Foran, *Sword in the Sand: U.S. Marines in the Gulf War* (Hong Kong: Concord Publications, 1992), n.p.

9. Gugiotta and Murphy, "Jets Roar," 1.

10. Engelhart and Foran, *Sword in the Sand,* n.p.

11. Mark Fineman, "Smoke Blots Out Sun in Bomb-Blasted Basra," *Los Angeles Times,* February 5, 1991.

12. John Balzar, "Road to Hell, Kuwait to Basra Road," *New York Times,* February 24, 1991, A1.

13. *Newsweek,* Commemorative Edition (Spring/Summer 1991): 97.

14. *Newsweek,* Commemorative Edition, 40.

15. "Excerpts from Schwartzkopf News Conference on Gulf War," *New York Times,* February 28, 1991, A8.

16. Kari Points, "Sexual Politics," 19.

17. Quoted in *Sports Quotations: Maxims, Quips and Pronouncements for Writers and Fans,* ed. Andrew J. Maikovich (Jefferson, NC: McFarland, 1984), 74.

18. Arnold J. Mandell, *The Nightmare Season* (New York: Random House, 1976), 25.

19. Quoted in *Sports Quotations,* 76 and 94.

20. Kevin Nelson, *Football's Greatest Insults* (New York: Putnam, 1991), 93.

21. The aphorism was coined by Red Sanders, coach of the UCLA football team, in 1955. Quoted in *Sports Quotations,* 100.

22. Quoted in *Sports Quotations,* 71.

23. Quoted in *Sports Quotations,* 100.

24. Thesis VII, "Theses on the Philosophy of History," in *Illuminations,* ed. Hannah Arendt, trans. Harry Zohn (New York: Schocken, 1978), 256.

25. Quoted in *Sports Quotations,* 102.

26. Ira Berkow, "The Savage Pleasure of Football," *New York Times,* November 26, 1991, B11.

27. John McMurtry, "Kill'Em! Crush 'Em! Eat 'Em Raw!" in *The Norton Reader. An Anthology of Expository Prose,* ed. Arthur M. Eastman, 7th ed. (New York: W. W. Norton & Company, 1988), 400.

28. Keith Nelson, *Insults,* 171.

29. Tom Friend, "Blood Sport. Are There Ethical Limits to Violence on the Field?" *Sport,* December 1992, 30.

30. Michael Walzer, *Just and Unjust Wars. A Moral Argument with Historical Illustrations* (New York: Basic Books, 1977), 140.

31. Quoted in *Sports Quotations,* 68

32. Friend, "Blood Sport," *Sport,* 34.

33. Elayne Rapping, *The Looking Glass World of Nonfiction TV* (Boston: South End, 1987), 84.
34. Eugene Bianchi, "The Super-Bowl Culture of Male Violence," *From Machismo to Mutuality: Essays on Sexism and Woman-Man Liberation*, ed. Eugene C. Bianchi and Rosemary R. Ruether (New York: Paulist Press, 1976), 54–69.
35. Joe Klecko, Joe Fields, and Greg Logan, *Nose to Nose. Survival in the Trenches of the NFL* (New York: William Morrow, 1989), 19.
36. David Kopay and Perry Deane Young, *The David Kopay Story. An Extraordinary Self-Revelation* (New York: Arbor House, 1977), 50.
37. Vide, Naomi R. Goldenberg, "On Hockey Sticks and Hopscotch Patsies," *Returning Words to Flesh. Feminism, Psychoanalysis and the Resurrection of the Body* (Boston: Beacon, 1990), 42–57.
38. Marc Alain Deschamps, "Pour une psychoanalyse du sport," *Études psychothérapiques* 20, no. 3 (October 1989): 168–74.
39. Klecko, Fields, Logan, *Nose to Nose*, 18.
40. Quoted in Kevin Nelson, *Insults*, 54.
41. Kopay, *David Kopay Story*, 57.
42. Fred Smerlas and Vic Carlucci, *By a Nose. The Off-Center Life of Football's Funniest Lineman* (New York: Simon and Schuster, 1990), 216.
43. Fred Smerlas and Vic Carlucci, *By a Nose*, 26.
44. Kopay, *David Kopay Story*, 53–54.
45. Bianchi, "Super-Bowl Culture," 55.
46. Quoted in *Sports Quotations*, 95.
47. Joseph L. Price, "The Super Bowl as Religious Festival," in *Sport and Religion*, ed. Shirl J. Hoffman, (Champaign, IL: Human Kinetics, 1992), 13–16.
48. Quoted in Richard Sandomir, "Where the Roman Numerals Dance with the Dollar Signs," *New York Times*, January 31, 1993, 1.
49. Eric Schmidt, "Patriots vs. Scuds: Iraqi Touchdown is Averted," *New York Times*, January 27, 1991, L13.
50. Steve Jacobsen, "What Makes It So Super?" *Sports Illustrated*, (January 14, 1991) (special advertising supplement), n.p.
51. Michael Novak, *The Joy of Sports. End Zones, Bases, Baskets, Balls and the Consecration of the American Spirit* (New York: Hamilton, 1988), 86.
52. Novak, *The Joy of Sports*, 82.
53. David Meggyesy, *Out of Their League* (Berkeley: Ramparts, 1970), 146–47.
54. Cam Benty, "Sport's Video Game Review," *Sport* (December 1992): 78.
55. Novak, *The Joy of Sports*, 80.

Chapter 4

Four

SCAPEGOATING THE EMASCULATED:
SOCIAL PSYCHOLOGICAL MODELS
OF AUTHORITARIANISM AND
SACRIFICIAL VIOLENCE

> Violence is frequently called irrational. It has its reasons, however,
> and can marshal some rather convincing ones when the need arises.
> Yet these reasons cannot be taken seriously, no matter how valid they
> appear to be.
>
> —René Girard, *Violence & the Sacred*

IN WATCHING THE LASER-GUIDED "smart bomb" close in on its target or the quarterback's "long bomb" into the end zone, the male spectator is infused by the excitement of the moment. He catches his breath in anticipation of success or in fear of failure. For those fleeting seconds, "reality" is intensified in a way that eclipses the transitory routine of everyday life. These moments of "showdown" in both war and football, these experiences that so characterize the male imaginary, signal the suspension or bracketing (*epoké*) of ordinary existence—a pause or a digression from the clutter of minutiae found in professional and domestic life. It is an emptying of the accumulated experiences of mundane time, an opening in the surface of everyday existence, and an intensification of male experience so deep and so dense with affect as to be almost inexpressible. Bathed in a mystical aura, football and war become the stuff of male camaraderie in conversations on the job, at bars, and in the living rooms of America. The power of these tales provides a cross-generational language between fathers and sons, grandfathers and grandsons. The experience cannot be communicated directly but only can be transmitted in the retelling of those moments, glorious and tragic, that trigger an empathetic identification of men with their heroes of the gridiron and battlefield.

107

The allure of war and football frequently is met with incomprehension by women. Why men feel drawn to such passionate emotions is something of an enigma—a peculiar idiosyncracy of the gender that many wives, girlfriends, and mothers indulge with a sense of humor. Specifically drawing on the analogy of war, many women lament their fate as "widows" during the football season, destined to spend their Sunday afternoons and Monday nights alone. The ritual of these male territorial games seems unintelligible, a cypher of the male psyche. The etymology of the term "cipher" helps to unveil the depth of this mystery to women. Traced to the Arabic *çifr*, meaning a nought or zero, this designation for an "empty place" is the translation of the Sanskrit *sunya* or void. It is a void that remains a mystery to those who are not initiated into the rites of comprehension. To many women, football's meaning is obscure. Its violence is meaningless, even when the rules are explained by male partners. The visceral thrill that men experience on the football field or the field of combat equally dumbfounds many women. Yet this cipher is most assuredly not an absence. To the Indian imagination, reflected in the Hindu and Buddhist traditions, this void is the very foundation of existence. It embodies another order beyond the *maya* or illusoriness of everyday life.

In the male imaginary, these territorial games are likewise of another order—one that seems to transcend the world of home and hearth shared with women and children. Such games are not marginal to the society-at-large; they are enfleshed in the interstices of the culture. The rhetoric of politicians and the roar of the crowd suggest that male territorial games have their reasons, but, as the brilliant critic René Girard has reminded us, "these reasons cannot be taken seriously, no matter how valid they appear to be." It is reiterated that war may be undertaken to vindicate the national honor, to uphold international law, or to punish aggression or that football is merely for fun, but the cathected nature of these games suggests that beneath the rhetoric is a silence that holds secrets. What secrets do the interstices in the language of patriarchal culture hold?

What is cut off from understanding, what is held a secret (Latin, *se*, "away," *cerno*, "separate") calls for a deciphering. The riddle of male territorial games has been a mystery (Greek, *myein*) to which many have turned a "blind eye." One male acquaintance warned me that too close an examination would take the joy out of the game, and, while it remained unsaid in that context, I have sensed the fear that such ruminations could take the pleasure out of war, the sweetness out of victory. The temptation exists to close the book and return to an uninterrogated enjoyment of male territorial games wherein a privileging of sight makes a spectacle of the Other—the enemy, the rival, the emasculated. As a male in this society, I have experienced this temptation to turn away, to close my eyes for the sake of male camaraderie; yet, I also find it deeply disturbing. I have an uneasiness about the pleasure that so many men derive from witnessing the domination and destruction of other human beings, regardless of the higher purpose invoked. Football may well teach discipline and endurance; war may be necessary in some cases to defend the innocent and achieve some semblance of justice. But why should the battering and rending of the human body be so relished? Perhaps a change of focus is in order. In lieu of the spectacle of the Other, men need to make a spectacle of themselves so that what is hidden may be made manifest.

In a technological age, however, specular inquiry is unfortunately identified with a technical process. The ubiquitous camera in postmodern America allegedly exhausts the field of vision. Nothing remains a secret to this "manmade" eyewitness. Televised football games are marked by the presence of numerous cameras, situated to maximize shots of the action from every possible perspective, including reverse angles. Network coverage supposedly "uncovers" the "reality" of the game by appearing to be everywhere simultaneously—filming the formations from the second tier of the stadium, taking close-ups of the quarterback, shooting the action from both sides of the stadium, gaining access to the private exchanges of coaches and players on the sidelines and the referees on the field, and comprehending the entire event through shots from blimps high above the stadium. So, too, did television cameras catch the action during the Gulf War, from the ground fighting at Khafji in Saudi Arabia and the SCUD missile attacks in Riyadh and Tel Aviv to the spectacular bombing of Baghdad. Although news reporting was subject to censorship under the rules set by the Pentagon, Americans had the opportunity to watch hundreds of broadcast hours, analyzing the conflict in military, political, and economic terms.

Unlike Vietnam, the Gulf War comforted us with the illusion that nothing could remain hidden. The camera testifies to a desire to know absolutely everything, to be absolutely everywhere—as if technical enhancements would flush out the secrets of existence. That illusion could not be sustained in the jungles of southeast Asia, and hence it was important to efface the memory of Vietnam because of what it hid—not about the enemy, but about ourselves. The trauma of Vietnam, played out in the cultural wake of the war through such movies as *Apocalypse Now* and *Platoon*, suggested that in the "heart of darkness" we were confronting something frightening in the constitution of ourselves. It is for that reason that the Gulf War could not be another Vietnam.

In the deserts of the Middle East we could avoid introspection; we could fix our eyes on the clearly visible; we could avert our eyes from the mystery of masculinist culture. We could avoid thinking about the war and the reasons why we felt so entranced by it. Like the camera itself, we could focus on our targets, our enemies, and relish his destruction out in the open where there are no ghosts to haunt us, no doubts to plague us. But the "Vietnam syndrome," as President Bush called it, has not been exorcised. The president wished to banish those deep-seated insecurities "for good." "I think it's that I want to see an end," he ruminated after the cease-fire.

> You mention World War II. There was a definitive end to that conflict. And now we have Saddam Hussein still there, the man that wreaked havoc upon his neighbors. We have people unaccounted for—I just need a little more time to sort out in my mind how we—I can say to the American people, it's over, finally. Last "t" crossed, last "i" is dotted.

Anxiety was clearly evident in the president's remarks. It was as if the president wished to allay a crisis of confidence by inarticulately asserting a longed-for mastery over the enemy, over language (every "jot and tittle"), over himself. In doing so he only succeeded in making himself a spectacle that betrayed his insecurities even at the very moment of victory. The failure of the Administration to "finish the job" by removing Saddam Hussein from power highlighted the uncertainty that rests as the foundation to the male bravado of power politics. Indeed a continued state of anxiety is the only certainty in this world. Under the guise of pragmatism, machismo, and militarism thrive on the inexorable existence of the enemy, the Other. Even before a shot had been fired, the conservative *New Republic* attempted to allay the fear that a world could exist without enemies. "[R]est assured," claimed the editors. "History is not ended. Another Saddam will be along."[1] Politicians and generals may try to comfort themselves with the knowledge derived from the Gulf War that they have definitively proved themselves the masters, and, if called upon, they can do so again. Yet the "Vietnam syndrome" has not disappeared; it is merely temporarily forgotten. The fears that the jungles of Southeast Asia conjured up are the fears that still exist in the construction of the masculinist psyche. And it is in this context that we need to examine the reflection in the masculinist eye: how and why the image of the Other as emasculated exists.

As the ground on which a masculinist culture is renewed, male territorial games are the reenactment of an originary violence which establishes the parameters of the patriarchal order. It might be commonly objected that both the rules of war and the rules of the game precede these instances of male violence or that man's "natural" aggression is channeled, articulated, and exorcised within an existing framework. From a postmodernist perspective, the practice of male territorial games produces its antecedent, creates the memory that founds the present on a legitimized past. It is a reinscription of a founding violence, of a violence that founds itself, which is legitimated precisely because of its iterability. The violence of male territorial games is justified, not because it has always been that way, but rather it has always been that way because it is so now. Appeals (like that of Michael Novak) to the "natural" aggression of males as an explanation for male territorial games function as alibis for an anagnoretic violence which, as a performative tautology, creates the fundamental law of the culture.

As Walter Benjamin argued in his classic 1921 essay on the "Critique of Violence," societal law is underwritten by a "law-making violence" (*die rechstetzende Gewalt*) and a "law preserving violence" (*die rechtserhaltende Gewalt*).[2] The latter most often appeals to the former as the primal act that legitimates the exercise of power; yet, an archeology of "law-making violence" is rarely undertaken. The lawless character it exhibits before establishing itself as the law is shrouded in mystery, hidden in political ideologies or in appeals to the natural order. Male territorial games celebrate this founding violence of patriarchy through the signs of aggression and blood. Violence therefore underscores the community of men, a covenant binding males in a "cutting." That covenant is alive, the agreement is cut, the men are marked only insofar as the law announces itself in violence. The law therefore is predicated on the performance of violence. Its reality is made known through the male territorial games of ritual reinscription.

In a world dominated by patriarchal societies, war serves as the reminder of that power which rests as the foundation of the international order. The distribution of power is determined by international law, but that law is legitimated by its enforceability, by the willingness of existing powers under the United Nations to use "law-preserving violence." If war functions to reinscribe the legitimacy of the international law of patriarchal societies, then football serves to reinscribe a gendered sense of national community among American males. Neither is natural; both are manifestations of cultural artifice. Yet, such violence is not bloodless, either physically or metaphorically. The reinscription of the social order requires a sacrificial victim, someone whose blood effaces the threat of lawlessness that haunts patriarchal culture. For it is in the blood of the victim that the sovereignty of the law is written.

TYPICAL OF A HIGHLY INDUSTRIALIZED SOCIETY
WITH IRRATIONAL AND ANTIRATIONAL BELIEFS

"You know what football is to me?" once pondered the San Diego Chargers' coach Sid Gilman. "It's blood."[3] Gilman's comment reflects an attitude common to many coaches and players, and although the violence practiced on the field is in some respects restrained, the intent to punish one's opponent and the physical injuries suffered testify to the brutal seriousness with which the game is undertaken. During one play-off game last year, a lineman whose face was covered in blood appeared on the television. John Madden, the "color" commentator, remarked that it was the way a football player should look and his co-host Pat Summerall heartily agreed. On the gridiron echo the same sentiments as those on the battlefield. "[T]here was the whole militaristic aura surrounding pro football," recalled Dave Meggyesy, a former linebacker for the St. Louis Cardinals. "It is no accident that some of the most maudlin and dangerous pre-game 'patriotism' we see in this country appears in football stadiums."[4] Although only a game, football is no less real to the male imaginary. It avows an adversarial mentality that seeks to dominate, humiliate, and vanquish the foe and restore wholeness.

But whereas in football the opponents are established, indeed scheduled, war creates its opponents. Each nation is a potential adversary or potential ally, as America itself experienced in the aftermath of World War II wherein our enemies, the German and Japanese, became our friends, and our allies, the Russians and the Chinese, emerged as our newly anointed foes. The construction of the Other as being not only an opponent but both different and a threat is the object of propaganda. Yet as blatant as the manipulation of propaganda appears to be, it is a lie that frequently resonates comfortably with our construction of the truth. The foe is depicted as being beyond the pale, lawless, deranged, subhuman, and evil. As Edward Said's work has pointed out, Islam has long played such a role in the psychic economy of the West and embodies what Jean Baudrillard has called an *altérité irréductible*[5]—an image bathed successively in sensuality and puritanism, in materialism and asceticism.

Invoking the call to *jihad* and the memory of the Islamic victor Saladin, Saddam Hussein took on the appearance of a madman in the eyes of the West. In the face of the Coalition's overwhelming technological superiority, this irreducible alterity seemed less than rational. And through the scopes of high-tech bomb sights and marked out in "kill boxes" by grid coordinates, the enemy seemed less than human. Along the highway to Basra, the notorious "Road to Hell," one American pilot compared the slaughter to "shooting fish in a barrel,"[6] And one Marine Lt. Colonel described the experience as akin to "flipp[ing] on the light in the kitchen at night and the cockroaches start scurrying."[7] As if to reinforce this image of Iraqis as insects, the American company Orkin Pest Control sent a shipment of "Bug the Thug" bumper stickers to affix to American military vehicles.[8] The imagined threat to the human "us" was evident in this comparison of the enemy to vermin who spread filth and disease. The metaphor holds the alarming implication that the enemy is deserving of extermination.

This psychological tendency to divide the world between "us" and "them" along ethnocentric lines bears a resemblance to the "authoritarian personality" model, devised by scholarly professionals in the 1940s and 1950s to test the American public for susceptibility to fascist propaganda. Designed to explore the relationship between personality and prejudicial attitudes and practices, the project received the support of both the American Jewish Committee and the U.S. government and was staffed by such social psychologists and sociologists as Nevitt Sanford, Else Frenkel-Brunswik, and Daniel Levinson as well as the renowned scholar of critical theory, Theodor Adorno. Through the development of survey instruments, the E (ethnocentrism) and F (fascism) scales, the model sought to explain the resultant break between the conscious and unconscious layers in the personality of the high scorer.[9]

It was believed that the secret to anti-Semitism and racism in general lay in what was hidden by the unconscious: the ego-alien needs of the personality. According to psychoanalytic theory, this legacy is based on two dynamics of the parent-child relationship. On the one hand, the child regards itself as failing to live up to parental expectations, to be unworthy of parental love and respect. By introjecting parental images of authority in the form of a ruthless superego, the child seeks to punish itself; yet, it can do so only by projecting its own image of weakness onto others. Thus, the child will fulfill parental expectations only by annihilating its own unworthiness, now embodied in the existentially Other. On the other hand, the resentment of the child toward its parents for its perceived rejection is too dangerous to express in the context of a parental-child relationship. That hostility can only be disposed of through the withering hatred of outside parties. Both identification and resentment are accommodated through the construction of the existentially Other.

"Projection of one's inner impulses, particularly of aggression, onto others," wrote Frenkel-Brunswik, "will naturally lead to a conception of a dangerous and hostile world and consequently to a general suspiciousness of others."[10] The Other is read as a stranger or interloper within the midst of the national or international community who embodies a living threat to the authoritarian's existence. In his classic 1908 essay Georg Simmel described this construct of the stranger as "an element of the group itself, not unlike the poor and sundry 'inner enemies'—an element whose membership within the group involves both being outside it and confronting it."[11] Citing the same metaphor that President Bush was to use to characterize a world with Saddam Husseins, Frenkel-Brunswik identified the authoritarian's fear of the Other with the image of the "world as jungle."

This fear produced by the projection of anxiety over one's own life divides the world between ingroup and outgroup in such a way that the outgroup is characterized by stereotyping and homogeneity. As a defense mechanism, projection ensures the ego against a self-awareness of what is considered by the subject to be character flaws, that is, weaknesses or immorality.

(The notion that members of an outgroup evidence objectionable traits and all members of the outgroup are the same has little relation to the "specific nature of its object."[12]) This defense mechanism does not eliminate anxiety; instead, it externalizes it in a concrete object. "[M]ost essentially," claimed Levinson,

> outgroups are seen as *threatening* and *power-seeking*. . . . But the conflict is seen as permanent and unresolvable; the only alternatives are dominance and submission; justice requires dominance by the superior group, and the subordinate group will always remain resentful and rebellious.[13]

Most often, this intrapsychic tactic used to keep the ego intact has social and political consequences. Blaming the Other as the source of anxiety results in an "extrapunitiveness." Although the practical threat of the Other may be exceedingly limited or, as in the case of European Jewry, none at all, the authoritarian personality perceives the outgroup as a constant source of danger. Ethnocentrism is therefore logically paired with a second set of personality attributes, employed by the ingroup to maintain a vigilant watch over its boundary with the outgroup.

These traits include emphases on power and "toughness," anti-intraceptive tendencies (opposition to the subjective, tender-minded, and imaginative), pessimism, and violence, and an excessive and prudish concern with sexuality. The outgroup is perceived as being an aggressor who consistently tests the strength of purpose of the ingroup. And it is only through force of will and outright violence that the outgroup may be resisted. Although the origin of this "enemy" may be found in the projective processes of the authoritarian mind, anti-intraception suppresses critical awareness of this defense mechanism. Mystical determinants, superstitious beliefs, and stereotypic images all inhibit rational perception and discourse, thereby negating the possibility of any evidence contrary to the individual's solipsistic view. The authors of the study also theorized that, in the mind of authoritarians, outgroups are the locus of sexual deviance—practices in which ingroup members had a keen interest because such activities embodied their own sexual fantasies.

Coupled with these characteristics is a decided turn toward conformity on the part of ingroup members, a submissiveness to its leaders, and a wrathful aggressiveness toward its enemies, both foreign and domestic. The quest for complete identification with parental authority suggests that the authoritarian draws strength not from an autonomous ego but from outside the self. As an adult the individual seeks a substitute for the parents and therefore draws ego strength through submission to hierarchical authority. Social approval is garnered through a vigorous public advocacy of conventional morality. Conformity guarantees the vitality of the ingroup and all its members. Those who exhibit idiosyncratic behavior risk social ostracism and even expulsion from the ingroup as racially, politically, or sexually deviant. The individual's hatred of his own alleged "flaws" causes an irrational compulsive hostility and authoritarian aggression toward "outsiders" on whom these "flaws" can be projected.

This psychodynamically created enemy frequently is depicted in what seems to be contradictory fashion. On the one hand, the enemy is stereotyped as an abstraction so that all members of the outgroup might be depicted as sexually deviant, power-hungry, or, as the infamous Nazi propaganda film *Der Ewige Jude* alleged, vermin. On the other hand, the outgroup might be collapsed into one symbol through "personalization." "Here, the term assumes a very definite meaning," argued Adorno,

the tendency to describe objective social and economic processes, political programs, internal and external tensions in terms of some person identified with the case in question rather than taking the trouble to perform the impersonal intellectual operations required by the abstractness of the social processes themselves."[14]

The complexity of international politics and economics is simplistically reduced to the childlike level of the schoolyard.

The original study conducted in the 1950s found a number of surveyed groups in America who showed a marked inclination toward authoritarianism, among them a group of San Quentin prisoners and a California Republican women's club. The authors noted that authoritarian women repressed any attribute that may have been regarded as male and practiced an authoritarian submissiveness toward authoritarian men. The male ego-ideal of ingroups, on the other hand, was represented by a repudiation of any sign of softness and passivity; indeed, any characteristic that may have been perceived as being "feminine" was projected onto the outgroup, for example, their sensuality, emotionalism, irrationality. To the authoritarian male, neither he nor any of his leaders could be called a sissy. "The typical high-scoring man," wrote Frenkel-Brunswik, "apparently has a particular need to conceive of himself as an ideal of masculinity."[15] This "pseudo-masculinity," claimed the authors, camouflaged a deep resentment, if not outright hostility, toward women, although such feelings were carefully hidden behind conventional platitudes of respect for womanhood. The authors further noted that authoritarian men tended to come from homes marked by a high degree of father domination, whereas those who scored low on the E and F scales were raised in domestic environments heavily shaped by maternal influence.

Although the study was criticized in the 1950s for a distinctly liberal-left slant,[16] this model might be useful in reconsidering the rhetoric of the Gulf

War conflict. There seems to be some similarity between the characteristics of the authoritarian personality and the language employed by the president, military leaders, soldiers, news reporters, and many members of the American public-at-large. The depiction of Iraqis as being uncivilized, animals, indeed, in some cases, vermin, conjures up the classic distinction between the ingroup as the normatively human and the outgroup as subhuman. The distaste for Iraqis tapped into the long-held antipathy of Americans for Arabs in general who were held responsible for the oil crisis of the 1970s and the economic hardships of that period. It wasn't surprising that the cross-over from national group to racial identity appeared from time-to-time among American troops in various forms, including an avowed resentment of Arabic cultural codes of behavior that restricted the troops' activities and a deep suspicion of their Arabic allies' military prowess. At a Fordham University teach-in in New York in February 1991, one American journalist who had recently returned from the Gulf related his shock on seeing a mural painted on one of the hangers at the Dhahran American air base: the depiction of an American Superman throttling a skinny figure, eyes bulging, in clearly identifiable Arab dress. Noting that "there was no interaction between cultures," a U.S. Marine helicopter pilot later reported on the American troops' lack of respect for their Saudi counterparts, exhibited at the battle of Khafji.

> Guys who supported them said the Arabs would roll up about 20 tanks, shoot one round, toward the Iraqis, take a little fire and the 20 tanks would stop, put it in reverse and start coming back. . . . It got to the point where we would move a Marine battalion up behind them and not let them come back. So we were in support of them, uh, well, not quite.[17]

Although this hostility could not be expressed directly toward their Arab allies, this avowed resentment and desire for revenge could be channeled into the vilification of a "legitimate" enemy as a focal point of hatred: Iraqi society. The callous disregard for the lives of noncombatants was evident in the aerial attacks on the cities which reduced postwar Iraq to a "premodern" existence as well as in the unrepentant bombing of the Al-Ameriyah civilian air raid shelter, targeted by an American "smart bomb" and scored as a "direct hit." The civilian death toll from aerial bombardment has been minimally estimated to be ten to twenty-five thousand, excluding the noncombatants among the twenty-five thousand killed along the "Road to Hell" in the retreat of the Iraqi army from Kuwait. Dismissed by the Shermanian adage, "war is hell," civilian casualties were not to stand in the way of American war aims. The Bush administration saw the conflict largely as a test of will, that America would not be intimidated, that it would not be blackmailed, that the Gulf would not be another Vietnam. The president seemed obsessed with the importance of an American display of power and toughness.

In his September 11, 1990 speech on a "New World Order," he called for unity, since "our ability to meet our responsibilities abroad depends upon political will and consensus at home." Similar to authoritarian concerns for the solidification of the ingroup, the president appealed to fellow Americans to fall in behind his leadership and not to break ranks. But that consensus was not always forthcoming as was evident from the antiwar protests around the country and the massive demonstration two hundred fifty thousand strong against intervention in the Gulf on January 26, 1991. Consequently, as in the Vietnam era, antiwar protesters were sometimes depicted as being less than American, as being traitors to the ingroup. I recall quietly standing at a rally in Times Square one cold January day in 1991, listening to an antiwar speaker, when a group of conservatively dressed businessmen began screaming at the crowd, "Faggots! Perverts! Fucking queers!" I was surprised by the unprovoked vehemence with which I and other listeners were attacked. It seemed as if the presence of the antiwar rally was taken as a personal affront to these men. To those individuals it was clear that anyone who would give an ear to antiwar arguments was, in their minds, sexually "deviant." It implied that those males opposed to the war were, like our Saudi allies, "cowards" and that "real" Americans, whether on the battlefield or in the barrooms, would have to do the fighting for us. That conclusion was articulated in the expression of homophobic fears over sexual dominance.

The *ad hominem* character of the attack was consistent with the tenor of discourse set by the administration. The president himself cast war rhetoric in personal terms: the enemy was symbolized by Saddam Hussein who was portrayed as the reincarnation of Hitler. The war became less a conflict over the international political order and the distribution of economic resources and more a metaphysical battle between the forces of good and evil. It was Saddam's army, Saddam's nuclear capacity, Saddam's chemical weapons, Saddam's rape of Kuwait. The rhetoric of the war implied that the president had little tolerance for diplomatic give-and-take, little understanding of the history of Iraq-Kuwait relations, little sympathy for the pressures on the Iraqi economy. Instead there would be no compromise. Saddam had simply gone beyond the pale of humanity—a fatal step that, in the mind of the President, had shown to the world what he really was: a monster to be destroyed.

All of these characteristics are reminiscent of the attributes of the authoritarian personality: the tendency to divide the world between "us" and "them"; to stereotype the outgroup; to homogenize individual members of the outgroup as all being the same; to personalize the enemy; to interpret conflict as a test of power and toughness; and to project the ever-present danger that the world represents to the ingroup. On the other hand, certain elements of the theory were conspicuous by their absence in the Gulf conflict.

Although the resentment against Arabs in general was widely felt in the American populace, the Bush administration took pains to distinguish between Arab allies and the Iraqis. The outgroup was not one constituted by race, but by nationality, and even this identification was further complicated by the administration's distinction between the Iraqi people and its leader. Although it may be argued that "surgical bombing" and "smart bombs" were alibis for the heinous destruction of the Iraqi socioeconomic infrastructure necessary for the continued existence of the Iraqi noncombatant population, the Bush administration and the Coalition field command claimed that the enemy was Saddam Hussein and his army, not Iraqi civilians. If the administration had been truly motivated by authoritarian compulsions, would it not seek the open bombing of cities, as the U.S. administration had done in Germany and Japan during World War II? Critics of the Bush administration claim that in addition to attacks on the Iraqi infrastructure (roads, bridges, water pumping stations, communication centers, power plants, and sewage facilities), the Americans also "intentionally bombed and destroyed civilian life, commercial and business districts, schools, hospitals, mosques, churches, shelters, residential areas, historical sites, private vehicles and civilian government offices."[18] Although the report alleges that the American military intentionally undertook indiscriminate bombing to terrorize the Iraqi population, the administration took shelter behind just war theory's "law of double effect": that the consequences of "collateral damage" were foreseen but not intended. Were these claims by the American political and military leaders disingenuous, designed to mislead the public about the war? Or were these claims, as questionable as they might be, sincere? If it were the former, could this disingenuousness be taken as evidence of authoritarianism? Would authoritarians attempt to camoflage their vilification of an outgroup, for example, an entire people?

Admittedly the president framed the confrontation with Saddam Hussein personally in terms of a test of will and did not exercise the patience to determine if economic sanctions would force an Iraqi withdrawal from Kuwait. Yet the ultimate aim of Operation Desert Storm was not the complete destruction and extermination of the Other. On the contrary much to the consternation of many Americans, the American military drive stopped short of the capture of Baghdad. And although the administration apparently had attempted to eliminate Saddam at the very beginning of the war and hoped that he might be in that Baghdad bunker in which over four hundred lives were lost, President Bush did not call for the unconditional surrender of Iraq or the execution of its leader. Such would not be the case with an authoritarian personality. "As long as anything different survives," wrote Adorno, "the fascist character feels threatened, no matter how weak the other being may be."[19] When the cease-fire was called in February 1991, Saddam Hussein was still in command and managed during the ensuing civil strife to consolidate his power. It seems that many of the classic characteristics of this social-psychological model were simply not present in the Gulf conflict. Moreover, does the theory of the authoritarian personality account for the castration and phallic imagery that pervades the discursive construction of male territorial games?

According to its designers, this model is "typical of a highly industrialized society with irrational and anti-rational beliefs."[20] Most would not argue with the claim that the discursive castration of the enemy is antirational — in fact, doubly so. It is not only that the rhetoric evidences an irrational compulsion to turn the enemy into a woman, but, since the rational faculty in the patriarchal West has been identified with *logos spermatikos*, that is, a gendered "seminal" reason, the "unmanning" of the foe transforms the enemy into a creature devoid of reason, a "woman." This patriarchal turn of phrase, this "unmanning," is therefore irrational in both form and content. It irrationally creates the irrational to legitimate its own masculinist prejudice. But can the emasculated Other—the enemy as "woman"—be classified as an outgroup according to the authoritarian personality schema? The feminist critic Susan Griffin seems to suggest as much in her book *Pornography and Silence: Culture's Revenge Against Nature*.

In lieu of the authoritarian personality, Griffin has substituted what she calls the "chauvinist mind." This chauvinist mind clearly thrives on the domination, enslavement, silencing, and death of women who serve as a screen for the projection of the male's fear of nature. In this respect Griffin's theory embraces a similar psychodynamic to the authoritarian personality model. "For the pornographic mind and the racist mind are really identical," she writes, "both in symbolic content and in the psychological purposes of the delusionary systems they express."[21] Griffin points out that pornography frequently enlists anti-Semitic and racial stereotypes to elicit a sexual response. Nazism is a particularly popular and prevalent signature in pornographic films. Women, like blacks and Jews, are often described as being physically and mentally inferior, cunning and untrustworthy, stupid and lazy, deserving of discipline, pain, torture, and even death. Perhaps the description of women as an outgroup can explain the psychodynamic reason for the discursive castration and domination of the enemy as a "woman."

Despite the temptation to explain the hostility toward women evinced in the constellation of domestic violence, football, and war through the application of the authoritarian personality model to American men, this conclusion suffers from certain flaws. Daniel Levinson argued that "Jews, Negroes, lower socio-economic classes, labor unions, political radicals, communists, catholics, artists, intellectuals, Oklahomans, Japanese, pacifists, Filipinos, Mexicans and homosexuals"[22] all have been perceived as being outgroups, but nowhere do the authors call women as a class an outgroup. Moreover the use of castration and phallic imagery by authoritarians is notably absent in their study. There may be repressed hostility toward women, but there is no evidence that the foe must *of necessity* be rhetorically turned into one in order that hostility be expressed through violence. It is true that the authors noted the excessive concern of authoritarians about "sexual goings-on"—a concern shrouded in moral disapproval, yet that description does not fit the lewd and vulgar language so common employed in male territorial games.

Although the authoritarian personality model has been a useful tool to detect antidemocratic sentiments in a formally democratic society, the model does not seem to fit the rhetorical character of male territorial games, perhaps in part because it preceded the "second wave of feminism" heralded by the appearance of Simone de Beauvoir's *Second Sex*. In that sense this theory seems somewhat anachronistic—a model that explains the psychodynamics of right-wing authoritarianism which threatened the world during the 1930s and 1940s but which fails to engage what was and remains the norm in American society: patriarchal culture. To be sure, times have changed. Patriarchal culture has been challenged intellectually and culturally through the advent of feminism(s), even if politically and economically women still remain largely disempowered. That shift suggests that an adequate social-psychological model must engage the male imaginary of contemporary American masculinist culture in which woman appears as the Other, the enemy, the living embodiment of the male's greatest fear, castration. In war and football the emasculated are held guilty as objects of hatred, as subjects to be dominated, as beings whose blood is to be shed. The constellation of battering and male territorial games requires a theory that explains the logic of a sacrificial victim.

IN DESTROYING THE SURROGATE VICTIM, MEN BELIEVE THAT THEY ARE RIDDING THEMSELVES OF SOME PRESENT ILL

In his 1972 work *Violence and the Sacred*, René Girard argues that violence is an inevitable part of social life. It embodies the power to maim and kill members of any society and threatens the very fabric of the social order. Violence cannot be suppressed; it can only be redirected. For the sake of the body politic, it must be vented in a way that expends its destructive power and terminates the potential for a never-ending spiral of violence. Due to the kinship structure of human societies, violations of the person or property of a clan member trigger a violent response by the victim's family of equal or greater proportion. This "reciprocal violence" obligates the family of the new victim/s to react in a like fashion, resulting in an ever-building crescendo of violence that threatens the very foundation of the society. The rule of reciprocity leads not to chaos and anarchy but rather to the inexorable logic of lawlessness.

Human society is caught in a double-bind: all members are bound by the essential "fairness" of retributive justice. It is not to be mistaken for the "law of the jungle," for that paradigm is founded on the appropriation of a Darwinian "survival of the fittest." The application of the Darwinian model to the human condition has an aura of amoral, aggressive individualism. Girard, instead, theorizes an essentially moral foundation to lawlessness. But that very moral obligation, undertaken to preserve the clan, menaces the welfare of the society as a whole and thereby undermines the clans that these violent actions seek to preserve. It is therefore the ethos of the culture that threatens its very destruction.

Human culture is thus presented with a fundamental challenge: how to uphold its essentially moral and deadly sense of obligation and yet preserve the life of the society as a whole. Girard understands this challenge as a structural, not a psychological, problem. "We are not dealing with the sort of repressed desires that everyone is really eager to put on public display," he argues.[23] He finds no need to have recourse to the "unconscious" of psychoanalysis nor do scholars have to create a "death instinct" (*Thanatos*) that Freud postulated in his 1922 work *Beyond the Pleasure Principle*. Violence is inevitable, yet its origin is not in an aggressive drive (*Trieb*) but in mimetic rivalry. Human beings are marked by their propensity to imitate. As children they imitate their elders in order to make a mature social pattern their own; as adults they imitate others who enjoy the respect of their peers and possess those attributes and goods that are valued in the society. Violence between societal members over status or possessions is not a product of desire, claims Girard, "rather, *the subject desires the object because the rival desires it*."[24] Violence therefore originates in social relationships marked by envy. Envy produces violence. Desire is a product or sign of that violence. Girard argues that the validity of this analysis is demonstrable from the fact that the spiral of violence in human societies far eclipses that which may be caused by simple animal aggression.

Precisely because it is not a result of instinctual aggression, this spiral of violence is potentially devastating. Using the language of a medical model, Girard names this violence an infection. And like any virus or bacteria, this infection has the possibility of becoming a contagion, raging out of control and destroying the cells that compose the body politic. Girard suggests that modern medicine has discovered in human biology a basic principle that has long worked in human societies: the infection is both the disease and the cure. For just as an inoculation can inhibit the spread of infection, so, too, can violence itself be a cure for violence as a disease. "Only violence can put an end to violence, and that is why violence is self-propagating. . . . The aim is to achieve a radically new type of violence, truly decisive and self-contained, a form of violence that will put an end once and for all to violence itself."[25] The structural problem of violence in human culture therefore can only be resolved by resorting to violence as a "preventive measure."

In Hebrew and Hellenic cultures, Girard found a form of social inoculation in the guise of the scapegoat or sacrificial victim (Hebrew la'ăzā'zēl or Greek *pharmakos*). In Hebrew folk culture, codified by the priestly tradition in Leviticus, the scapegoat is one of a pair, chosen by lot, ritually burdened with the transgressions of the people and released into the wilderness of the demon Azazel (Lev. 16). It is believed that the animal was driven over a cliff to its death in order to expiate the sins of the community. The scapegoat therefore was created in the stead of those individuals, bound to the covenant, who in transgressing the law deserved death. Through the sacrifice of the scapegoat, "society is seeking to deflect upon a relatively indifferent victim, a 'sacrificeable' victim, the violence that otherwise would be vented on its own members, the people it most desires to protect."[26]

Most assuredly, the scapegoat functions as a surrogate for the originally intended victim, held to be guilty in the eyes of those whom s/he has violated. But the substitution of a surrogate for the original transgressor is more than the proxy for an isolated act of vengeance. As a social inoculation to prevent a societalwide contagion, the sacrificial victim bears the guilt of all transgressors and is subject to "hostilities that *all the members of the community feel for one another*."[27] This social catharsis of violence was also evident in Hellenic culture, according to Girard, where the animal was replaced by a human being. The *pharmakos*, or sacrificial victim, was publicly displayed and dragged through the streets as if to absorb the animosities that pervaded the society. Girard points here to the etymology of *pharmakon* which in classical Greek means both poison and remedy. As the carrier of social transgression, the *pharmakos* signified the source of reciprocal violence that poisoned the entire *polis*. It was only in the expiation of transgression and the expulsion of violence through the murder of the sacrificial victim that a remedy could be found. The substitution of the scapegoat (*le bouc émissaire*) for those originally villified signifies more than the transference of affect; it is "a veritable system of representation"[28] which ensures the integrity of the community itself.

Scapegoating as a structural mechanism functions magically in two ways. As an object of homeopathic magic, the surrogate victim must bear the markings of the original transgressor. Without sharing the signs of the mimetic rival, the scapegoat is an unsuitable substitute for the transfer of affect. As the *Doppelgänger* for the original transgressor, the *pharmakos* not only bears the responsibility for specific transgressions of the mimetic rival; the scapegoat becomes the essence of transgression itself. Once this substitution has taken place in the imagination of the populace, the original contagion is both reversed and transformed. Whereas violence had spread throughout the body politic from the site of infection, that is, the original transgressor, it now recedes in the wake of the murder of the surrogate victim, and the contagious magical power of social immunization spreads throughout the society, thereby guaranteeing the health of the community.

The effectiveness of this collective exercise in magic is contingent on a precarious balance of anamnestic memory and amnesia. On the one hand, the scapegoat must appear to have the same characteristics as the original transgressor. Significant divergence might make the exchange of the surrogate victim for the original transgressor unrecognizable, and therefore the sacrifice would not be an efficacious substitute. On the other hand, any consciousness of this act of exchange must recede. In other words, the visceral sense of the surrogate's authenticity must necessarily eclipse awareness of this ritualized sleight of hand. *Too much memory* defuses the expression of the original violence. The victim is recognized as a phoney. If then the substitution is too obvious, the power of collective outrage dissipates. *Not enough memory* desymbolizes the surrogate victim. The scapegoat becomes just another individual. "Sacrifical substitution," claims Girard,

> implies a degree of misunderstanding. Its vitality as an institution depends on its ability to conceal the displacement upon which the rite is based. It must never lose sight entirely, however, of the original object, or cease to be aware of the act of transference from that object to the surrogate victim; without that awareness no substitution can take place and the sacrifice loses all efficacy.[29]

The violent unanimity of the community is therefore contingent upon the selection of and attitude toward the surrogate victim. The victim must appear similar to the original transgressor by bearing or being made to bear similar characteristics. These signifiers are recognized in the person of the scapegoat; however, if the scapegoat is too similar to the original transgressor, the community risks the return of reciprocal violence and the social inoculation will fail. Thus, the scapegoat must also be recognizably different— that is to say, no links between the surrogate victim and the society-at-large can exist. To insulate the community from the risk of a return to reciprocal violence, a further step is taken.

The second, the only truly "ritualistic" substitution, is superimposed on the first. It is the substitution of a victim belonging to a predetermined sacrificial category for the original victim. The surrogate victim comes from inside the community, and the ritual victim comes from outside; otherwise the community might find it difficult to unite against it.[30]

Most often the social estrangement necessary for the efficacy of the sacrifice is ensured by drawing the ritual victim from categories designated as alien to the normatively human community, that is, those comparable to animals. Girard points to such classes of human beings in ancient societies as slaves, foreigners, criminals, women, and children. Once these categories of sacrificial victims are established, the selection of the particular victim can be made.

Girard's theory suggests that woman as the scapegoat in patriarchal cultures is neither accidental nor reducible to male biological aggression. The victimization of women serves the purpose of siphoning off the violence among men that would otherwise threaten the well-being of the homosocial community. Women qua women, as the embodiment of both transgression and difference, are *chosen* as targets of male violence. The life's blood of patriarchal culture is therefore predicated on the spent blood of its women or those metaphorically regarded as such. But in order to apply Girard's model to the misogynist practices of war, battering, and other sports, several questions need to be addressed. How does the death of the scapegoat have the power to redeem the homosocial community from its transgressions? Why have women become the primary category of sacrificial victim in modern, secular societies? And what is the connection between the depiction of "woman as the enemy" in ritualized male territorial games and the battering of women in American homes?

LES CHOSES CACHÉES

Although the scapegoat may be charged with a particular crime, the victim is guilty by virtue of being a member of a sacrificial class. "The persecutors," warns Girard, "do not realize that they chose their victim for inadequate reasons, or perhaps for no reason at all, more or less at random."[31] The scapegoat may or may not be guilty of the particular crime, but that judgment is irrelevant to the function that the victim plays. The scapegoat is mythically guilty and therefore in the eyes of the community is in fact guilty. The community-at-large comes to believe that the scapegoat is a "troublemaker" and that the violence that pervades the society is his or her responsibility. The victim therefore gets what s/he deserves. Once the victim is identified as a member of the sacrificial class, little or no evidence is needed by the community to be convinced of the allegations. Indeed evidence to the contrary is irrelevant; the scapegoat is tautologically guilty. "In destroying the surrogate victim, men believe that they are ridding them-selves of some present ill. And indeed they *are*, for they are effectively doing away with those forms of violence that beguile the imagination and provoke emulation."[32] In the eyes of the community, the relief that the ex-orcism of violence brings confirms their illusory suspicions of the scape-goat's guilt. This thinly veiled yet arbitrary process for the selection of the surrogate victim ensures that the scapegoat will symbolize the object of hatred for the entire community.

As a liminal creature of the communal imagination, the scapegoat both establishes the boundary between similarity and difference, identity and otherness, and passes back and forth between these states of being. The admixture of these two states—an impossible possibility—simultaneously induces feelings of both fascination and revulsion. Insofar as the victim transcends the normatively human, this offspring of the imagination is a "monstrous double,"[33] an abomination whose very being exudes transgres-sion. At the same time, the scapegoat's very inhuman qualities mesmerizes the community. As a monster (Latin *monstrum*), it wields the authority of the divine. It is a suspension of the "natural law," that is, one predicated on reciprocity. It is a miracle that redeems the community from its own vio-lence, which does what the community itself cannot do, by making that violence its own. "Because the victim is sacred, it is criminal to kill him—but the victim is sacred only because he is to be killed."[34] In that murder the spiral of violence collapses in on itself and is extinguished.

This performative tautology hallows the scapegoat as the *numen,* the di-vinely transcendent whose power is based on its own violation, its own sacredness. The attitude toward the victim undergoes a reversal, for the sa-cred is reverenced as well as condemned and feared. As the sacred, the victim's holiness lies in its woundedness. The scapegoat is made holy through the spilling of his or her blood. The ritual victim is therefore the sine qua non of the community for, without the substitution of the scapegoat's vic-timization for the reciprocal violence of mimetic rivalry, the community could not survive. The punishment of transgression through the sacrifice of the ritual victim establishes the very law of transgression that is binding on each and every member of the social order. It is a law inscribed in the blood of the victim and in the consciousness of every human. The human being is still motivated by mimesis, but in the aftermath of sacrifice it is an inverted imitation, one oriented toward not doing what the sacrificial victim allegedly did. The murder of the ritual victim is the foundation of the ethos of a revitalized culture. The ritual slaughter of the victim is therefore not a barbaric residue of inhumane superstition but the very essence of a human-izing social mechanism: religion. Religion without the shedding of blood is no religion at all because it cannot save humanity from its own destructiveness. It only "humanely" condemns the community to the descent into a ceaseless barbarism of mutual slaughter. It is more than the "empty" belief in a transcendent dimension, for its transcendence is made real, its saving power is manifest, only in the sacrifice of its victim. It cannot be rationally understood for to do so demystifies the magical relations of substitution and contagion on which its power is based. Religion is therefore real only insofar as it is misunderstood. Its effectiveness is predicated on ignorance.

In the context of Western culture, it is only logical that Girard's theory leads inevitably to a form of Christian triumphalism. For the promise of religion—the exorcism of violence—is manifest in the *Agnus Dei*, the sacrificial lamb, who as the Christ of the Western theological tradition, died *pro nobis*. (John 1:29: "The next day, seeing Jesus coming toward him, John said, 'Look, there is the lamb of God that takes away the sins of the world.'") As Girard argued in his 1978 book *Des choses cachées depuis la fondation du monde,* Christianity reveals the fundamental truth of all religions: the central role of the scapegoat. Although it may sound sacrilegious to some Christians, Girard suggests that the part played by Jesus as the "lamb of God" is not unique. The passion narratives of the synoptic gospels repeat an ancient pattern, albeit one that human beings have hitherto not understood. It is a pattern "hidden since the foundation of the world," in the very structural dynamics of human culture.

The Hebrew scriptures relate paradigmatic stories of this dynamic, for example, the Genesis myth of Cain and Abel. This story mythically recounts the "first murder" precipitated by the jealousy of Cain. As a nomadic shepherd, Abel sacrifices to God the blood of the first-born offspring from his flock of sheep which allegedly is deemed more pleasing than the agrarian Cain's offerings of the fruit of the earth. In a rage Cain murders his brother. From the standpoint of *les choses cachées,* the blood relation of Cain and Abel indicates that both came from the same community. But where Abel's sacrifice of the lambs is depicted as the cause of violence, the myth may be reread through the lens of ritual sacrifice as its effect. The blood of the lamb is Abel's—a victim of collective violence by the clan associated with Cain. Although the persecutors hold the victim *qua* victim guilty, the narrative serves the function of projecting and eliminating the transgressions of the community. The murder or blood sacrifice frees the community from the conscious burden of its guilt, hidden from view by its mythic expiation. Because the death of the victim is the sine qua non for the reconstituted and now innocent historical community, the remembrance of these events is shrouded from conscious awareness by the communal identification with the innocent victim rather than his guilty persecutors. Redemption from communal transgressions depends on a forgetting of the mechanics of expiation. Girard concludes that "Abel is only the first in a long list of victims exhumed by the Bible and exonerated of culpability which is often imputed to them by the entire collectivity."[35]

In recalling the blood of the innocent Abel, as reported in Matt. 23:35, the Jesus of early Christian portraits compares his own impending fate to that of the first victim—unjustly accused by the community-at-large. The victim is held to be guilty, condemned by representatives of the body politic (Pontius Pilate and Herod) and the religious authorities of his own community (Pharisees and Sadducees). Of course, these charges of treason and blasphemy on their face are false. The victim is, in this sense, innocent. However, Jesus becomes the screen on which transgression—or what the gospels call "scandal" (Greek, *skandalon*)—may be projected.[36] Girard interprets scandal as the "stumbling-block" of mimetic rivalry (envy, jealousy), whose private character metamorphosizes into public controversy by virtue of the displacement of anger from the mimetic rival to the ritual victim. Jesus as the Christ is a scandal because he is made to be so. He is made to embody all scandals, all instances of mimetic rivalry, which are interchangeable and impersonal. But it is this very dynamic, contends Girard, that is satanic. He interprets this cosmological figure, introduced as "the adversary" in Job 1:7, as "the Accuser." Satan therefore metaphorically embodies the communal projection of mimetic rivalry onto the innocent victim. It is the satanic power of human culture—indeed, the very nature of the human political order—to dispel its violence unjustly. It is the Satanic power of human culture to depict the victim as guilty, evil, indeed as Satanic, as the bearer of accusations. The text of Job (1:12) promises that the power of Satan is not unlimited, that the innocent will be redeemed; however, it is clear that the redemption of the innocent only occurs *ex post facto,* after the victimization has occurred. Be it Abel, Job, John the Baptist, Jesus, or countless others, named and unnamed, victimization exorcizes the violence that threatens to burst asunder the entire community.

According to the Christian tradition, Jesus' guilt is true in another sense. For although Jesus may not be guilty of the political or religious crimes of which he is accused, that is, the usurpation of political and religious authority as "King of the Jews," he is in the Christian theological tradition guilty of being "fully human." The new covenant that binds the Christian community together is based on a blood sacrifice called for by the failure of humans *qua* humans to fulfill the Mosaic law. The Sinai covenant (*berith*) was "cut" with a divine warning of sacrifice: just as the blood of the sacrificial animal is shed, so shall it happen to those who disobey the law (Exod. 24:8). The blood of the Christ does not restore the old covenant but rather establishes the new for it is an originary violence. In that he is God-man, the Christ is both similar and different: similar in that he is "fully man"; different in that he is "fully God." He bears all the markings of the human and drinks the cup of suffering to its dregs; yet his radical difference ensures against reciprocal violence. His sacrifice makes members of the Christian community holy and thereby obligated to avoid the transgressions for which he has already paid with his life. The nonviolence of the Christian community is therefore written in the blood of the savior. "Once you were alienated from God and were enemies in your minds because of your evil behavior. But now he has reconciled you by Christ's physical body through death to present you holy in his sight, without blemish and free from accusation" (Col. 2:21–22).

The political and religious orders are based on untruth: the alleged guilt of the innocent. But, through the blood sacrifice of the victim, they are redeemed despite themselves. According to Girard, the Christian faith, on the other hand, is based on truth: the forgiveness of all transgression and the injunction to go and sin no more. Truth redeems humanity from untruth. "To follow Christ," Girard concludes, "is to renounce mimetic desire."[37] It is a truth not of this world, not of the extant political and religious orders. But whereas in pre-Christian religions the dynamic of substitution is shrouded in mythology, the Christian orthodox reading of the Bible demythologizes religion and makes plain what had been obscure. The story of the risen Christ exposes to light that which has been "hidden from the foundation of the world"—the mechanics of mimetic expiation. Girard's Christian triumphalism is not merely the overpowering of Satan. Jesus is *Christus Victor* because he undoes the power of Satan which is contingent on shrouding the dynamic of scapegoating in secrecy. Because the message of Christ exposes the untruth of scapegoating, it breaks the hold of mimetic rivalry. It is a revolutionary knowledge because human beings can no longer vow their ignorance of the victim's innocence. By revealing the lie of satanic persecution, it is incumbent upon human beings to change, to give up the flawed morality of retributive justice and to aver mimetic rivalry. It is for that reason that Satan tempts Jesus with "all the kingdoms of the world" (Matt. 4:8) for to compromise Jesus would be to undermine his authority in exposing the lies of the "Accuser." But, as Girard argues, it is Jesus' resistance to temptation that establishes his authority—an authority that Jesus preserved through his willingness to be the last scapegoat and which he granted to his disciples in the Great Commission (Matt. 28).

IF YOU THINK FOOTBALL IS A VIOLENT LITURGY, REFLECT UPON THE EUCHARIST

This triumph of Christianity encountered certain risks. The power of ritual sacrifice, including Christ's own, to exorcise violence was predicated upon a degree of misunderstanding. The victim was identified with not only the original transgressor but all transgressors in the community—in fact with the very meaning of transgression itself. Moreover the violent nature of the ritual sacrifice ensured both the exorcism of violence and the transfiguration of the victim. Conscious awareness of the process of substitution tends to undermine the collective transfer of affect onto the ritual victim. In articulating the course of substitutionary atonement, the Christian theological tradition risked the very principle that it embodied. The rational explanation of the Logos held forth the temptation to mistake reason for the performative *metanoia* of sacrifice. Together the theological exposé of scapegoating and the decline of Christian ritual in an increasingly secular West exposed the social order to the illusory dream of rational control over mimetic rivalry and reciprocal violence, evident in Enlightenment ideals and the scientific/technological revolution. It tempted human beings with the thought that they could do away with scapegoating altogether, *including* its paradigmatic explanation in the Christian doctrine of substitutionary atonement. But banishing the memory of the scapegoat mechanism without changing the societal structures of mimetic rivalry invited the return of the repressed. Even though Girard claimed that Christianity exposed the lie of Satan, unjust accusation, the danger existed that a "this-worldly" order might not want to abandon what had proven to be so effective in eliminating violence from the body politic. The "revelation" of Christianity might be intentionally forgotten, although this amnesia has been shrouded in the rhetoric of rationalist, scientist, or specifically anti-Christian rhetoric. As a result Girard argues that the rejection of the Christian message by an increasingly secular Western culture did not bring about more humane social orders. On the contrary it turned those societies back toward the magical world of the scapegoat mechanism. In lieu of the ritualized remembrance of Christ's crucifixion, Western societies would find other scapegoats whose persecution would be legitimated by pseudo-rational appeals, for example, racist, homophobic, and misogynist ideologies.

Because mimetic rivalry remains intact in contemporary Western culture, this "rapid disintegration of the last sacrificial practices" produced a crisis.[38] Violence needed to be expressed, and it has found ready outlets in the persecution of Jews and blacks, gay men, lesbians, and women in general. Inspired by the ideal of equality in democratic societies, the reform movements of the post–World War II era have sought to reduce the level of violence against these groups. In Girard's view, these secular social changes, which result in the decline of difference, have a potentially devastating effect. The well-being of the society-at-large is contingent upon the expulsion of violence, but such an exorcism is only possible through its transfer to an Other. The political ideology of equality, whether in conservative or liberal guises, mitigates against the maintenance of categories from which may be drawn surrogate victims. It is particularly evident in the reformist struggles against anti-Semitism, racism, sexism, and homophobia. Girard has noted how prejudicial statements about ethnic groups and those physically challenged are no longer commonly expressed, at least in the mainstream mass media. Social progress on this front has certain disadvantages in a culture that has failed to abandon the dynamic of mimetic rivalry. Although political and cultural reforms may be motivated by the desire to humanize social relations, they leave in their wake an unresolved legacy of violence that manifests itself in other ways. Violence is endemic to contemporary American society, whether it be found in muggings and drive-by shootings on the street or murders on American television shows. Coupled with the proliferation of firearms throughout society, from Saturday night specials to the most sophisticated automatic weapons, American everyday life has become bathed in blood. Reciprocal violence is not only a possibility; it is an integral part of American consciousness.

From the Girardian perspective, the feminist challenge to the androcentric bias of Western culture has been particularly problematic for this traditional means to exorcise violence. The cultural pattern of gender difference ascribed the normatively human to the male and made the "weaker sex" contingent upon the "stronger." But the feminist revolution has lead increasingly to a "destructuralization" of the patriarchal social order, not only in terms of the body politic but also in the sphere of private lives. "A dynamic force seems to be drawing first Western society, then the rest of the world, toward a state of relative indifferentiation never before known on earth, a strange kind of nonculture or anticulture we call modern."[39] Without difference there can be no sacrificial victim, no expiation of transgression, no redemption from reciprocal violence. Girard seems to suggest that this disappearance of difference and, with it, sacrificial categories could be accommodated if the West still embraced the Christian myth of the God-man as ritual victim. Christian triumphalism makes the elimination of difference based on social distinctions and the establishment of a just social order viable possibilities. In a rather eccentric way he implies that Christianity is the *sine qua non* for feminism and all other political movements that seek to set the captive free. But the erosion of *both* Christianity *and* social differentiation threatens to plunge Western societies into an endless spiral of violence.

In the wake of the decreasing importance of religious, sacrificial rites in modern culture, the fading of gender difference threatens to remove one of the most powerful vehicles for the exorcism of violence. It should not be surprising therefore that in our secular society the move toward de-differentiation has met opposition in the form of male territorial games. As a means to resist the principles of equality embodied by modern social reform movements, they are as regressive as many women fear. Both football and war reinscribe gender difference in masculinist consciousness. The mimetic rivalry among men is expiated and an increasingly secular society is preserved through the victimization of those rhetorically conceived as the emasculated. Indeed emasculation seems to be a prerequisite for the effective interdiction of violence that would otherwise beset androcentric society-at-large. The emasculated Other, conceived either metaphorically or literally, emerges as the primary vehicle for the expiation of aggression in contemporary secular, democratic America. Woman is reverenced for her power to save the homosocial community from the internecine consequences of mimetic rivalry. She is divine, but not because she is put upon a pedestal in modern American culture. She is divine because she is unjustly tormented, brutalized, terrorized, and killed. *She* is the victim of a "fatal attraction," doomed by her difference to bear the weight of all transgressions. In a competitive androcentric society, the exorcism of violence from the homosocial environment has become a cultural obsession with men. And when and where women cannot be victimized literally, their absence is filled by the figure of the emasculated Other manifest in male territorial games, that is, war and football.

Because they play a salvific role, these games are regarded by both participants and observers alike with a certain reverence. Although football is thought to be merely a "pasttime," it is regarded by both its practitioners and fans with a seriousness that eclipses its role as mere amusement. In his work *Joy of Sports: End Zones, Bases, Baskets, Balls and the Consecration of the American Spirit,* Michael Novak dubbed sports the "natural religion" of Americans. Likewise, the humorist Russell Baker once argued that the opiate of the people in America is sports. Sports allow Americans to find solace away from the world of work and denial. The spreading popularity of professional sports identified the viewing of games with the redemption of the human spirit and the rise of physical fitness with the resurrection of the human body. Any suggestion that some sports ought to be banned because they are too violent is routinely met with vehement objections. The domestic consumption of televised sport has generated the proliferation of sports cable stations and a subculture of sports bars that formally specialize in what had become a popular informal activity in taverns throughout the United States. In particular football has become so hallowed and revered in American culture that the traditional day of rest—the Sabbath, the day of the week on which the ritual victim of Christianity was resurrected—has been identified with the mass viewing of these professional games. Critics of the game attack its disturbing emphasis on violence, but Novak defends football by arguing that it is no worse than religion. "If you think football is a violent liturgy," he argues, "reflect upon the Eucharist."[40]

If religion has traditionally functioned as the "safety valve" for societal violence, it would be difficult not to find something religious about football.

Like the sacrificial rites of organized religion, organized, professional football regularly schedules highly ritualized public exhibitions of violence, eliciting
cathartic exhortations from spectators who transfer pent-up emotion onto
the participants. In the struggle for ball possession—the control of the phallus, male bodies are bruised, bloodied, broken, and sometimes even perma-
nently damaged. Those with marked athletic prowess are regarded as mythic
heroes whose public celebrity is heralded in television commercials and print
advertisements and whose memory is safeguarded in the "Hall of Fame."
They achieve the standing of demigods who suffer and triumph. In what has
confounded some commentators and overwhelmed some players, they are
made to be role models whose activities on and off the field are expected to
embody the victory of good over evil as in the war on drugs.

Although football functions as a metaphorical game of sacrifice and cathartic violence, the autotelic legitimation of football screens this underlying dynamic. It plays an ideological function similar to the forgetting, be it
intentional or unintentional, that shrouds the exorcism of mimetic rivalry in
the Girardian interpretation of religion. It may be taken that Baker's obser-
vation means more than the relative importance of football in modern American
society. It points out that football plays an ideological function similar to
that of religion according to the Marxist critique: that it hides a process of
alienation. But whereas Marx argued that religion fails to fulfill its promise
of the redemption of humanity, Girard's model suggests that, absent Christianity, rituals of sacrifice, and cathartic violence like football are essential
for the preservation of society. Indeed it is the very misunderstanding of
this dynamic by sports spectators that is essential to its success. The symbolic castration and domination of the opponent serves to expel violence,
but conscious awareness would impede the transfer of affect. It would take
both the thrill and the pleasure out of the game. Yet football is not the only
possible avenue for the expulsion of violence.

Since the criteria for the choice of a sacrificial victim is that s/he be
drawn from a category of human beings who have no social links with
society-at-large, no group fits that description better than the foreigner. The
shedding of the foreigner's blood allows for the expression of violent emotion with little repercussion within the social order. In the context of modern societies, nationalism or patriotism becomes the vehicle that maintains
the sharp boundaries between victor and victim and ensures against reciprocal violence. In his speech "Toward a New World Order," President Bush
appealed to Americans to close ranks as the tensions with Saddam Hussein
increased during the initial phase of Operation Desert Shield. This ideological vigilance was regarded as necessary if the nation was to achieve its war
aims, and so it is if the aim is to expel violence from the society. "We see
here the principle behind all 'foreign' wars," claims Girard, "aggressive ten-

dencies that are potentially fatal to the cohesion of the group are redirected from within the community to outside it."[41] Although there may be other justifications for warfare—indeed some may be compelling reasons—the underlying psychosocial impetus for war is its role in the maintenance of domestic societal equilibrium.

Because the killing of the sacrificial victim is an essentially religious act, all foreign wars are, culturally speaking, "holy wars." Of course politicians are quick to refer to the "sacred duty" of all men in going to war. War-making is heavily ritualized: from the legal declarations that mark its temporal boundaries of beginning and end to the victory celebrations and mourning of the hallowed dead. Modern Western commentators and politicians escoriated Saddam Hussein's call for *jihad* and have criticized the Islamic doctrine in general; yet the pronouncement of "holy war" is no more than the acknowledgment of what war against the foreigner means. President Bush himself did not hesitate to invoke the name of God in his address launching Operation Desert Storm in January 1991 or in his live message at Superbowl XXV. Fighting the war against Saddam Hussein was the "sacred duty" of Americans and so those actions received the theological *imprimatur* of the leader of American civil religion. The shedding of blood was no escalation of violence for petty political or economic reasons but rather had a "higher purpose": to defend the honor of the nation and to redeem its principles. Although the "sacred" character of the war allegedly permitted the shedding of blood, a Girardian reading of the conflict suggests that it was the shedding of blood that made the war holy.

Sacrificial victims are made holy in a foreign war by virtue of being maimed or murdered. As symbols of transgression they are reviled, but as bloodied martyrs or witnesses to the ritual exorcism of violence they are feared. In this context it is altogether fitting that Saddam Hussein identified the Iraqi effort with Islam. American commentators may have disparaged Saddam's invocation of Islam, but the religious designation of the opponent is strangely appropriate in the Girardian model. For just as the victim is a transgressor, so, too, is Islam according to the traditional view of the West. It is allegedly a heinous repudiation of the Christ, his crucifixion and resurrection, and his blood sacrifice which rests as the foundation of Eurocentric culture. But ironically, as Christian pacifists are quick to point out, war against the foreigner, the Arab, the non-Westerner, does to the Muslim what, according to Christian theology, humanity did to Jesus. The Islamic repudiation of the Christian tradition enables Americans to place Muslims in general and Iraqis in particular outside the parameters of "civilized" community. For the West's "holy war" not only expels violence from its own societies, it compels the Other to turn against itself by submitting to its enemies rather than to its God. From the Western perspective, its *raison d'être* becomes solely to satisfy the need of the Western economy—be it political (oil) or psychic (sacrifice). "Fanatical" Islam—Islam taken at its most extreme, that is, at its word—will be made to comply with Western needs through the shedding of their own blood. Their cries and their corpses, however, are a source of some anxiety, for they testify to the release of rage and the destructive potential of weapons that frighten and awe even members of the American military establishment. Iraqi bodies are marked by this violence, mute testimony to a power that American society might otherwise turn on itself.

If we take the president and the Coalition military leaders at their word, Saddam Hussein personifies this enemy. He stands as the "Accused," the bearer of all transgressions; in short, he is projected as satanic. As is evident from the rhetoric of the Gulf War, his metaphysical standing as the incarnation of evil dwarfs the historical controversy over the Iraqi dispute with Kuwait. And as the "adversary," as the sacrificial victim, the marks of violence ought to be found on his body. And so it is. The rending of the flesh is already effected in the imagination of American leaders from the very outset. The tool of rape—his army—is to be cut off. His eyes—the Iraqi air force—are to be put out. His guns are to be silenced and his missiles are to be shot down. He is to be rendered weak, defenseless, and "militarily castrated." The game of war, like the game of football, portrays the overpowering, domination, and emasculation of the enemy. The token of his power, of his being as a man in a patriarchal world, his phallus, is excised in various and sundry images. In the male imaginary, castration—the process of unmanning—transforms the enemy into a woman.

This pattern of violence in male territorial games seems to fit Girard's theory of sacrificial double substitution. Because mimetic rivalry within the American homosocial community cannot be directly expressed without threatening the equilibrium of the society-at-large, the expression of violence is siphoned off onto a surrogate victim, a male opponent or enemy, who replaces the original transgressor. In order to ensure that the sacrifice of the surrogate victim does not threaten to spillover into the society-at-large, the expression of male aggression is directed toward a ritual victim, doubly removed from the original transgressor and secured by the ritual boundaries of male territorial games. The ritual victim is drawn from categories designated by the game theory of sports and war, either from "inside" or "outside" the American homosocial community. "Drafted" from the homosocial community-at-large, football players reiterate the mimetic rivalry of male spectators in everyday life on the football field. And in order to underline their categorical separation from everyday life, they assume mythic identities drawn from membership with totemically designated teams, for example, Bears, Lions, Giants, etc. In identifying with either team (usually chosen by proximate geographical location), spectators adopt one totemically designated group as their own homosocial community. The opposing rival team, rotated according to schedule, constitutes the ritually identified "outside" group on which is projected the hostility based on mimetic rivalry in everyday life. Although in one sense the game is not "real"—as was emphasized repeatedly in commentaries on the Superbowl during the Gulf War, it is treated every bit as if it were, from the adoption of the rhetoric of war to the use of physical violence on the "field of combat." In this sense football is the ritualized domestic analogue to "real" war in which the enemy is not only metaphorically vanquished and perhaps even physically maimed but also killed. In war, as in football, the enemy embodies the double substitution for the original transgressor in mimetic rivalry. Although war, unlike football, may have "real" causes (conflict over honor, commerce, natural resources), it serves as a vehicle by which the anger toward one's personal rival may be safely expressed in the vilification of the enemy, designated as an alien group and personified by its leader. The American political order seems to have a particular penchant for personalizing the enemy, be it Hitler, Tojo, Mussolini, and Stalin, or, most recently, General Manuel Noreiga or Saddam Hussein. And while war, unlike football, does not have an established schedule of opponents, all foreign groups have the potential to become the enemy at any given time.

WHAT CRIME, WHAT TRANSGRESSION, DID WOMEN COMMIT?

Insofar as the enemy is identifiably male, the ritual victim bears enough similarity to the original transgressor to sustain the transfer of affect from mimetic rivalry to the ritualized male territorial game. However, argues Girard, "this resemblance must not be carried to the extreme of complete assimilation, or it would lead to disastrous confusion.[42] He fears that in cases where the sacrificial victim is too similar to the original transgressor(s), "violence will overflow its channels."[43] Mimetic rivals within the homosocial community may become the victims of this spillover, thereby undermining the very purpose of male territorial games. But insofar as the enemy is, through castration imagery, identifiably female, the ritual victim is sufficiently different to ensure the insulation of the homosocial community from direct expressions of violence among its members. Although it might be argued that the linguistic transformation of man into woman is merely an incidental consequence by virtue of the removal of the phallus as a sign of masculine power, the consequences of castration in the male imaginary, are not. The absence of male power is a frightening image in a patriarchal society. The thought of emasculation produces the fear that in turn both legitimates and motivates aggressive action. In a world of mimetic rivalry skewed by the phallic metaphor for power, competitors contemplate their rival's emasculation rather than their own. Rhetorical castration is therefore a sign of the ritual victim who exists as an interloper in a homosocial community. The feminization of the enemy is therefore not incidental but rather essential to the social dynamic of sacrificial violence in a patriarchal social order. The enemy is woman because she is what men are not but fear they might become. Ritual victimization of the enemy as female confirms male identity. Male territorial games prove that men are men—to men—and ensure the solidarity of the homosocial community.

If the enemy is "woman," then the ritual victim as the surrogate for the mimetic rival bears the signs of womanhood. In the sacrificial context the linguistic construct "woman" both shoulders and betokens the violence that would otherwise be expressed in the domestic community *among men*. Violence against women would therefore appear to be incidental—a displacement of aggressive male rivalry. But what would trigger this incidental violence against women? Why would women, out of all possible categories of sacrificial victims, be chosen? Girard surmises that "[a]ny bloodletting is frightening. It is only natural, therefore, that menstruation should awaken fear . . . it is in many societies regarded as the most impure of impurities."[44] Blood may be read as the sign of violence, and therefore insofar as a woman is a woman, insofar as she bleeds, bled, or will bleed, her very physiology suggests her role as the sacrificial victim.

> We ought, however, to go further: to inquire whether this process of symbolization does not respond to some half-suppressed desire to place the blame for all forms of violence on women. By means of this taboo a transfer of violence has been effected and a monopoly established that is clearly detrimental to the female sex.[45]

Yet, the explanation of the "natural" origins to woman as victim seems satisfactory only in a limited fashion. To acknowledge bleeding as a natural, "womanly" phenomenon does not explain why it *necessarily* signifies the designation of woman as sacrificial victim, as evidenced by male territorial games. Although Girard acknowledges that women may be ascribed to a sacrificial category because of their physical weakness, relatively speaking, and marginal social status, he also notes that historically they have oftentimes been conspicuously absent from the ranks of sacrificial victims. Although he does not speculate on the reason for this anomaly, it is apparent that women are often viewed primarily as the mothers or material foundation of homosocial community. Women may also be protectively shrouded by taboo—beyond the reach of the social mechanism for the alleviation of violence. Hence, the role that women play may be assumed by men who are conceived as the enemy in football and war. But, if such is the case, why is the enemy depicted in the rhetoric of these games as emasculated, as female? Is the coincidence of menstrual blood and the blood of the sacrificial victim alone sufficient to explain the construct of the emasculated Other as the enemy? Do not men also bleed? Perhaps, on the other hand, violence against women is no coincidence. Perhaps it would be useful to reconfigure the application of Girard's model to male territorial games and domestic violence.

According to the Girardian model, violence within the body politic signifies the locus of the original transgressor(s) in the eyes of their rivals. That violence has been interpreted as violence between male mimetic rivals in a homosocial community. If male territorial games frequently coincide with domestic violence, it suggests that battered women as women bear a resemblance to the emasculated Other portrayed in war and football. Domestic violence is therefore a form of collateral damage, falling on the heads of unintended victims. The violence was originally intended for males but safely vented by displacing it on ritual victims who were both similar to the original male transgressors yet different from them through the marks of emasculation. Women literally embody the sign of difference that ensures that the ritual victim cannot be mistaken for the male mimetic rival. The spillover of violence from the field of combat to the domestic setting would therefore be unintended because the original target was male rather than female. But there seems to be something terribly wrong with this interpretation of the Girardian model. Such reasoning both excuses the spillover from male territorial games and conflicts with the literature on domestic violence in the United States.

The figures for battering in the United States—particularly Lenore Walker's conclusion that nearly half of all women will be emotionally and/or physically abused by their intimate partners at sometime in their lives—mitigates against reading violence against women as incidental. The testimony of experts specializing in the study of domestic violence indicates that battering is intentional. Battered women are simply not the victims of collateral damage. Batterers directly intend to do them harm. If battered women are the intentional victims of male violence, it is not because they resemble the difference of the ritual victim from the original mimetic rival—it is because they resemble the similarity of the ritual victim to the original mimetic rival. In other words, *batterers and other misogynists perceive women (mothers, wives, girlfriends, daughters), not men, as their mimetic rivals.* Women inspire the jealousy of these men, but not because they are the object of desire evinced by male rivals. Instead women must embody what they want to become and possess what they desire. Yet, if the enemy *qua* sacrificial victim is made to look like woman, what crime, what transgression, did women commit?

If the sacrificial victim bears the marks of castration and those cuts mark the site of the original transgressor, Girard's model does not explain why women and men are bound together in mimetic rivalry. Why do men wish to mime women? To take their place? What object is made desirable by its possession by women—so desirable that it evokes male *ressentiment* and leads to the vilification of woman as enemy? Perhaps it is something that men desire but the sight of which scotomizes their vision, as if it were too bright to comprehend. In any case, the answer to these questions lies far beyond the scope of Girard's sociological aetiology of the scapegoat. It requires an explanation of the masculinist psychic economy itself for which we must seek elsewhere.

NOTES

1. "The Guns of August," *New Republic,* September 3, 1990, 11.
2. Walter Benjamin, "Critique of Violence," in *Reflections*, ed. Peter Demetz, trans. Edmund Jephcott (New York: Harcourt Brace Jovanovich, 1978), 277–300. Vide, the postmodernist commentary on Benjamin's essay, Jacques Derrida, "Force of Law: The Mystical Foundation of Authority," *Cardozo Law Review* 11 (July-August 1990): 919–1045.
3. *Sports Quotations: Maxims, Quips and Pronouncements for Writers and Fans*, ed. Andrew J. Maikovich (Jefferson, NC: McFarland & Co., 1984), 91.
4. David Meggyesy, *Out of Their League* (Berkeley, CA: Ramparts, 1970), 147.
5. Jean Baudrillard, *La guerre du Golfe n'a pas eu lieu* (Paris: Galilée, 1991), 100.
6. *Washington Post,* February 27, 1991, 1.
7. "The Terrible Toll," *Newsweek Commemorative Edition* (Spring/Summer, 1991), 82.
8. Jack Andersen and Dale Van Atta, *Stormin' Norman: An American Hero* (New York: Kensington, 1991), 163.
9. T. W. Adorno, Else Frenkel-Brunswik, Daniel J. Levinson, and R. Nevitt Sanford, *The Authoritarian Personality* (New York: W. W. Norton, 1969), 442–67.
10. Adorno et al., *Authoritarian Personality*, 411.
11. Georg Simmel, "The Stranger," *Georg Simmel. On Individuality and Social Forms*, ed. Donald N. Levine (Chicago: University of Chicago, 1971), 144.
12. Adorno et al., *Authoritarian Personality*, 612.
13. Ibid., 148.
14. Ibid., 665.
15. Ibid., 393.
16. Respondents with left-wing political sympathies most often scored much lower on the E- and F-scales leading one American sociologist, Edward Shils, to denounce its "Leninist" bias. Although Theodor Adorno had Marxist sympathies, he could in no way be described as a "Marxist-Leninist" or even a sympathizer with Soviet communism. In a personal conversation, Nevitt Sanford remarked to me that he was caught somewhat by surprise by the criticism, "being a life-long Republican from Georgia."
17. Quoted in Tony Engelhart and Pat Foran, *Sword in the Sand, U.S. Marines in the Gulf War* (Hong Kong: Concord, 1992), n.p.

18. Ramsey Clark, et al., *War Crimes. A Report on United States War Crimes Against Iraq* (Washington, DC: Maisonneuve Press, 1992), 15.

19. Adorno et al., *Authoritarian Personality*, 632.

20. Ibid., ix.

21. Susan Griffin, *Pornography and Silence: Culture's Revenge Against Nature* (New York: Harper & Row, 1981), 158.

22. Adorno et al., *Authoritarian Personality*, 147.

23. René Girard, *Violence and the Sacred*, trans. Patrick Gregory (Baltimore; Johns Hopkins, 1972), 318.

24. Ibid., 145.

25. Ibid., 26–27.

26. Ibid., 4.

27. Ibid., 99.

28. René Girard, *Le bouc émissaire* (Paris: Grasset, 1982), 63.

29. Girard, *Violence and the Sacred*, 5.

30. Ibid, 102.

31. *Violent Origins: Walter Burkert, René Girard and Jonathan Z. Smith on Ritual Killing and Cultural Formation*, ed. Robert G. Hamerton-Kelly (Stanford, CA: Stanford, 1987), 78.

32. Girard, *Violence and the Sacred*, 82.

33. Ibid., 271.

34. Ibid., 1.

35. René Girard, *Des choses cachées depuis la fondation du monde* (Paris: Grasset, 1978), 225.

36. Ibid., 573–92.

37. Ibid., 592.

38. Girard, *Violence and the Sacred*, 139.

39. Ibid., 189.

40. Michael Novak, *Joy of Sports: End Zones, Bases, Baskets, Balls and the Consecration of the American Spirit* (New York: Hamilton, 1988), 91.

41. Girard, *Violence and the Sacred*, 249.

42. Ibid., 11.

43. Ibid., 39.

44. Ibid., 34.

45. Ibid., 36.

F i v e

DESCENT INTO THE MASCULINIST PSYCHIC ECONOMY:

BATAILLEAN AND IRIGARAYAN MODELS OF INTERPRETATION

> There is in understanding a blind spot: which is reminiscent of the structure of the eye. In understanding, as in the eye, one can only reveal it with difficulty. But whereas the blind spot of the eye is inconsequential, the nature of understanding demands that the blind spot within it be more meaningful than understanding itself. . . . to the extent that one views in understanding man himself, by that I mean an exploration of what is possible in being, the spot absorbs one's attention; it is no longer the spot which loses itself in knowledge, but knowledge which loses itself in it.
>
> —Georges Bataille, *Inner Experience*

> The blind spot of an old dream of symmetry
>
> —Luce Irigaray, *Speculum of the Other Woman*

PERHAPS NO MAN HAS been more willing to address this scotoma of the male gaze than Georges Bataille—an enigmatic figure whose work is shrouded in the mysteries of French cultural politics between the world wars. Raised an atheist, Bataille converted to Catholicism in 1914. Beset by a crisis of identity, he then recanted his conversion following a retreat with the Benedictines in 1922. His was a passionate atheism that conflated the sacred with the *ek-stasis* of sexual experience: the transcendence of the self in the bursting forth of orgasm, in the rending of physical and spiritual boundaries. As an *habitué* of Parisian intellectual circles between the wars, Bataille was active in the surrealist movement, praising Dali's painting in his essay "The Lugubrious Game" (1929) and sharing its distain for bourgeois cul-

140

ture. But while he was to embrace the Marxist thought of the late 1920s and early 1930s, which became so much a part of an "orthodox" surrealist movement, Bataille himself was rejected by its father, Jacques Breton, in the "Second Surrealist Manifesto" (1929). Breton was repulsed by Bataille's "excremental" philosophy, as evidenced by the libidinal anality of the latter's "Solar Anus" (1927).[1]

Although Breton saw violence as an inevitable analogue to the surrealist dream, for example, "the simplest Surrealist act" of shooting a pistol indiscriminately into a crowd, Breton's disdain for the bourgeoisie was balanced by a vision of the transcendent, marked by an aspiration for purity. To Bataille, on the other hand, violence was an inevitable part of social excess and sexual degradation."To be sure," writes Girard,

> Bataille is primarily inclined to treat violence in terms of some rare and precious condiment, the only spice still capable of stimulating the jaded appetite of modern man. Yet on occasion Bataille is able to transcend the decadent estheticism he has so fervently espoused.[2]

Violence was not merely a vehicle for private pornographic pleasures and sadomasochistic fantasies but rather was a basic philosophical principle. To Bataille there was no "beyond" to transcend to, but its very absence drew man—in Bataillean literature, the normative human being—to seek his own destruction and defilement in the rending of the self. Ecstasy was identified with abasement. Bataille claimed that the "the most *human* part of the human body"[3] was the "big toe," an appendage sunk deep into the mud yet essential to the erection of man. The fetish of the "big toe" in the Bataillean credo is thereby unmistakably identified with the phallus. "[S]urrendering to an inexorable movement, whose violence he can feel acting on the most remote areas of his being with a rigor that frightens him,"[4] man embraces a Nietzschean "joy before death," an explosion of phallic sexuality conflated with libidinal anality. "Only a shameless, indecent saintliness," he writes, "can lead to a sufficiently happy *loss of self*."[5]

Rather than an outcome of a "natural" (or, for that matter, "unnatural") physical desire, this "apotheosis of the flesh," this sanctification of the impure, was conceived by Bataille to be a cultural fiction. It is the human, (read male) imagination that establishes the boundaries of transgression, which is the *sine qua non* of violence itself. Barbarism is a byproduct of civilization, and although violence might be construed as that which is excluded from civilized behavior, it is just this very distinction that creates violence as such. "[A]ll civilised men are capable of savagery," Bataille reminds us.[6] Transgression becomes the hallowed practice of the earth-bound mystic.

In the Bataillean world, the violence of male sexual transgression that rends the practitioner and convulses his partner is revered as a holy ritual.

For men mired in the profane world of everyday life, it is the means by which one may transcend the homogeneity of mundane time and space, not to elevate oneself to a higher plane but to descend into the maelstrom of excess and degradation. It is a release, a total divorce from the confines of reason, an undoing of the self. As the mirror image of apophatic Christian mysticism, Bataille's schema sacrifices human knowledge in the burning desire for ecstasy—a standing outside of oneself. He called this sensual "cloud of unknowing" a heterology or science of the sacred.

> In that way it [heterology] leads to the complete reversal of the philo-sophical process, that ceases to be the instrument of appropriation, and now serves excretion: it introduces the demand for the violent gratifications implied by social life.[7]

In a world governed by the principle of utility, the virtue of heterology—its manly truth—lay in the irruption of the social fabric, in its essential unproductiveness. It has no purpose other than its own existence.

Like the *mysterium tremendum* that awakens the individual from the slumber of daily existence, the heterologous sexual experience has the force of a shock wave which shakes the subject to his very foundations. It is a power that induces both dread and fascination—and a passionate desire to witness one's own demise. For it is only in an awareness of one's impending disso-lution that a man knows the value of his own life. Although the homolo-gous boundaries of the bourgeois social order are defended by traditional theism, heterology attacks those conventions of sexuality and morality which, according to Bataille, anaesthetize both body and soul. The transgressive male sexual act, which transcends social and physical boundaries, creates a community of men who are hallowed by their very actions. "WE ARE FERO-CIOUSLY RELIGIOUS," declared Bataille, but this faith was not to be con-fused with that of the bourgeoisie. His was a holy war against piety.

> Man has escaped from his head just as the condemned man has escaped from his prison. He has found beyond himself not God, who is the prohi-bition against crime, but a being who is unaware of prohibition. Beyond what I am, I meet a being who makes me laugh because he is headless; this fills me with dread because he is made of innocence and crime; he holds a steel weapon in his left hand, flames like those of a Sacred Heart in his right. He reunites in the same eruption Birth and Death. He is not a man. He is not a god either. He is not me but he is more than me: his stomach is a labyrinth in which he has lost himself, loses me with him, and in which I discover myself as him, in other words as a monster.[8]

To the profane world this transfigured man, resurrected from dead, is horri-bly disfigured, a grotesque vision. But in the eyes of Bataille, he is some-thing marvelous to behold. He is someone above the law, a true revolutionary, a totally free man whose libertinism redeems men from sanctimony.

De Sade's "sovereign man" epitomizes this religious creature. In his missive "The Use Value of D. A. F. de Sade," Bataille excoriates those who would rehabilitate de Sade in order to fetishize him as a precious literary commodity. Like the sacred itself in bourgeois society, de Sade had become that which was excreted, excluded, and exiled from modern, profane existence as if to circumscribe his effect on the social order. But like all that is expelled from the human body and the body politic, (excrement, semen, the mad, libertines), the *ek-stasis* of scatology promised a revolutionary e-sc(h)atology. The person of de Sade embodied the advent of a qualitatively different reality. That revolution would organize society around orgiastic and murderous rituals that indulge in the play of excretion and rupture as an antibourgeois but nonetheless sacred enterprise. The difference between a pre- and post-Sadean human history is that de Sade embraced the heterogeneous, the deviant, the eruptive as a basic principle of moral philosophy. Enthralled by the language of Nietzsche, Bataille was later to describe de Sade's position as "a reflecting and rationalised will to violence."[9] Violence would no longer appear at the margins of society but would rather be recognized at the very heart of the social order. The collective effervescence of war and ritual blood-letting, rape and murder, would become celebratory feasts. De Sade pointed the way to a society in which "[t]he man subject to no restraints of any kind falls on his victims with the devouring fury of a vicious hound."[10] This "sovereign man" would affirm his masculinity and his humanity in the rending and penetration of the body, both his own and his victim's.

THE TABOO IS THERE TO BE VIOLATED

To Bataille, the distinction between man and animal was not to be found in either intelligence, as Darwin held, or in the repression of animal instincts per se, as Freud thought, but rather in the cultural construction of taboo. The creation of taboos insulate human beings from death, manifest in the powers of violence and sexuality; yet the very establishment of taboos creates desire. It offers to fulfill the yearning of man to transcend himself and his world and simultaneously interrupts and intensifies that desire. The taboo, claimed Bataille, is there to be violated.[11] This mutually reinforcing binary opposition—the no and the yes—engenders the inner experience of eroticism with a power that eclipses mundane existence. The rational construction of boundaries for the preservation of the species induces a sense of vertigo, an anticipation of letting go, even though the risk be death itself. The taboo is brought full circle from insulation and prevention to temptation and self-destruction. Taboo unwrites itself, and though its original impetus was to distance man from the animal, the vertiginous centrifugal force explodes taboo and closes the gap between man and animal.

Taboo produces desire that is expressed sexually; thus, in the Bataillean psychic economy, human sexuality is not a "natural" phenomenon. "Transgression itself is organized," claims Bataille.[12] The physical orgasm is a metaphor for the social transgression of taboo. Hence, transgression is born of taboo and has no independent existence. Rapture exists only in the wake of rupture—a rending open of the membranes of the social body. The rupture of bodily boundaries therefore is not immediate; it is mediated by the violation of normative boundaries. Prohibitions against incest, sodomy, sadomasochism, bestiality, necrophilia, and extra- and premarital sexuality impart an erotic aura to those acts. *Interdicta* all fall by the wayside in their consumption, but the acts themselves are indelibly marked by these taboos. They remain an echo even after they are violated.

"The transgression does not deny the taboo but transcends it and completes it."[13] If, by establishing the frontier of transgression, *interdicta* create physical desire, then the violation of cultural boundaries inevitably is fulfilled in the violation of physical ones. Consequently, male sexuality is the undoing of both. In the eye of man, the act of coitus, with its images of physical exertion and penetration, replicates the image of bodily violation, of an opening and spilling forth of bodily fluids, that symbolizes wanton injury, murder, and anarchy. "For the truth is," confessed Bataille, "that between death and the reeling, heady motion of the little death [*petite morte*] the distance is hardly noticeable."[14] The metaphors of love and death, that is, to lose one's head, to be slain by love, a dying to love, are not mere hyperbole but an apt description of the essential characteristic of eroticism.

Love and death serve as the bridge to a utopian existence—a nowhere where the image of pleasure and eternal happiness exercise a power that does not exist. This image promises human fulfillment through what Bataille refers to as the "continuity" of the cosmos—human undoing, death, nothingness. But the allure of continuity only exists in the eye of the discontinuous, in the man who, *qua* man, is separated from others and from himself. The image of continuity only can be seen through the lens of discontinuity and disappears at the moment when discontinuity surrenders itself, that is, at the moment of sexual consummation or death. The transition from discontinuity to continuity unmasks pleasure and eternal happiness as an abyss, a bottomless maw that swallows up the male imaginary in sexual orgasm and man himself in the erotic thrill of war.

Eros itself is seduced by the image of death that beckons its undoing. It is at this point, when the social conditions of taboo and transgression are intact, that physical passion is loosed on its path of self-destruction. "Two things are inevitable: we cannot avoid dying nor can we avoid bursting through our barriers, and they are one and the same."[15] Bataille's theory suggests that what passes for the "natural" sexual appetite exists only insofar as the consciousness of sexuality's cultural construction is repressed. It is but a pale imitation of the discursive construction of violence that is sexuality, of the discursive construction of sexuality that is violence. "If I only gain access to the simple intensity of inner movement, it goes without saying that discourse is only rejected for a time, that it remains at bottom the master."[16] That truth for Bataille can be plainly seen.

According to this oculocentrism, *"the mind is an eye."*[17] Enthralled by the forbidden object, man scans above and beyond the horizon of desire with a "pineal" eye—an organ attuned not to the horizontal plane but to the vertical. In this grotesque metaphor, the exorbitant organ allows man to look outside of himself, to look himself outside, into the sun, the source of light and life. Its image burns itself into the retina as a blind spot, a point that marks the overwhelming of the optical senses, a void that invites a man to extinguish himself. Marking the climax of male erection, the pineal eye "appears in a kind of nimbus of tears, like the eye of a tree, or, perhaps, like a human tree. At the same time this ocular tree is only a giant (ignoble) pink penis, drunk with the sun and suggesting or soliciting a nauseous malaise, the sickening despair of vertigo."[18] Reminiscent of Jung's dream of the phallic tree in the cavern below ground,[19] Bataille's ocular phallus embodies the male gaze as the very meaning of existence. Its aim is not domination *per se* but rather its own bursting apart. Phallic hegemony therefore takes pleasure in watching its own dissolution.

Male coitus is a ludic act that culminates in the spent self. "This great burning head is the image and the disagreeable light of the *notion of expenditure.*"[20] The purpose is to lose oneself by bursting into and merging with this totality, with this infinite continuity for it is only in the loss of the self that its meaning can be savored. Like the image that remains on the retina after the burst of light is gone, man experiences himself in his own disappearance. Only then can he feel the boundaries of himself that have been melted in the heat of ecstasy. Bataille reads this principle of loss as the basis of human societies. Even primitive cultures, he argues, are faced with the problem of material abundance and excess. The social order is designed to accommodate the need for expenditure through the practice of potlatch. The earth itself as well as the human organism parodies this social need. Magically the rotation of the earth mimes these coital movements of human beings. "The earth sometimes jerks off in a frenzy, and everything collapses on its surface."[21]

Man, as microcosm, is a part of the whole yet desires to be the whole. His desire is his anguish. It is anguish that drives him to become all-in-all, to become one with the cosmos, to be indistinguishable from the totality.

And it is this desire that fuels the passion of two discontinuous creatures to overcome their separation, to exceed even the summation of their parts, in sexual orgasm. They allow themselves to be carried aware by the illusion of continuity, a conjunction of one flesh; yet this aim of male sexual desire is ultimately destined to fail. For copulation, like the mystical copula, does not succeed in embracing the totality. The pineal eye can no more have the sun than the earth's eruptions can reach the heavens. The orgasm is momentary, and discontinuity rendered unconscious returns to plunge the individual once more into the anguish of desire.

Loss affirms this fundamental truth: all creation is insufficient. Bataille's sexual mysticism promises the unity of the cosmos in the final, fatal act of continuity, but it turns back upon itself in the *satori* awareness that man is a cosmic joke. His paltry efforts toward the intellectual appropriation of and physical merger with the cosmos fall comically short. Like the punch line of the riddle, he reveals the truth about himself in all his pretensions. The bourgeois man is scandalized by this sexual truth, but for Bataille the sovereign man laughs at himself. And it is a cruel laughter that takes no pity on him who wishes to escape his fate as the victim of his own self-destructive pleasure or another's remorseless will. The madness that surely follows is embraced by the sovereign man willingly as a way of life.

Few follow the path of the sovereign man who savors his own destruction as well as that of his victims. For those who choose otherwise, the metaphor of desire that lusts after totality gives way to frustration. The transitory pleasure of orgasm is displaced by the reappropriation of desire: desire for a continuity that can never be inhabited. Only death is a state of permanent continuity, perhaps to be accepted by he who dies in a few brief moments before expiring. For the observer, however, the contemplation of both orgasm and death can be held longer. The male gaze of the voyeur may savor the rending of physical boundaries by observing the visage of one who is penetrated. And whereas the contemplation of one's own impending death is compromised by its momentary nature, the male observer vicariously may linger over the pleasure of rupture in the death throes of his victim. In the wake of violent death, the onlookers experience an almost mystical silence—an eerie and powerful absence that symbolizes the exhaustion of rupture, the departure of life, and with it, the cessation of discontinuity. Men are brought together in death.

Ultimately the consciousness of pleasure derived from the contemplation of orgasm and death will dissipate like the evaporation of bodily fluids and the escaping body heat of the corpse. Continuity remains ever elusive but ever demanding as the alpha and omega of desire. Like the endless wheel of life and death, discontinuity and continuity destine men to a life of repetition-compulsion in that they can do no other than to desire what is forbidden and to lose what has been illicitly won. In this play between taboo and transgression, discontinuity and continuity, the masculinist imaginary conceives male activity as a game. It is regarded as a source of enjoyment and pleasure, a respite from work, but nonetheless it is deadly serious. Its rules are shaped by the utilitarian economy of desire: to maximize continuity while retaining discontinuity. The aim is to experience continuity—the oneness of death and sexual orgasm (*la petite morte*)—without surrendering simultaneously the capacity to observe it, that is, without dying. The bodily integrity necessary for life is ensured if the ruptured body is not one's own. The pleasures of rupture and self-annihilation are available by proxy: in "woman" as victim. The male gaze vicariously makes the rupture its own. Taboo and transgression, discontinuity and continuity thereby manifest themselves in two locations for male activity: in war and in sexual relations.

A MAN CANNOT USUALLY FEEL A LAW IS VIOLATED IN HIS OWN PERSON

Like the image of the torn body in Ludwig Meidner's painting *Apokalyptische Landschaft* (1913) (See Figure 5.1), that which is rent asunder marks the eruption of ecstatic time into everyday life. Exposed bodies and corpses, nakedness and blood heighten the excitement that courses through the male body. The allure of violation infuses the imagination with desire to a maddening degree.

> I imagine human movement and excitation whose possibilities are limitless; this movement and excitation can only be appeased by war.
> I imagine the gift of an infinite suffering, of blood and open bodies, in the image of an ejaculation cutting down the one it jolts and abandoning him to an exhaustion charged with nausea.[22]

This desire to expose one's body to violence—the manly virtue of courage—takes hold in a fit, seeking to sacrifice others and even oneself as a violation of taboo.

Like Girard, Bataille identifies foreign conflict as a locus for ritual sacrifice, common to many cultures. Whereas the violation of taboo within the society risks social ostracism and even death, war serves as a vehicle to experience both the taboo and its transgression without repercussion of social condemnation. In the context of foreign conflict, murder and rape are instruments of war. Even in modern Western societies, governed by the canon of international law, murder is justified (if the victim be a combatant or deaths of noncombatants are foreseen but not intended). Although rape is recognized as a war crime, it is rarely punished. Permission to rape frequently has been used to reward the efforts of soldiers, and it has not been

FIGURE 5.1   *Apokalyptische Landschaft*, 1913 by Ludwig Meidner. Oil on Canvas, 80 × 196. Nationalgalerie, Berlin. Reprinted by permission.

uncommon to employ it as an instrument to terrorize and subdue a population, as is evident in the allegations surrounding the rape of nearly twenty thousand women, largely by Serbian soldiers in the recent Balkan conflict. Apart from its political or military uses, rape and murder are forms of transgression that are enjoyed in the collective effervescence of war fever. Nothing is so gratifying, suggests Bataille. "I AM MYSELF WAR."[23]

War as a social form embodies the psychic reality of the male imaginary. Every man is capable of killing and raping. According to Bataille, it is his desire whether or not he has the courage to assume the mantle of the sovereign man. Ritual sacrifice allows that desire to burst forth, to burst the bounds of the human body and human consciousness. A holy madness descends upon him who contemplates such desires that are consummated in an ecstatic expulsion of bodily fluids, for example, vomit, urine, semen, blood, and excrement. The excitement may even become so all consuming as to incite auto-mutilation: lacerations of the flesh, the severance of fingers and other ablations, castration, or enucleation. That which is cut-off, excreted, and marginalized becomes sacred, infused with the power of the holy, objects of fascination and revulsion. Like the Civil War general who donated his amputated leg, lost at Gettysburg, to the Army War Museum so as to be able to visit it regularly over the remaining years of his life, they testify to the power of self-destruction and the pleasure derived from its contemplation. Yet, to what extent may self-mutilation be pursued? If the passions stop short of death, how can the ultimate disgorging be savored?

> I would not have been able to recognize myself open to the winds of the outside since all knowledge would be dissolved in me as soon as my heart would have ceased to beat. In order that in me this existence given to men cease to be unprofitably closed and *communicate*, it was necessary that another die before me.[24]

No animal can take a man's place, according to Bataille, for an animal is incommensurate with a human being. Only human flesh and human agonies can render this "pleasure."

Ritual sacrifice embodies a surrogate human victim in the cathartic *agon* of rupture. The executioner identifies with his victim, not because he takes pity on him, but because he is his victim, the subject of his own violation. In the Bataillean imagination, the murderer who disembowels the Other, guts his own viscera and watches his own life spill onto the ground. He knows no reason. He is lost with his victim. He experiences the violent convulsion of his own body, of his own organs. He dies in and through his victim. Yet in the sacrifice of his surrogate, he vicariously enjoys his own boundlessness. He sees a freedom that otherwise would remain elusive to him. But unlike his victim, he is resurrected from the dead—in order to do what? To suffer the anguish of discontinuity and to know the desire, the bloodlust, for violation. Thus war, like the male sexual act, is by nature cyclical.

It is not only that the victim makes it possible for the sacrificer to witness the agonies and pleasures of rupture, evident in writhing bodies and contorted faces, it is also that, according to Bataille, most men are overwhelmed by the thought of their own violation. The experience of holy transgression must therefore be mediated by the Other in order to take effect. Transgression rests on the social construction of taboo, and the reality of its violation is contingent on its perception in the body of the Other. As the Other in a gendered world, women embody both the taboo against rupture and its transgression. They are the "no" and the "yes." Like other tabooed holy objects, their bodies hold power insofar as they can be violated. In this Bataillean world, for a man to come to himself, to know himself in his dissipation, he must transgress the taboo that is called woman. Such is the case in eroticism where "the female partner . . . was seen as the victim, the male as the sacrificier, both during the consummation losing themselves in continuity established during the first destructive act."[25] As the one whose rupture is culturally reiterated in the signification of a woman's genitals, woman disappears before the assault of men. Her person dissolves into his in the act of penetration which affects the identification of the sacrificer with his victim. Her dissolution proleptically anticipates his own orgasm that momentarily annihilates the boundaries of man and woman, sacrificer and victim.

Like Girard, Bataille argues that women biologically are prototypical victims because of their menstrual flow. "Blood in itself is a sign of violence," he argues.

> The menstrual discharge is further associated with sexual activity and the accompanying suggestion of degradation; is one of the effects of violence. Childbearing cannot be dissociated from this complex of feelings. Is it not itself a rending process, something excessive and outside the orderly course of permitted activity?[26]

At first glance Bataille's suggestion that menstruation and childbearing are "excessive" seems absurd. Yet it is precisely the taboo that marginalizes these functions in bourgeois society which establishes the threshold of transgression. Menses and afterbirth excites the male imagination with images of the penetrable body. Both might be read as the effect of which the male subject is the cause. If blood is read as the sign of violence and if women naturally bleed, ergo women are natural victims of violence. But whereas for Girard blood signifies the accidental relationship between women and victimization, Bataille reads women's discharges as a sign necessitating victimization.

As the synecdoche for woman herself in colloquial language, the "cunt" or vaginal opening is a paradigm for the rending of the body and its penetrability. In Bataille's eyes it is an object of envy, for men are beset by castration anxiety that both evokes a fear of continuity, death, and otherness, yet at the same time tempts men with the allure of self-ablation. This mutilation that woman *qua* woman embodies is disembodiment in the male imagination—the first step toward the frenzy of mystical ecstasy. "Man achieves his inner experience at the instant when bursting out of the crysalis he feels that he is tearing himself, not tearing something outside that resists him."[27] Because the violent dissolution of body and self must be witnessed to be enjoyed, the substitution of the Other for the male subject prolongs the anguish of pleasure/the pleasure of anguish. Although through orgasm a man may experience the opening of his own body, his identification with the victim also permits him to experience the fantasy of penetration and self-mutilation, once deferred, without the finality of total continuity, that is, death. She is simultaneously a hole and a mirror, he may both penetrate her flesh and read in her eyes the concretization of his desire for the rending of his own.[28]

The cultural construction of sexuality and violence betokens that, although women may be indelibly marked in the male imaginary by the morphology of their genitals, penetration need not be vaginal nor, for that matter, does the Other have to be a biological woman to be "womanly." Thus, anal or oral copulation, even with a man, may produce a similar experience of disgorging. In the Bataillean model, "woman" is a way rather than a type of being. If woman is the paradigm of penetrability, any penetrated body may be constructed as "female." Both de Sade and Bataille's novels are replete with such instants. Men may appear as desirable, penetrable bodies in the Bataillean psychic economy and therefore may function as "women." (Although clearly many heterosexual males share this view in circumstances where biological women are unavailable, that is, the widespread evidence of "homosexual" rape by otherwise "heterosexual" males in prison, homosexuality awakens in heterosexual men an isomorphic identification with the bodies of gay men and raises the fear of penetration and gender confusion. Most often they insulate themselves from conscious awareness of this unconscious desire for rupture by having female sexual partners.)

Bataille therefore reads man's quest for meaning in the cultural construction of "woman" who must be necessarily dominated and effaced in order for a man to sense his own uniqueness, his own freedom, and his own holiness. She plays an essential role in the very structure of the male psyche. When the potential victim "acts like a woman," the sacrificer is tempted with the pleasure of his own demise. It is both frightening and fascinating. The nakedness of a woman excites a man with the anticipation of rupture in that he loses himself in her body. Yet how she exercises such power remains unclear to him. Woman remains shrouded in mystery, the blind spot in man's eye, replete with meaning, yet beyond understanding, beyond self-reflection. Woman holds the secret to man's psyche, but it is unclear to Bataille whether she is capable of divulging that secret, whether it is better for both to remain speechless. For it is in the silence of sexuality as violence, violence as sexuality, that he can blindly achieve his own transcendence. Just as the earth spews forth its flow unto the sun, so, too, does man ejaculate himself into this sign of violation. "The *solar annulus* is the intact anus of her body at eighteen years to which nothing sufficiently blinding can be compared except the sun, even though the *anus* is the *night.*"[29] Knowledge blissfully loses itself in the knowing of a "woman."

Bataille's model suggests that violence against women is the urtext for the reading of male violence. "S/he" is the gateway to the transcendent—a world of both unutterable ecstasy and degradation. This mystical attitude toward violence and sexuality echoes the attributes of male territorial games. Both war and football are looked upon by their participants and spectators as tantamount to sacred male activities. Both are indelibly marked by a will to violence. Both ritually act out victimization of the opponent/enemy, conceived as being the Other. And although the level of physical violence in football does not reach the threshold of that in war, they are imbued with a similar language. Rupture of the enemy's lines and the dialectic of phallic and ground possession reiterate Bataillean themes of sensuous, mystical, and masculinist violence. Even though the opponent/enemy may be biologically male, the language of these blood sports transfigures the Other into "woman" whose being is opened up to the subject and made available for penetration, domination, and dissolution. Victors need the vanquished in order to burst with pride and revel in male glory. The "losers" are most often depicted as those "open to defeat," and thereby shamed and humiliated, bearing the signs of "womanly" submission. Among those who survive is the gnawing anxiety that they are not "real" men, that in defeat they have lost a part of themselves. As in the Bataillean image of coitus in which the female dissolves into the male, only the conqueror remains, sole possessor of the field, proprietor of the vanquished's territory. In victory is manhood. Those who have put up a "good fight"—who have valiantly resisted the physical imposition of the discursive signs of womanhood—are accorded honor in defeat, but respect for the defeated is rare. For the victorious partisan, be he participant or spectator, war on the field of combat elicits the pleasures of discursive and physical rupture and the climatic thrill of affective release. As pointed out by the GI who compared killing Iraqis to having sexual intercourse with women, war embodies the desire to impale the enemy with phallic weaponry, whether it be bullets, rockets, or warheads, in an orgy of violence. Experiencing combat for the first time is often compared to losing one's virginity, only it can in no way be mistaken for love. It is a loss of innocence—a sign in Western culture that consummation of male desire does not come without its cost. And whereas the "blood sport" of football stops short of killing, the experience of war on the battlefield offers the certainty that life, in the aftermath of death and destruction and in the warm glow of victory, is good.

Even though the president vouchsafed the reasons for going to war, those reasons had far more to do with the dominant cultural ethos of American identity than political and economic necessities. In a sense, they had to be felt rather than comprehended. Why does conflict on the battlefield or the gridiron have such a hold on the American imagination? Political and sociological explanations fail to account for the pleasure and excitement derived from these games of violence, nor do they explain the rhetoric of castration and phallic penetration or the image of women as the linchpin between these games and the male psyche. Men frequently deny that this language has any meaning whatsoever or contend that they don't mean what they say. Yet it is very clear from the muscled language of threats and taunts that their words have very precise and unmistakable meanings to their opponents and enemies. The role that "woman" as a cultural construct in the rhetoric of castration and phallic penetration plays is essential, yet it is as if men are hardly aware of its effect on its victims—women and those regarded as being effeminate.

In this regard the theoretical models of René Girard and Georges Bataille help to illustrate the structural relationship of violence, sexuality, and male territorial games: Girard depicting the scapegoat as the enemy, picked for no good reason except to exorcise violence; Bataille showing how the enemy as Other is necessarily "female" and must be penetrated in order to vicariously experience rupture. Yet neither answers the key questions that lie at the heart of the masculinist psychic economy. Although women may be viewed as "natural" surrogate victims due to the reading of menses as the sign of transgression, the Girardian model does not explain what crime women allegedly committed according to the male imaginary. Why are they regarded as the mimetic rivals of men? What do they possess that men desire? And even though women's bleeding may paradigmatically signify the penetrable body, Bataille's work does not answer why men are so obsessed with the sundering of bodily boundaries, both their victim's and their own. Both are blind spots in the male gaze, impervious to self-reflection. Perhaps like a scotoma that results from the scarring of the retina some lesion of the masculine psyche is responsible for this obfuscation of gender dynamics.

To seek answers for these questions requires the help of psychoanalytic maps that explore the structures of the masculinist psychic economy. But to do so also demands some distancing from the masculine voice that finds it difficult to articulate what it cannot see, what remains unfathomable to the male gaze, what is the "blind spot of the old dream of symmetry."[30] In this context, the feminist psychoanalyst Luce Irigaray has argued that Freudians and Lacanians need to hear another voice in a different language—that of woman. Although cross-genderal communication is beset by many problems, for example, male solipsism, translation, etc., woman's voice yields a perspective that is not apparent in the masculine discourse of popular culture or in that which dominates the academies. Irigaray's work psychoanalytically deconstructs the discourse of both and suggests an aetiology of male violence that identifies why men regard women as their rivals and why they are so fixated on castration and phallic imagery.

Patriarchal Culture Is a Culture Founded on Sacrifice, Crime, War

According to Irigaray, women sacrifice their bodies and are sacrificed by men as the offering that founds patriarchal culture. It is society that reproduces itself materially through women's bodies and exercises control over women's reproductive organs through the regulation of sexual intercourse, contraception, and abortion. To be sure women undergo gender-specific physical dangers in reproduction, but they are also victimized by a culture that treats women as things, that denies them the right to moral agency, that all too frequently brutalizes them. They are the psychological as well as the material foundation to a patriarchal culture. They exist for the sake and at the pleasure of the masculinist psychic economy. Empirical evidence shows that physical and emotional abuse, incest, and rape are the fate of many women in our society, and for those who escape such treatment, the threat always remains just below the surface to terrorize them. "How can we define the madness in which women are placed?" asks Irigaray. "You often need something of language, some delusion to signal that you are living in madness. Women do not in fact suffer from delusions. If they could, it would protect them. They suffer in their bodies. An absolutely immense bodily suffering."[31] It is their bodies and their blood that are the substance of American society, even though their contributions are rarely recognized by the "real world" of androcentric culture—the world of male socioeconomic and political elites. They are taken for granted as "natural resources" of an androcentric order that sees in women or those treated as such the means by which men can know their own power.

Her vilification as the castrated and powerless suggests that woman serves as the sacrificial body whose very rending makes men whole and holy. If the imaginary body in Western culture is normatively male as Freud, Lacan, and Irigaray all suggest, woman's allegedly defective body becomes the means by which men know their perfection. Her wounding is his blessing (Old English: *bletsein,* to wound). As the surrogate victim, she is castrated in his place so that his anxiety may be allayed. Accordingly, in the masculinist psychic economy, the phallogocentric world stands astride the bodies of women. "Mutilated, wounded, humiliated," writes Irigaray,

> overwhelmed by a feeling of inferiority that can never be "cured." In sum, women are definitively castrated. Their guilt would remain mute: active, of course, but unutterable, ineffable, to be expressed only by the body. They would give themselves up to be punished—by the accomplishment of castration without knowing what they had done wrong.[32]

To men who read gender difference reductively, woman's "crime" is ineffable, fused with her very being, her very body. She embodies transgression and is, by nature, guilty. But if, on the other hand, woman is not read as being a category of nature but rather a cultural fiction, that is, a way of being imposed by heterosexist society, we must revive the question that Girard's model posed: What crime did woman allegedly commit?

Surely it must be more than the tautology that women are not men. Although it might be argued that men project their own crime of violence onto their victims (for example, women are "asking for it"), neither answer really explains why, in the minds of men, women deserve their fate. Girard's model suggests that women and men are mimetic rivals who contend with one another over the object of desire. If, as Freud argues, the male child models himself initially after the mother and the mother is assumed to be the possessor of the phallus, then the object of mimetic rivalry is the phallus itself. In contrast to the Freudian theory that inscribes the figure of the father/superego with the power of castration, Irigaray suggests that men conjure up the vision of their mothers as the castrator. Inasmuch as male children suppose that all human beings possess the phallus and then later discover that their mothers have none, they assume that mothers have brought castration on themselves. Because Girard's account of hostility toward the rival is based on mimesis, the mother-woman symbolizes to the male the temptation of self-mutilation, that is, the loss of the phallus, echoing Bataille's depiction of the masculinist psychic economy. The need for rupture mimics the mother's "crime" of self-mutilation, but the substitution of women (or those placed in "womanly" roles) for the male subject allows heterosexist men simultaneously to fantasize rupture as well as preserve what the masculinist psychic economy considers the object of desire—the phallus.

Reading football and war through the lens of the Irigarayan model, it is apparent that male territorial games are the substance of this patriarchal culture. They recapitulate male identity in ritual performance. Football, like war, is not merely a tangential activity in the life of this culture but rather—as virtually any American male will tell you—is very much a part of who he is as a man. The rhetoric of these games articulates the unspeakable: the severance of the phallus from the body and the struggle for its possession. Men can both fantasize what it is like to be the mother, to be a woman, and resist that temptation. For in losing the phallus, losing the game, losing the war, they lose themselves as men. And for this frightful thought they punish their enemy, desire revenge against the mother, and seek to destroy her image as woman. "Patriarchal culture," declared Irigaray," is a culture founded on sacrifice, crime, war."[33] That is to say that patriarchal culture is established on the victimization of women *qua* woman.

Their sufferings contrast sharply with the excitement and interest generated by male territorial games that allegedly bring out the best in men. The trials of combat and celebrations of victory transfix Americans who, whether in the streets or their living rooms, vicariously participate in the euphoria of their proxies—in the deserts of the Middle East and on the playing fields of football stadiums all over the country. The inexorable escalation in the Gulf, just like the passing weeks in the NFL schedule, heightened anticipation for an emotionally charged culmination of tensions. As participants and spectators, men exuded confidence in the rationale for these male territorial games. "We know why we're there," President Bush assured the Congress and the nation in his State of the Union address of January 1991. But the allegation that American males, like other men, take pleasure in war is met with denial. "This nation has never found glory in war," insisted the president. Supposedly the war was an unpleasant task thrust upon the United States and its armed forces. Yet the response of both the population and the government, evident in the victory parades in Washington and New York City, belies the president's claims. Football fans need not be so disingenuous. They unapologetically revel in the excitement of the gridiron and the seemingly endless media coverage of Superbowl week and Superbowl Sunday.

It is not expected that women should understand the esoteric logic of these games or the visceral response that they elicit in men. All that is necessary is that women accept these practices as instinctual or natural. In that way, men neither have to explain nor justify the reasons for these passions that would require a metalanguage that legitimates androcentric discourse. To those women who become accustomed to these male passions, clichéd in the phrase "A man's gotta do what a man's gotta do!", acquiescence seems to be an inevitable consequence. But to those who are not privy to the cultural meaning of the American homosocial community, it seems incomprehensible. One Marine commander recalled a conversation with his four-year-old daughter just before he left for the Gulf. "When I left, she was crying and telling me she did not understand why I had to go. It really got to me."[34] Of course it is not only children who don't understand this compulsion for male territorial games. Antiwar demonstrators and Monday Football widows share in this consternation. And even the participants and spectators themselves find difficulty in articulating the reasons for their passions, the method to their madness. The President himself shrouded the ultimate explanation in mysticism. "We are Americans," reflected the president, "part of something larger than ourselves."

The work of Luce Irigaray suggests that the reason for their obliviousness may be that, in the modern patriarchal social order, discourse itself is androcentric. Language is constructed from the male perspective, and if that perspective contains a "blind spot," so, too, will its discursive expression. The rhetoric of male territorial games therefore is not remarkable because it is marked by the presuppositions common to the language of the culture. Of course it is not only in modern times that language has been informed by androcentrism. Western societies have certainly been influenced by the Stoic doctrine of language as *logos spermatikos* and long even questioned whether women were capable of reason. Based on the classical and medieval assumption that women served as only the source of unformed biological material seminally stamped with the divine image of the *logos,* this premodern misogynist conception of language was dispelled by modern science. But that does not mean that language was freed from the *imprimatur* of patriarchal social relations.

According to psychoanalytic models of the modern era, language is gendered male but not for philosophical or theological reasons. Instead the character of discourse is founded in early childhood. As the father of modern French psychoanalysis Jacques Lacan has argued, language itself is synthesized with the sense of sight. The aetiology of discourse lies in the verbalization of what appears within the field of vision. An object takes on linguistic significance "because it can be seen, because it is erected. There can be no symbolic use for what is not seen."[35] Lacan suggests that the male child's fascination with its own genitals results in the phallus being regarded as the primary signifier of language, the signifier of desire. Cultural reality is constituted by the gaze of the male as both subject and object. For Lacan language is therefore phallogocentric in the same way that Freud argued that libido is masculine.[36] Both the human being and human language are normatively male. But whereas Freud's hydraulic conception of cathexes is based on the satiation of biological needs, Lacan's semiotic construction renders desire unending. The signifier of desire, the phallus, is free-floating, released from dependence on the signified, the penis. In the Lacanian linguistic edifice, it is the phallus that speaks in and through language.[37] This patriarchal construction is inscribed in social reality not only in the paternal name which legitimizes offspring but in law itself—the customs, habits and codes that defend the rights of males by tradition or by force, if necessary. Irigaray notes that even the neutrality of the law most often is a screen for the exercise of masculine power.

Lacan's semiotic interpretation of Freud thus leaves little room for women. Without the phallus, their access to language and power is limited.

> Women's castration is defined as her *having* nothing penile, in seeing that She has No Thing. Nothing *like* a man. That is to say, *no sex/organ* that can be seen in a *form* capable of founding its reality, reproducing its truth. *Nothing to be seen is equivalent to having no thing. No being* and *no truth.*[38]

Man's existence is therefore predicated on this difference from woman. He possesses what woman lacks: the phallus, language, a human culture. In the Lacanian world, women not only face the abyss; they are the abyss. They are the "lack," the hole into which everything, along with the phallus, disappears. Women betoken nonexistence. Lacan consequently argued, in what has now become his famous dictum, that *"la femme n'existe pas."*[39] Obviously women physically exist, but Lacan's point is that, in a culture mediated by androcentric language, woman as a separate entity or "essence" does not. Thus, Western culture puts women in an anomalous position: since to Lacan "there is no pre-discursive reality,"[40] they physically exist but they are not real.

Hence, women have no discursive reality—indeed, no reality at all—other than that given them by men. As Irigaray described the rather frightening implications of Lacan's thesis, they live "only within models and laws devised by male subjects. Which implies that there are not really two sexes, but only one."[41] In this unisexual, monological world, it cannot be said that they exist in the same way that men do. On the contrary, like the biblical story of Adam's rib, women are derivative of the prototypical human: the male. They are an imperfect imitation of men and, as is widely reasoned in patriarchal society, can never truly take his place. To do so would efface the original on which they depend for their very existence. Women exist at man's pleasure, that is, only insofar as they serve the need of the masculinist psychic economy.

According to Irigaray, women serve two functions in the male imaginary: first, they are the means by that men can touch themselves.[42] Like his own hand or the solipsism of language, a woman's body allows a man to feel his own phallocentric reality. Secondly, woman serves as a mirror to unify the male subject. Lacan's paper on the "mirror stage," presented before the International Congress of Psychoanalysis in 1949, argued that, due to the immature physical development of the newborn's motor system, a baby experiences a bodily dehiscence that inhibits the formation of its self-image. That identity only emerges in the "mirror stage," a development over the first eighteen months, during that the child uses its own reflection, in a mirror or in the physical response of persons in the immediate environment, to constitute itself as an "Ideal-I." This "armour of an alienating identity" never rests secure either in the body or in the dialectical relationship with other "I's."[43] The unified self is therefore an ontological fiction that always threatens to melt away. Irigaray asserts that males learn to use females as a mirror to reinforce their own sense of identity. They need to see themselves reflected in the eyes of women to compensate for their own insecurity—most often, claims Irigaray (citing Virginia Woolf's *A Room of One's Own*), so that their egos are inflated to twice their size.

For women, on the other hand, no mirror is available to use as the means for unifying their own subjectivity. In the patriarchal context of Western society, mirrors reflect only the pure exteriority of woman and therefore serve to reinforce her role as a plane or surface on which man can see his own reflection.[44] She is appearance, not substance. Androcentric culture leaves women not only speechless but scattered as well. Her own reality is composed of what Irigaray calls the "scraps, uncollected debris"[45] of the female imaginary. She is constituted not by her own reflection but by the male gaze. "[O]ne might begin by being surprised, being suspicious, that it should be necessary to *become* a woman."[46] In Western societies women are not born; rather females must learn how to be a woman. She is a woman in a man's eyes.

> Out of this difference will be lifted one of two terms—but determined in relation to what?—and this term will be constituted as "origin," as that by whose differentiation the other may be engendered and brought to light. *The same remarking itself*—more or less—would thus produce the other.[47]

Gender relationships therefore primarily benefit the male in the sense that he experiences his own identity reflected in the admiration, fear, etc., that a woman feels for him. She is the means by which he inscribes himself with his own image. Woman, on the other hand, is a surface with no depth, an echo, a fiction wholly contingent upon androcentric reality. Accordingly, she is therefore construed as the other of the same.[48] She has no reality on her own—at least no separate reality perceptible to men. There is, Lacan insists, "no Other of the Other."[49] Without the Name of the Father and his Laws, she might well not exist at all.

In the Irigarayan model, woman is abandoned, left in a state of *déréliction*. Exiled from androcentric discourse, she speaks in fragments—the fragments of her self/ves—condemned to stuttering and stammering in a language not her own. Learning to become a woman, to be "the other of the same," brings her out of her self/ves into an alien land where she must learn to speak this foreign tongue. But it is precisely this marginalized existence, to which she is condemned, that draws suspicion from her male counterparts. Freud himself described woman as the "Dark Continent"[50] for, like colonized peoples who live on the boundaries of Eurocentric patriarchal civilization, she, too, is conceived as being dark, dangerous, unknown, and perhaps unknowable. It is assumed that she needs to be domesticated, to be taught the conqueror's language—one that she will never master, although she may be able to understand her master's wishes. Irigaray suggests that women are taught to abandon any desire to represent themselves—in effect, they are taught to abandon themselves to men's representations. She must learn to speak the language of desire of/for the phallus. This metaphor conjures up images of oral and genital rape, for, as Irigaray has implied by her controversial metaphor, the phallus separates the lips that keep a woman in touch with herself. Colonizing the minds and bodies of women in order to reproduce himself and his culture, "[h]e envelops her within these walls while he envelops himself and his things in her flesh."[51]

Yet just as the imperial powers of a century ago always feared the threat of insurrection, so, too, do men in modern patriarchal culture fear the rebellion of women. Woman is seen as the boundary of androcentric language, as the border of the known world. Although, like other colonized peoples, she may be intimidated, ridiculed, or even subjected to the most cruel violence, she remains a source of perennial anxiety. Perhaps she is even more dangerous, for whereas those subjugated by the imperial powers lived physically at the farthest reaches of the empire, women live amidst patriarchal culture, in the very homes of men. As the crease in the allegedly seamless masculinist symbolic, woman is the portal to the boundless, the infinite, and the irrational, and hence woman as absence is conflated with ultimate power and death. She is both the foundation on which man builds his identity as well as the force that can reduce it to rubble. She is paradoxical for her power lies in what she does not possess. She lacks the phallus and thereby symbolizes his own nonexistence.

Every woman is potentially each man's nightmare. She is a living reminder of his own castration, for without the phallus—the primary signifier—he is neither lucid nor articulate. He is struck dumb at the sight of her genitals. Freud argued that the Greek myth of the Medusa illustrated this dimension of the male psyche. Her decapitation was a thinly veiled allusion to castration. The head, adorned with snakes rather than hair, reiterates this loss because "the multiplication of penis symbols signifies castration."[52] Here is the "blind spot" in his vision. He cannot see it, but not because it is not within his capacity. He cannot see it because he dare not. He must avert his eyes for the sight of the sightless, of the blind spot that dares to return his gaze, is his own demise. It is a sight whose meaning is too terrible to contemplate, whose meaning is the absence of all meaning. In the male imaginary, a woman's genitals are not only a gash in the body; they are a void that beckons man to his own self-destruction. "Beneath this shining light of the sky, today, justice aside," wrote Bataille,

> this sickly existence, close to death, and yet real, abandons itself to the "lack" that its coming into the world reveals.
>
> Completed "being," from rupture to rupture, after a growing nausea had delivered it to the void of the sky, has become no longer "being," but wound, and even "agony" of all that is.[53]

The wound remains open in the male psyche, a constant reminder of the maw of nonexistence, hidden by garments but never banished. It is a wound "that rarely heals of its own accord," confides Bataille.[54]

In horror, the male spectator, nonetheless, turns stiff—a psychophysical response of erection by which the man comforts himself that the loss is not his own. The horror recedes in the shift of attention to the phallus. And there he finds shelter from the naught which is woman. In that the shape of a woman's vagina is the inversion of the phallus, the woman is no longer boundless but conforms to the morphology of the male, not only physically but also psychologically. The threat of her genitals is kept within bounds. She is no longer an infinite void, and men therefore dare to take pleasure in what may be their own undoing. Within the framework of the male psyche, sexual intercourse is therefore far more complicated than the response to only a sexual need. According to Lacan, it is a desire for totality or complete immersion in the Other, even though the imputation of omnipotence to the Other induces a certain anxiety.[55] It is as if man is attempting to make woman yield the impossible: to fuse a finite, unified self with an infinite sense of all-in-all. Men would be as gods. Hence, man experiences "the desire to force entry, to penetrate, to appropriate for himself the mystery of this womb where he has been conceived, the secret of his begetting, of his 'origin.'"[56] He is redeemed with the eternal return to the womb wherein lies his own apotheosis.

A "Symptom" of Man

It is apparent, however, that this construction of woman is charactererized by a strong ambivalence. On the one hand, woman, who functions as a mirror to unify the masculinist subject, holds forth the promise of the infinite, a world before the advent of boundaries, an "oceanic feeling" of almost mystic sexuality. On the other hand, woman symbolizes his own dissolution in the morphology of her own genitals, a world devoid of androcentric language and culture, the demise of his own existence as a man. As Irigaray noted in her "Poverty of Psychoanalysis," some analysts of the Lacanian tradition would therefore consider woman a "symptom" of man—a neurotic manifestation of some deeper disturbance.[57] Some even suggest that this psychopathology is inevitable and unalterable, that it is the only way woman can exist. Like the ascetic martyr of Christian antiquity, she must acquiesce to this suffering for her existence otherwise has no meaning. In contrast Irigaray finds that this discursive construction of woman should not be cast in the light of predestination. Women exist in the flesh as prediscursive realities, and it is in their potential as the "other of the other" that they can escape the imposition of male hegemony, both linguistic and physical.

A woman on her own is a threat to man because without the mirror that unifies the self, he has no self-consciousness as the man of patriarchal culture. It becomes imperative to "keep a woman in her place," for otherwise he will not know his own. Thus, the maintenance of masculinist identity demands the control of women in order to keep an eye on them, not only so that they don't stray but also so that they do not rebel. Because women also embody the dissolution of the masculinist self through the image of castration, they must be insulated from feeling their own power which threatens the foundation of phallogocentric authority. How is that possible? Irigaray suggests that man displaces the fear of the abyss-that-is-woman with his own phallus. Women cannot feel their own power if they are conceived as the "other of the same," if they are culturally born as women, if they conform to the phallocentric ethos in the same way that their vaginal walls conform to the shape of the phallus. Hence, the anxiety that castration imagery engenders is allayed by the imagery of phallic penetration. As the living embodiment of the metaphoric penetrable body, woman remains the linchpin of the masculinist psyche.

Because male territorial games reiterate masculinist identity through the homosocial experience of male bonding, it is not surprising that the rhetoric of castration and phallic penetration plays a prominent role in them. The phallus, as the primary signifier, is the guarantor that the masculinist subject "means what he says." The brandishing of phallic weaponry in war, whether it be missiles, bombs, rifles, knives, or countless other arms, threatens the opponent with castration: a state devoid of one's own autonomous meaning in which one's existence, like that of a woman in patriarchal culture, is dependent upon the sole possessor of the phallus. The surrender of the enemy is not only the surrender of his weapons and his autonomy but of his manhood as well. In the masculinist psychic economy, the defeated feel humiliated, emasculated—a humiliation similar to that described by Freud as the shame that a woman "naturally" feels about the inadequacy of her own genitals. Without access to phallic imagery, the vanquished remains in disarray, speechless, compelled to pay tribute and recognize the hegemony of the victor. The victor even sees himself in the look of the vanquished, as in the eyes of a woman, and knows himself to be "a virtuous, courageous and manly conqueror."

The glory of war in that men revel, in which they know themselves to be men, however, does know bounds. Men have written of the horrors of war— the ghastliness of death that can be read into the burned corpses along the "Highway of Death" from Kuwait City to Basra. War reduces men to mangled bodies and destroys the pretense of civilized ways. It is a ghastly sight that, if seen through the Irigarayan model, bears a resemblance to the sight of woman in the masculinist psychic economy. For she is not only the vehicle by which men know themselves, she also signifies the abyss, the maw of nonexistence. Death is a woman who beckons a man beyond his own bounds. Tempted to feel his own power, he runs headlong into war that reveals the fate that awaits him. The mangled bodies of his victims, like the "mangled" bodies of women as *castrati,* proleptically anticipate his own loss of self, perhaps as a warrior, but certainly as a man. The warrior as man/the man as warrior is warned not to look too closely at the bodies of his victims, for the euphoric passions of war, like sex, give way to nightmarish fears.

The Gulf War largely insulated the American public against the redounding of this castration imagery. Although the mass media were inundated with rhetorical and even pictorial representations of the enemy's emasculation, the Pentagon's censorship policies ensured that the wounded and dead among American and coalition forces would not appear on national television or on the front pages of the morning newspapers. And even the ten thousands of dead and wounded Iraqis were largely excised from the conscience of American viewers by the networks who exhibited restraint on the grounds of "good taste."

Like the psychophysical response to the "Medusa's Head," described by Freud, castration fears were supplanted by signs of phallic penetration. The ever-present images of the Nintendo war afforded viewers the opportunity to engage in a vicarious gang rape of the enemy. The irresistible thrust of American airpower was met by weak and altogether inadequate defenses by the enemy. The confidence with which pilots carried out their mission was characterized as their professionalism and dedication to "just doing a job"; yet, no one could disguise the excitement with which both the pilots and the viewing public, in newsrooms, barrooms, and living rooms all over America, thrilled to the destruction of their targets. Viewers became so accustomed to the sequence of events in the bombing runs that they even anticipated and savored the imminent explosion in the buildings below, following the release of the bombs/themselves.

Removed from the consequence of those actions, the bombing runs themselves become a pure sign of dominion—a sanitized castration and rape of the enemy. Indeed the American military itself argued that the operation was designed to ensure the impossible: a virtually bloodless war. Reassured by the American media, the public was told that the war was fought according to the logic of collateral damage. The deaths of civilians were ancillary; certainly they were not intended. And in light of the mass surrenders of Iraqis troops along the front, deaths of human beings would be kept at a minimum. Both guilt and the terrors of war would be kept at bay. The political and military objectives of the Coalition would be achieved with minimal suffering, and the country would enjoy the psychological benefits of an American national renewal through the prosecution of a successful war—a war without the haunting specter of human annihilation. Its success ensured that American power, the ethos of the masculinist psychic economy, would remain unquestioned and unchallenged.

This unbridled celebration of Americanism was echoed in the coincidental timing of the Superbowl which, like the Gulf War, uses the rhetoric of castration and phallic penetration but insulates the American public from the fear that castration portends. As a cultural fiction that recreates the psychological dynamics of war, football is the struggle of two sides for exclusive possession of the phallus. It reiterates the boundaries of the homosocial community by defining sexual difference based on victors and vanquished, winners and losers. Ball possession/possession of the phallus distinguishes between those who control the course of action and those who don't. As the primary ball-handler, the quarterback is identified through contagious magic with the ball/phallus itself. And whereas the defense attempts to sack the quarterback and strip the ball, the quarterback attempts to penetrate the defense through the use of his surrogates, that is, ball carriers and receivers. When the defense is successful in either stopping the offense's drive or in forcing and recovering a fumble of the ball/phallus, the sides undergo a transformation. The offense becomes the defense (ball-less), and the latter comes into possession of the ball/phallus. Although the defense is in the more vulnerable position, ascribed in sexual difference to the female, the defensive players attempt to unwrite this rule-created disadvantage by acting in a very aggressive manner. They want to do to the other team's offense what has already been done to their own. But whereas war frequently illustrates the loss of the phallus, for example, defeat and death, in the most horrifying and bloody ways, football spares the spectator this unpleasant reality. The language of mutilation and murder is frequently employed by coaches, but disfigurement and death are rarely seen on this playing field. It is a game that limits the physical manifestations of men's nightmarish fear of women.

The play between offense and defense, phallus-bearers and *castrati,* thus reflects the perennial play of the masculinist psychic economy in everyday life. Adult men as well as adolescent males feel constantly challenged in the society-at-large to prove their masculinity to other men and to women. Control of one's identity is played out in the control of the phallus as the primary signifier of androcentric language whether it be read in any of the myriad phallocentric signs: money, power, social status, automobiles, "trophy women." But whereas that game is drawn out over time, and indeed may be a game that many men will not win, the experience is telescoped through football into an intense time-space continuum of four 15-minute segments that the male viewer vicariously enjoys. It is a drama of the self—his own self. His identification with his team's quarterback suggests that through his proxy he has his fate in his own hands. He is not only the quarterback; he is the ball—vulnerable to attack and loss yet infused with the potential for triumphant dominion on the field and in life itself. Victory inflates his own sense of mastery of self and others, mutually acknowledged in the homosocial community of fellow partisan fans. Defeat, on the other hand, is never direct. The devastation that the loss of the phallus presents is always mediated by the fact that football is "only a game," that it is "not real life," but most importantly that there is always next week or next year.

But whether it be war or football, the game is really endless. The phallus as that which is both erected and seen is always in danger of being lost. That is its nature, for in the gestalt of sexual identity in the masculinist psychic economy, that which is seen rests on the field of that which is not. As the naught that informs and shapes the phallus and its self-consciousness in man, woman is the ever-present threat. For either her withdrawal or her ingestion of the phallus into boundless, infinite Otherness could happen at any moment. The phallus must be reaffirmed and reinforced through the obsessive compulsive ritual of male territorial games in that woman, the enemy, is eternally vanquished, and the place of man in the cosmos is reassured. War and football thus embody *"the same re-marking itself"*—a gesture that reflects the insecurity that rests at the heart of man in patriarchal culture.

WHAT THE *ORESTEIA* DESCRIBES FOR US STILL TAKES PLACE

Although male territorial games seem to be rooted in castration anxiety, the fear of the power of woman is not simply about the preservation of the male's phallus. According to Irigaray, castration anxiety is a palimpsest that covers an original writing which nonetheless bleeds through. She insists that the fear of castration hides another cutting—that of the umbilical cord. Thus castration anxiety is a displacement of separation anxiety. The blind spot in his field of vision is revealed as a scarring of the male psyche. The mother is the one who has separated herself from her offspring; she has cut him off. Yet, in the male imaginary, where the umbilical cord once rested now stands the phallus. Whereas the male child initially assumes all human beings are endowed with the phallus, he becomes aware of the mother's lack of the phallus that he assumes is now his own/his self. Accordingly the male imaginary holds that in separating herself from him, she has rent her body—a form of auto-mutilation—on which his very being is predicated. To be male is to be paradoxical. On the one hand, his mother's "self-castration" is the *sine qua non* for his existence. As the bearer of the phallus, he is the beneficiary of maternal sacrifice. On the other hand, the image of castration infuses his body with the fear of nonexistence, for to be without the phallus, that is, the surrogate for the umbilical cord, is to be without the basis for his physical and cultural being. And it is not simply that the maternal power of castration or the temptation of mimetic self-mutilation haunts him. The mother-woman as absence creates an image of boundlessness, limitlessness, which far exceeds the power of the phallus to fill. The thought of castration therefore engenders a profound sense of ultimate impotence among men. Thus, he simultaneously honors his mother for her sacrifice but reviles her power over him.

Although women learn to overcome separation anxiety by virtue of their isomorphic identification with their mothers, men have no such alternative. To be male is to devise strategies by which he can live this paradoxical existence. He can overcome these deep-seated fears by unwriting separation anxiety through either appropriating the womb for himself or by eliminating woman's existence. The drive to penetrate or force entry is not simply a matter of sexual pleasure or aggressiveness but rather an attempt to return to the womb, to his own origin. Here he feels safe in a world restored to the innocence that never was. The act of returning to the womb is simultaneously a restoration of what had been lost to the mother in his birth—the phallus—and a pouring forth of himself—a self-rending gesture—that is his undoing. The triumph of the phallus in its return is a gift of fantastic self-mutilation in which the erection as primary signifier is lost in the *mater/*material world. Perhaps in placing the seed in her womb he can even give birth to himself—an offspring that is securely founded on his own phallic affirmation rather than on castration anxiety. The psychological desires of the masculinist psychic economy produce a politics that seeks to control woman's reproduction. But neither orgasm nor a fantasized return to the womb are permanent. The security of the preoedipal, prenatal existence is fleeting, and the male only comes to himself in the reappropriation of his alienated phallocentric identity.

Alternatively a man may want to eliminate the threat that woman embodies by marginalizing, disempowering, or even effacing her being. He may do so by restricting her access to phallogocentric power, for example, sexual discrimination in education and jobs, or perhaps, in the minds of some men, she should be punished through battering, rape, or even death. In those cases she must pay for her transgression, fictively constructed as the crime of castration—the alibi for separation anxiety. She must be made to pay for his being born. The woman-mother is therefore read as the enemy. The rhetoric of castration and phallic penetration herald a return to the womb, to undo the damage that the woman-mother has done to her son, which can only be accomplished if he extracts what is owed him: blood. Irigaray suggests that this strategy entails the need to "make the blood flow again"[58]— a sign of intrauterine existence which predates separation and the *Angst* of male phallogocentric existence. The shedding of blood therefore serves two purposes: it punishes the woman for her transgression, while at the same time returning to him what is his—her life/blood/life's blood. Violence against women, then, from the standpoint of the Irigarayan model stems from the desire for revenge against the mother-woman in the masculinist psychic economy. Battering, incest, rape, and the like cannot be attributed to such superficial causes as incompatibility or miscommunication, nor can its widespread appearance be caused by severely disturbed men alone. Ostensibly "normal" men have shown a propensity toward domestic violence, and while alcohol and drug abuse may serve as alibis for violence, they do not account for its origins. Instead the Irigarayan model sees it as a consequence of a patriarchal social order in which male identity is predicated on phallocentric anxieties. Of course this pattern is not merely the product of modern Western cultures but is a symptom of all patriarchal social orders. Unlike Freud who speculated in *Totem and Taboo* that originary violence is found in the killing of the primal father, the Irigarayan model suggests that violence against women recapitulates the primal crime of all patriarchal social orders: the murder of the mother.

Although Freud found the oedipal trilogy dispositive in the description of the triad of mother-father-child, Irigaray sees a definitive account in Aeschylus's *Oresteia*. In that trilogy Agamemnon, the king of Athens, sacrifices his own daughter, Iphigenia, as a propitiation to ensure a fair wind for the Hellenic fleet bound for Troy. After a decade of warfare Agamemnon proves victorious and returns a conqueror to his native Athens; his wife Clytemnestra, still mourning the death of Iphigenia, kills Agamemnon. At the behest of the oracle of Apollo, Orestes, their son, decides to avenge his father's death by murdering his own mother. Although the patriarchal order hallowed the ritual sacrifice of Iphigenia, Orestes condemns Clytemnestra for her act of retributive justice with the verdict, "Unholy was your crime, unholy shall be your punishment."[59] In the last play of the cycle, *The Eumenides*, the Furies, holdovers from the pre-Olympian matriarchal religion, demand the life of Orestes, who is tried for the heinous crime of matricide. Through the intervention of Olympian patriarchal deities—Apollo, the god of reason and harmony, and Athena, the virgin goddess of wisdom and courage—Orestes is spared condemnation.

The origin of this spiral of violence lay in the shedding of blood of a woman's body, Iphigenia's, whose sacrifice ensures the success of men in war. Iphigenia is depicted as an innocent, unblemished victim whose voice cannot be heard in the ears of men.

> *Heedless of her tears,*
> *Her cries of "Father!" and her maiden years,*
> *Her judges valued more*
> *Their glory and their war . . .*
> *Rough hands tear at her girdle, cast*
> *Her saffron silks to earth. Her eyes*
> *Search for their slaughterers; and each,*
> *Seeing her beauty, that surpassed*
> *A painter's vision, yet denies*
> *The pity her dumb looks beseech,*
> *Struggling for voice*[60]

Her sacrifice is regarded as necessary if the Athenian homosocial community is to fulfill its duty as a warrior caste. Without the sacrificial blood of Iphigenia, they would be less than men. The murder of a woman is reiterated in the revenge-taking of Orestes who believes that his mother has taken away his father. From the son's perspective, the act of killing the father is of an altogether different magnitude than the death of the woman-daughter-mother. In both Iphigenia and Clytemnestra's cases, the murders of these women are justified as either necessary or just. The killing of the father, however, is a crime. As is made plain by Apollo's address to the tribunal, a woman has very little to do with creation, serving only as a vessel for the seed that seminally stamps the son in the image of the father. Father and son are one substance so that to kill the father-husband is to undermine the very foundation of the son's existence.

For Irigaray, Aeschylus's tragedy articulates the castration anxiety experienced by the son. The mother has the power to rend the male body, to emasculate it, and to leave it dishonored. The murder of Agamemnon by Clytemnestra serves as a literary alibi which legitimates Orestes' desire for revenge against the mother. "What the *Oresteia* describes for us," warns

Irigaray, "still takes place."[61] The fantasized murder of mother-daughter, whether it be in the guise of Clytemnestra or Iphighenia or in the women of contemporary culture, becomes the *sine qua non* for homosocial community in patriarchal culture. All too often domestic violence brings "non-punishment of the son, the burial of the madness of women—and the burial of women in madness . . ."[62] The rhetoric of revenge—castration and phallic penetration—enters into male rituals which, as culturally endogamous bonding processes, ensure the safety of its participants from the threat of woman by engaging in fantasies that render women harmless.

THE DESCENT OF MAN

From the perspective of the Irigarayan model, castration and phallic imagery are not simply forms of male aggression but rather are the manifestations of men's deep-seated alienation in a patriarchal culture. This culture does not offer them the means by which they can truly overcome the trauma that they experienced at birth. Instead they settle for games that reenact that separation (through the castration of the opponent/enemy) and redeem that which has been lost (through penetration). The euphoria of victory in football and the glory of triumph in war both reflect a mystical bond among men in which they have achieved, if only for a moment, a wholeness that they have missed most of their lives. And although women are, by and large, conspicuously absent from the performance of these rituals, the metaphor of woman is noticeably present as the means by which men may vanquish their enemy and secure their redemption. In the midst of victory, in the glory that shrouds the champion, man stands alone—at one with the cosmos and himself. Here there is no distinction, not even the "other of the same"—only an eternal sameness. But the glory is fleeting, even though men go to extraordinary lengths to preserve these reified moments of history, so revered in historical monuments, trophies, testimonies, and other signs of remembrance. They are memories of what has been lost and what men would like to find again. And so in the masculinist psychic economy, men go in quest of what proves elusive even when they experience it.

As a form of repetition-compulsion, football continually reiterates this same game. Although each season and virtually every game guarantees a victor, the cycle is as endless as masculinist sexual desire which is but temporarily sated. Each return, each score is never sufficient because the construction of the masculinist psychic economy never permits a permanent state of rest. The reappropriation of the womb by the male warrior always culminates in his inevitable expulsion. Victory over one team always gives way to challenges by the next. Champions must always defend their titles. Yet frustration, like victory, is also only temporary. Without finality this male territorial game is not just a means to establish homosocial identity. The process itself is a way of life. And so football players and fans live an existence whose very endlessness gives meaning to their existence.

This game of football, this game of life, finds articulation of its primary signifier, the phallus, through the metaphor of the penetrable body. But Girard has pointed out, when the surrogate victim is too closely identified with the original transgressor, violence overflows its channels. For many men who involve themselves as spectators in the game of football, the strategies and counterstrategies of castration, penetration, and resistance pass from the metaphor of the penetrable body, "woman," to flesh-and-blood women. Although spectating offers the vicarious thrill of victory, it disempowers the spectator from directly affecting the performance. Disappointment and frustration on the field and on the television screen can be acted on in different venues—albeit apart from the rules of the game which adjudicate the boundaries of the penetrable body. The violence can therefore at times be virtually unrestrained. The metaphor comes alive in the physical presence of wives, girlfriends, daughters, etc., whose proximity allows for the immediate resolution of hyperreal frustrations.

The descent into the masculinist psychic economy is therefore more than a game; it is deadly serious for women who, although innocent bystanders, are deemed guilty by men. But it is not only biological women who are victimized; it is also all those who enflesh the metaphor of the penetrable body: gay men and wartime adversaries. Those identities were often conflated during the Gulf War in the person of Saddam Hussein. This configuration was aptly illustrated in a cartoon "The Descent of Man" (See Figure 5.2), reprinted from the *New York Times* in the 1991 edition of Sam Keen's classic work *Faces of the Enemy*. Scanning "The Descent of Man" from left to right, the reader is regaled with a mock reversal of Darwinian evolution. The cartoon begins with the portrayal of Clark Gable as the epitome of "mankind," whose figure is indelibly identified in American popular culture with that claim of androcentric narcissism, "Frankly my dear, I don't give a damn." From this icon of masculinity, we cross the boundary that separates the human from nonhuman, from man to ape. Following in the brute's footsteps is the chimpanzee who quizzically scratches his head as a symbol of the descent into prediscursive reality. And what is the nature of this prediscursive reality? The contiguous image of the snake/viper/cobra incarnates the notions of cold-blooded deceit and evil. The metamorphosis is completed by the eye settling on the image of Saddam Hussein, cut off at the waist, the stump of his body resting in what appears to be simultaneously a pool of blood/oil/faeces/urine, with flies buzzing about his head. Quite consciously, the narrative uses the *double entendre* of "descent" facetiously to twist the Darwinian allusion by replacing the origin of species

FIGURE 5.2   "The Descent of Man" by David Levine. Copyright © 1991 by The New York Times Company. Reprinted by permission.

with the degeneration of "man," personified by Saddam Hussein.

In his updated prologue written to reflect the American experience in the Gulf War, Keen intuitively stated that "like demon-possessed lovers . . . , we seemed lost without our enemies."[63] Despite the book's reflections on the "hostile imagination," his commentary is remarkable for what remains unsaid. According to Keen the cartoon bears witness to the persistence of war propaganda in the construction of the faces of the enemy: a greedy stranger, an aggressor, barbarian, criminal, torturer, rapist, beast, reptile, insect, enemy of God—in short the embodiment of transgression. But despite Keen's recognition of the gendered character of war propaganda and the pervasiveness of "phallic assertion," it is limited to abuse of the "enemy's women" as a sign of domination. What is missing, however, is any reference to the enemy as woman herself. For this cartoon can be doubly read, not only as the "Descent of Man" into the subhuman but also as the transmutation of male into female. The devolution successively charts: the disappearance of androcentric, cognitive discourse; the identification of this loss with the snake—long recognized as a sign of matriarchal spirituality; and finally the symbolic castration of the enemy, mired fixedly in libidinal anality. The message is clear: Saddam Hussein is "less than a man"—subhuman, castrated, woman.

Irrational, emotional, lawless, this unmanned figure had conjured up the power of maternal wrath, but the "mother of all battles" was treated with derision, as indeed are all females in war. Hussein is regarded with the same horror and disparagement that Freud claimed was the universal response of men to the sight of women's genitals. Hussein is marginalized, shamed, silenced, but above all guilty—not for what he is but for what he is not. For he is not a man. Cut off at the waist, Hussein is definitively a woman who enjoys the rights of the vanquished—none at all. As a cosmogonic narrative of masculinist sexuality, the cartoon portrays castration, not as the consequence of political judgment and moral condemnation but as their prerequisite. Hussein is not judged in order to be castrated but castrated in order to be judged. Why?

Without the figure of castration/castrated figure, there could not be the notion of phallomorphically conceived difference on which the masculinist psychic economy is predicated. Hussein is characterized as incoherent and lawless for the sake of discourse and morality, for without him or ones like him, that is, discursively created women, there would be no androcentric self-consciousness, no ground from which phallic assertion rises, no patriarchal civilization. Yet, at the same time, the very backdrop of Otherness, the outside, the unknown and unknowable, and the primitive menacingly seeks to envelop and consume phallic hegemony. Here the figure of castration/castrated figure threatens to turn back on the wielder of power. The castrated figure must be dominated and controlled, and if necessary, attacked and destroyed, lest the masculinist subject suffer the fate intended for the victim.

Saddam Hussein is made an example. The stump of his severed body sits in a pool of blood/oil/faeces/urine. *Inter faeces et urinam nascimur*, wrote Augustine. "We are born between faeces and urine." Freud argued that in the world of the male imaginary, the penis-substitute or (normatively male) baby is identified with feces. Marked by blood as the sign of castration and thereby mired in anality, women receive the phallus/fetus as a gift from the father and excrete it. Although born of the mother, it is marked with the name of the father as a sign of his ownership, his property, as the incarnation of himself. Women are therefore incidental to the production of the same: phallus/fetus/language/law. Similarly, in the cartoon as in the Gulf War, the "militarily castrated" (Nixon) and penetrated Saddam Hussein yields blood/feces, that is, his oil, which is not his own, but belongs to "real men"—the Americans who wield the force of logic, law, and phallic weaponry.

The fallout of male territorial games—battering and bombing, incest and rape—therefore simultaneously invents "woman" as the enemy and attempts to subdue her. For by overcoming her resistance, Otherness disappears. Violence produces harmony. War produces peace. The bomb or pregnant phallus alluded to in the reference to the Dhahran signing ceremony marks the Other ("Mrs. Saddam") as the same. And the anal penetration of the castrated Hussein with a SCUD missile destroys his manhood and reinscribes our own on/in his body. Men can "feel good" about the war and ourselves for in war "we" are reborn.

Perhaps the most difficult question in studying the relationship of war, battering and other sports is not why, but why now? What triggered this disturbing response of the American patriarchal social order? It has been suggested by a number of critics that the end of the cold war shifted the alignment of world tensions from East-West to North-South, and that the Gulf War opened the era of the "New World Order." Such a crisis would precipitate the invention of a new enemy with its attendant psychodynamics. Thus, the Gulf War was not a reaction to a threat to the "New World Order" but rather this new era's founding act of violence: the positing of a new facade to a reality as old as patriarchal culture itself. Saddam Hussein became the face of a new enemy to replace the one to which we had become so accustomed. And although domestic sport offers a vehicle for men to express their desire for revenge, its sublimated forms of bloodshed do not provide the same release as the "real" thing. The new post–Gulf War era therefore has not brought the peace that was promised by the Bush administration, because it is predicated on the exercise of violence to control those who embody rebellion within the old male order, both foreign and domestic. It would seem that the battles of Baghdad and Basra were in some very significant ways the recapitulation of what has happened in countless foreign wars waged by patriarchal cultures over the centuries. But perhaps even more disturbingly it reflects what has happened and continues to happen daily behind closed doors in America. And that war is not over.

NOTES

1. Vide, Allan Stoekl, "Introduction," in Georges Bataille, *Visions of Excess: Selected Writings, 1927–1939*, ed. Allan Stoekl, trans. Allan Stoekl, with Carl R. Lovitt and Donald M. Leslie, Jr. (Minneapolis: University of Minnesota, 1985), ix–xxv..

2. René Girard, *Violence and the Sacred*, trans. Patrick Gregory (Baltimore: Johns Hopkins, 1977), 222.

3. Georges Bataille, "The Big Toe," *Visions of Excess: Selected Writings, 1927–1939* ed. Allan Stoekl, trans. Allan Stoekl, with Carl R. Lovitt and Donald M. Leslie, Jr. (Minneapolis: University of Minnesota, 1985), 20.

4. Georges Bataille, "The Practice of Joy Before Death," *Visions of Excess: Selected Writings, 1927–1939* ed. Allan Stoekl, trans. Allan Stoekl, with Carl R. Lovitt and Donald M. Leslie, Jr. (Minneapolis: University of Minnesota, 1985), 235.

5. Ibid., 237.

6. Georges Bataille, *Erotism. Death and Sensuality* trans. Mary Dalwood (San Francisco: City Lights, 1986), 186.

7. Georges Bataille, "The Use Value of D. A. F. de Sade," *Visions of Excess: Selected Writings, 1927–1939* ed. Allan Stoekl, trans. Allan Stoekl, with Carl R. Lovitt and Donald M. Leslie, Jr. (Minneapolis: University of Minnesota, 1985), 97.

8. Georges Bataille, "The Sacred Conspiracy," *Visions of Excess: Selected Writings, 1927–1939* ed. Allan Stoekl, trans. Allan Stoekl, with Carl R. Lovitt and Donald M. Leslie, Jr. (Minneapolis: University of Minnesota, 1985), 181.

9. Bataille, *Erotism*, 191.

10. Ibid., 167.

11. Ibid., 47–48.

12. Ibid., 108.

13. Ibid., 63.

14. Ibid., 239.

15. Ibid., 140.

16. Georges Bataille, *Inner Experience*, trans. Leslie Anne Bold (Albany: State University of New York, 1988), 114.

17. Ibid., 118.

18. Georges Bataille, "The Pineal Eye," *Visions of Excess: Selected Writings, 1927–1939* ed. Allan Stoekl, trans. Allan Stoekl, with Carl R. Lovitt and Donald M. Leslie, Jr. (Minneapolis: University of Minnesota, 1985).

19. C. G. Jung, *Memories, Dreams, Reflections*, ed. Aniela Jaffé, trans. Richard and Clara Winston (New York: Random House, 1963), 12.

20. Bataille, "The Pineal Eye," 82.

21. Georges Bataille, "The Solar Anus," *Visions of Excess: Selected Writings, 1927–*

1939 ed. Allan Stoekl, trans. Allan Stoekl, with Carl R. Lovitt and Donald M. Leslie, Jr. (Minneapolis: University of Minnesota, 1985), 8.

22. Bataille, "The Practice of Joy Before Death," 239.
23. Ibid.
24. Bataille, *Inner Experience*, 194.
25. Bataille, *Erotism*, 18.
26. Ibid., 54.
27. Ibid., 39.
28. As Berkeley Kaite has observed, both hard- and soft-core heterosexual pornography stress the look of anguish/ecstasy on the face of the female subject. Berkeley Kaite, "The Pornographic Body Double: Transgression Is the Law," in *Body Invaders: Panic Sex in America*, ed. Arthur and Marilouise Kroker (New York: St. Martin's Press, 1987), 150–68. The heterosexual male obsession with the female orgasm reflects this need to experience and appropriate his surrogate's bursting of boundaries.
29. Bataille, "The Solar Anus," 9.
30. Luce Irigaray, *Speculum of the Other Woman*, trans. Gillian C. Gill (Ithaca: Cornell University Press, 1985), 11–129.
31. Luce Irigaray, "Women-Mothers, the Silent Substratum of the Social Order," *The Irigaray Reader*, ed. Margaret Whitford, trans. David Macey, (Oxford: Basil Blackwell, 1991), 48.
32. Irigaray, *Speculum*, 88.
33. Luce Irigaray, "Une chance de vivre," *Sexes et parentés* (Paris: Les éditions de minuit, 1987), 200.
34. Chris Hedges, "Finding Life's Meaning in Winds and Rains of War," *New York Times*, January 24, 1991, A13.
35. Jacques Lacan, *Seminar, Book II: The Ego in Freud's Theory and in the Technique of Psychoanalysis, 1954–1955*, ed. Jacques-Alain Miller, trans. Sylvana Tomaselli (New York: W. W. Norton & Co., 1988), 272.
36. Sigmund Freud, *Three Essays on the Theory of Sexuality, Standard Edition* of the *Complete Psychological Works of Sigmund Freud*, ed. trans. James Strachey (London: Hogarth, 1874), VII, 219: "Indeed, if we were able to give a more definite connotation to the concepts of 'masculine' and 'feminine,' it would even be possible to maintain that libido is invariably and necessarily of a masculine nature, whether it occurs in men or in women and irrespectively of whether its object is a man or a woman."
37. Jacques Lacan, "The Signification of the Phallus," in *Écrits: A Selection* trans. Alan Sheridan (New York: W. W. Norton & Co., 1977), 284.
38. Luce Irigaray, *Speculum of the Other Woman*, 48.
39. Jacques Lacan, "God and the Jouissance of Woman," in *Feminine Sexuality. Jacques Lacan and the école freudienne*, ed. Juliet Mitchell and Jacqueline Rose, trans. Jacqueline Rose (New York: W. W. Norton & Co., 1982), 144.
40. Jacques Lacan, *Le Séminaire, livre XX, Encore, 1972–73* (Paris: Seuil, 1975), 33.
41. Luce Irigaray, *This Sex Which Is Not One*, trans. Catherine Porter with Carolyn Burke (Ithaca: Cornell University Press, 1985), 86.
42. Irigaray, *This Sex Which Is Not One*, 24.
43. Jacques Lacan, "The Mirror Stage," in *Écrits: A Selection*, trans. Alan Sheridan (New York: W. W. Norton Co., 1977), 1–7.
44. Luce Irigaray, "Femmes divines," in *Sexes et parentés* (Paris: Les éditions de minuit, 1987), 77.

45. Irigaray, *This Sex which Is Not One*, 30.
46. Irigaray, *Speculum*, 22.
47. Ibid., 21.
48. Ibid., 321.
49. Jacques Lacan, "Subversion of the Subject and Dialectic of Desire," *Écrits: A Selection*, trans. Alan Sheridan (New York: W. W. Norton & Co., 1977), 311.
50. Sigmund Freud, *The Question of Lay Analysis,*" *Standard Edition of the Complete Psychological Works of Sigmund Freud*, ed. and trans. James Strachey (London: Hogarth, 1974) XXI: 241.
51. Luce Irigaray, "Sexual Difference," in *The Irigaray Reader*, trans. Seán Hand (Oxford: Basil Blackwell, 1991) 170.
52. Freud, "Medusa's Head," *Standard Edition*, XVIII: 273.
53. Bataille, *Inner Experience*, 80.
54. Bataille, *Erotism*, 104.
55. Lacan, "Subversion of the Subject and the Dialectic of Desire," *Écrits: A Selection*, trans. Alan Sheridan (New York: W. W. Norton & Co., 1977), 311.
56. Irigaray, *This Sex Which Is Not One*, 25.
57. Irigaray, "The Poverty of Psychoanalysis," in *Irigaray Reader*, trans. David Macey with Margaret Whitford (Oxford: Basil Blackwell, 1991), 89.
58. Irigaray, *This Sex Which Is Not One*, 25.
59. Aeschylus, "The Choephori," *The Oresteian Trilogy*, trans. Philip Vellacott (New York: Penguin, 1959), 137.
60. Aeschylus, "Agamemnon," *The Oresteian Trilogy*, trans, Philip Vellacott (New York: Penguin, 1959), 50–51.
61. Irigaray, "The Bodily Encounter with the Mother," in *The Irigaray Reader*, trans. David Macey (Oxford: Basil Blackwell, 1991), 37.
62. Irigaray, "The Bodily Encounter," 37.
63. Sam Keen, *Faces of the Enemy: Reflections of the Hostile Imagination* (San Francisco: Harper, 1991), 7.

S i x

THE MEN'S MOVEMENT:

AN ALTERNATIVE TO "ACTING OUT" MALE HYSTERIA?

[W]e are trapped within modern, masculine madness.
—Sam Keen, *Fire in the Belly*

AS FREUD ARGUED IN his essay "'Civilized' Sexual Morality and Modern Nervousness" (1908), certain disorders like hysteria and obsessional neuroses are rooted in complexes derived from the repression of sexual desires, most often experienced in childhood. Hysteria has been generally associated with women, appearing usually in adolescence, although symptoms may be exhibited later in life. Typical of the biological reductionism of nineteenth-century neurology, the term hysteria was etymologically derived from the Greek *hystera*, meaning "uterus." Symptoms may be of the conversion type in which neurological malfunctions are common, such as anesthesia, paraesthesia, paralysis, seizures. Although the conversion type with its severe physical manifestations frequently is accompanied by diffidence (*la belle indifférence*), a deep-seated anxiety may produce a histrionic personality in which the subject shows excessive affect, such as, being overly sentimental and easily excitable, lacking self-confidence, exhibiting nervousness and gullibility.

According to Freud's understanding of the oedipal complex's effect on females, the origin of hysteria lies in the relationship of little girls to their parents. They hold their mothers responsible for their lack of a phallus, and as a consequence of "penis-envy," turn their attention to their fathers as a love-object. In place of their very own phallus, they substitute the wish for a child. Through their incestual desire for the father, they can acquire both the phallus and penis-surrogate. Yet whereas the passing of oedipal desires in young boys allegedly occurs through the little boys' castration fears of their fathers, no such threat exists with little girls because, according to the Freudian model, they have already suffered that traumatic fate. Incestual desires are repressed—but without the coercive power of the ever-present father who looms in the boy's consciousness as the superego—only to reemerge after the latency period. Social custom in bourgeois society, which sought to suppress any expression of female libidinality before or outside of marriage, made the transfer of affection from the father to the lover/ husband all the more difficult. Given the social norms of a patriarchal society, Freud confessed that he was not at all surprised by the appearance of hysterical symptoms among women who had to negotiate on their own the metamorphosis of desire from an incestual to an exogamous relationship. Yet in a society dominated by a phallic psychic economy, it was only logical that Freud ascribed to himself the role of saving women from themselves.

As overbearing as Freudian male egotism may be, this psychoanalytic model, despite itself, exposes the undercurrents of a society in which female sexuality is defined as aberrant and male sexuality as normative. Although it is assumed that women must struggle with a largely unresolved oedipal complex, men's "higher" moral character, underwritten by castration anxiety, results in the sublimation of these energies into the formation of human culture, for example, economic, social, and political activities. Freud admits that not all men are capable of such sublimation. Some act out their sexual desires in what he considered "perverse" activities; others attempt to suppress their desires but fail to do so adequately, resulting in the development of psychoneuroses evidenced in their behavior. Yet patriarchal society as a whole has, in Freud's scheme, successfully overcome the Scylla of "perversions" and the Charybdis of neuroses. Through their alleged moral integrity and strength of character, men have secured a stable, bourgeois society that not only provides the basis for Western civilization but assists the "weaker sex" in attaining some sense of equilibrium.

Despite Freud's claims about the inherent superiority of male psychosocial development, it is apparent that hysteria as a female-specific disturbance is a consequence of a patriarchal social order that denies women the right to moral agency and autonomy and uses them as the means to fulfill its own phallocentric desires. Although women do suffer—a great bodily suffering as Irigaray argues, the aetiology of female hysteria is not in their "natures" but rather in the masculinist psychic economy. Men use women or those conceived as women to discharge their own unresolved incestual desires. But where the patriarchal social order problematizes the discharge of such desires by women—what appeared to Freud as the troubled, private world of female sexuality, the sublimation of male incestual desires is institutionalized as public norms. This distinction reflects the tautological and arbitrary definition of neurosis in the Freudian model. Neuroses are not simply surrogate sites of libidinal discharge but rather those sites which are deemed asocial.

[The sexual instinct] places extraordinarily large amounts of force at the disposal of civilized activity, and it does this by virtue of its especially marked characteristic of being able to displace its aim without materially diminishing its intensity . . . In contrast to this displaceability, in which its value for civilization lies, the sexual instinct may also exhibit a particularly obstinate fixation which renders it unserviceable and which sometimes causes it to degenerate into what are called abnormalities.[1]

In a male-dominated society, it should not be surprising that men regard male activities that serve as surrogate sites for libidinal discharge to be socially and psychologically normative. Not benefiting from the "moral strength" derived from castration anxiety, women, on the other hand, express libidinal discharge in "abnormal" ways, such as, hysteria. Despite the obvious release of affect in male territorial games, men frequently justify them as serving a noble aim (securing peace, guaranteeing freedom, defending national interests), a pedagogical purpose (building character), or simply as an autotelic activity undertaken for "pure" fun.

A rereading of Freud, however, suggests that men in general should not be taken at their word. If, as Irigaray argues, castration fears are really a displacement of men's separation anxiety, then male activities such as territorial games are the product of unresolved desire for and aggression against the mother—conflicts that are too dangerous to express in the childhood home. The overly sentimentalized elevation of mothers not only embodies the taboo on incestual relations, as described by Freud, but also veils an abiding resentment toward them for the expulsion of the son into an alien environment, vulnerable and exposed to physical and psychic dangers. As desperate attempts to unify a decentered masculine subject in what is regarded as an essentially hostile world, male territorial games embody forms of institutionalized male hysteria—not a "suffering of the womb" but rather a suffering from the loss of the womb. The degradation of women—be it battering and rape or in ritualized expressions of territorial games—is more than a device to overcome the incestual impediments to sexual desire, as Freud suggested.[2] It is a way to work out hostility toward the mother. Ironically male territorial games that shroud hostility toward women in the arcane rules of homosocial activities frequently are revered in much the same way as motherhood. Desire and fear of women in general and mothers in particular can be acted out without violating incest taboos. Because war and sports seem to be common enterprise to most men, indeed, a defining moment in what it means to be a man in our culture, participation in territorial games is not looked upon as being aberrant. In a patriarchal social order the very opposite is true. The refusal to partake of institutionalized male hysteria, with its attendant emotionality, violence, sentimentality, and romanticism, is taken as evidence of effeminate, that is, deviant, behavior.

Although female hysteria is notably idiosyncratic according to the Freudian model with symptom-formation tied to individual experience, male hysteria has been collectivized and ritualized into the institutions of the military and modern sport. The routinization of hysteria through the rules of war and rules of the game control what might otherwise be anarchic discharges of emotional cathexes. Its obsessive compulsive character imposes a method to the madness in which repetitive, irrational, involuntary expressions of violence directed toward the enemy as woman/woman as enemy are codified into periodic release of aggression and desire. The rhetoric of castration and phallic penetration betray the underlying purpose behind these activities which to many, particularly women, seem senseless. To men instilled with a culturally determined male hysteria, the emotionally cathected locations of womb and phallus appear in the language of male territorial games where men can act out their fantasies toward the mother-woman. The ideological justification for these male activities hide from consciousness their underlying purpose—a purpose that, in my discussions with men about football and war, is most often so vehemently denied that it surprises even the respondents themselves. Whereas according to Freud women have great difficulty in working through their infantile aggression and incestual desires, it would seem that the Freudian construction of female sexuality is a displacement of men's own deeply held hostility toward and incestual desire for their mothers. The Freudian model of female sexuality therefore acts as a screen on which to project the anxiety that remains the very foundation of male sexuality in an androcentric culture.

Although the Freudian model refuses to recognize the essentially neurotic character of male behavior, patriarchal culture evidences strategies to contain this free-floating male aggression and libidinality. As loci for the expression of what might be otherwise uncontrolled, male territorial games offer prescriptive frameworks by which men can learn to channel their hostility and desires. Aggression and libidinality are habituated in order to experience the fantasized emotional release that men seek and to serve as pedagogical models for their sons' initiation into manhood. Although men may disagree on many issues, most often the bonding of male brotherhood surfaces in the common experience of male territorial games, be they war or sport. Although oedipal hostilities may even divide fathers and sons, it is these games that bring the generations together in a "men's way of knowing." Despite the effectiveness of these games in the discharge of emotionally cathected ideas, they remain symptoms of unresolved separation anxiety. Release is only temporary and sublimation is an ongoing process. Its repetitive, cyclical character guarantees that war, like football, will continue to thrive as a way of life in patriarchal culture. Without addressing the root cause of institutionalized male hysteria (the desire for and animosity toward the mother), the enthusiasm of American men for football and war, as well as for domestic violence against women, will not abate in the near future.

WE ARE ALL WAR-WOUNDED

It has been suggested in some circles that American culture is undergoing a marked transformation, that from the crysalis of the newly born men's movement will emerge a postsexist utopian social order based upon mutual respect between men and women. Although it has been mocked by the mainstream media (including its parody on the CBS sitcom *Murphy Brown*) and has been regarded with deep suspicion by many feminists, some see hope among this new breed of "sensitive men"—largely white, middle-aged, and middle to upper-middle class—who, unlike icons of previous generations that embodied silent, repressed men of action, are willing to talk about and among themselves.[3] In what at first glance appears to be a parallel to the women's movement in the 1960s, these men are committed to a course of emotional exploration—what leaders of the movement call "inner work"—to uncover and reevaluate what it means to be a man in this culture.

The social movement and its academic analogue, "men's studies," is rooted in the spontaneous formation of small men's groups across the country during the early 1970s, in part inspired by the crisis in patriarchal society due to the feminist revolution. A generation of men raised on the civil rights struggle and opposition to the war in Vietnam began to attend to the concerns of the women's liberation movement that had shattered the illusionary world of static sex roles inherited from the 1950s. If it was deemed that women were quite justifiably challenging this legacy from the age of conformity, then young middle-class, white males needed to redefine themselves, particularly when their fathers' generation, comfortably accustomed to the practices of sexism and racism, demanded the ultimate sacrifice of their sons in Southeast Asia for ill-defined purposes. In many respects, these men's groups were politically liberal, supportive of both feminism and, in a few cases, the gay revolution.

Nineteen Seventy-five marked the first year for a "National Conference on Men and Masculinity"—a meeting held annually—and academics have established a "Men's Studies Association." The movement has been accompanied by an explosion of periodicals dedicated to men's issues, including such publications as *Man! Men, Relationships, Community* (Austin Men's Center), *Man Alive!: New Mexico's Journal of Men's Wellness, Ho! A Men's Journal, The Talking Stick: A Newsletter about Men, Transitions, Men's Rights, Inc., Journeymen NetWORK* (National Congress of Men), and *Men's Studies Review*. Through these publications men learn about the hundreds of workshops, wilderness retreats, drumming ceremonies, vision quests, conferences, and other assorted "men's gatherings" in virtually every corner of the country. Spokesmen like John Lee, Michael Meade, Robert Moore, James Hillman, and Tom Daly tour the country, speaking on the emergent concerns of the "new man." *Wingspan: Journal of the Male Spirit*, a newspaper with a reported circulation of over one-hundred thousand, reports that one or two new men's groups form each week in the United States. Of course it would be foolish to assume that the proliferation of men's groups embodies the upsurge of a monolithic perspective. Like the feminisms of the women's movement, the positions of the men's movement represent a number of different theoretical points of view. Some are pointedly feminist and fight homophobia, as in the National Organization of Men Against Sexism. But perhaps what is most telling about the orientation of our culture is that neither feminist and gay men's groups nor books like John Stoltenberg's *Refusing to Be a Man* have captured the imagination of the mass media. Rather the focus has been on those groups inspired by two books, Sam Keen's *Fire in the Belly* and Robert Bly's *Iron John*, which have sold hundreds of thousands of copies and have served as lightning rods to a largely self-absorbed and heterosexual men's movement.

Although as spokesmen for the men's movement these two authors proselytize for a revitalized masculinity in modern culture, they both were vocal critics of the war in the Gulf. Robert Bly opposed the war from the very outset and called its culmination in the massacre of retreating Iraqi troops along the road to Basra this generation's My Lai. Allegedly he even compared the American military adventure in the Gulf to Agamemnon's sacrifice of Iphigenia.[4] And long before the Gulf War, Sam Keen was critical of what he called a "war system," which results in the dehumanization of the enemy and the wanton destruction of manhood. Keen warns that "we are all war-wounded."[5] Even though the actual number of men who go to war as well as the number of such wars is small, our patriarchal society inculturates all boys with the consciousness of the warrior caste. No male child can escape the mass culture of the past fifty years from John Wayne to Rambo, whether the little boy plays soldier in the schoolyard or the little boy in the adult male acts out his childhood fantasy in the deserts of the Middle East. Keen laments this warrior consciousness which has become synonymous with the male psyche in modern America. He enumerates its characteristics which include heroism, the primacy of will over reason, a passion for danger, paranoia, simplistic dichotomous thinking, hierarchical social ranking, and misogyny.

But whereas Keen and Bly criticize what they regard as the senseless slaughter in war, both affirm the men who are willing to undergo deprivation, risk their lives, and in many cases sacrifice themselves for the welfare of the society as a whole. They ascribe this selflessness to the nobility of men which can be diverted from its true purpose by the manipulations of jingoistic politicians. But although they disapprove of the cynical exploitation of this male virtue by both men and women, they vehemently deny that they would substitute a passive and pacifist new man. That would be neither preferable nor even possible. "Warrior energy," as Bly calls it, is an intrinsic part of the male psyche and must be dealt with in some way. "If a culture does not deal with warrior energy—take it in consciously, discipline it, honor it—it will turn up outside in the form of street gangs, wife beating, drug violence, brutality to children, and aimless murder."[6] Domestic violence therefore is not so much a consequence of individual psychopathological case histories as a cultural failure to provide an adequate vehicle to express this "warrior energy." It is something that transcends the individual male and may well escape control if the bulwark against its eruption is not reinforced and properly channeled by society-at-large. Bly's "warrior energy" is in some respects reminiscent of Klaus Theweleit's study of Germany's Freicorps, *Male Fantasies,* in which he cites Ernst Junger's reflections on "struggle as an inner experience."

> It is stronger than we are. A nebulous thing lies within us, driving its enigmatic being across the troubled waters of the soul at times like these. . . . Only now do we recognize how little at home we are with ourselves. Something slumbering deep down, drowned out by frenetic daily routine, rises up and, before it has even taken form, flows away into gloomy sadness.[7]

Even the man who is ostensibly successful and stable may be tempted to give in to his "darker side" if that which slumbers within his psyche is not expressed in a socially productive fashion.

Although Keen seemingly regards this conception of manhood as a cultural construct subject to change, preferably toward some rational end, Bly understands the "warrior" as a biologically immutable characteristic of men. He argues that the structure of the male psyche has never changed and that modern and "primitive" man are much closer in nature than most imagine. Thus, masculinity is not merely a cultural construct as Keen holds, but rather biological males are men biologically through and through. "Geneticists," notes Bly, "have discovered recently that the genetic difference in DNA between men and women amounts to just over three per cent. That isn't much. However, the difference exists in every cell of the body."[8] This irreducible difference suggests that men and women are rather like different species of the same genus. He also suggests that, despite protean cultural manifestations, females at bottom are "real" women who fit the "template in [men's] genetic memory."[9]

Whereas Keen at times seems to reject Bly's notions of biological essentialism, but he, too, is suspicious of changing cultural forms. Even though he is unwilling to claim that "biology is destiny," he nonetheless prefers to hold to the belief that underlying appearances are real differences between men and women—differences shrouded in mystery. "So what's the difference between a man and a woman?" he writes. "I can't say, but that doesn't mean that I can't recognize the difference."[10] Keen is the philosopher of the movement as Bly is its poet, yet it seems that his philosophical prowess has fallen short of articulating this basic distinction. Although woman remains impervious to male logic, she is not hidden from the male gaze. Keen indicates that he, as a man, can instinctively intuit his binary opposite: the essentially feminine. Like Bly, Keen believes that this gender difference can best be expressed through recourse to mythologies. "Stories shape our biology as much as our biology shapes our story."[11] The existentially real is read through the lens of the essentially mythological.

Philosophy is limited to what he regards as the one unshakable fact about gender relations: that men and women mutually define one another by exclusion. Unlike Bly's embrace of the Jungian rubric of anima-animus, Keen holds to a structuralist binary opposition of the genders anchored in biological sex. "As nearly as I can tell, I, being a man, have nothing feminine about me."[12] Male and female are two sides of a Möbius strip, inextricably intertwined yet always opposites. Keen's conception of gender relations is therefore entrenched in what Luce Irigaray regards as the androcentric construction of sexuality of patriarchal social orders: that women constitute the "Other of the Same." His utopian vision is a far cry from Irigaray's poststructuralist analysis which argues that "one sex is not entirely consumed by the other. There is always a remainder."[13] But in Keen's schema there is no room for the "Other of the Other." There seems to be no other alternative but a latter-day "battle between the sexes." The deconstructive approach is deemed illusory and destructive to the welfare of men in quest of the holy grail of masculinity. As Bly argues this path is taken by academics with "pins in their necks"[14]—a metaphor for intellectual somnambulism caused by the "Great Mother" who wishes to subvert men's work.

[M]EN HAVE . . . CEASED TO SWALLOW THE BLAME IMPUTED TO THEM BY FEMINISTS AND MINORITIES

Although the men's movement was historically associated with the shift in gender identities arising from the feminist challenge to traditional sex roles, representatives of the movement have been quick to disclaim responsibility for the oppression of women. Rather than admit and work through the guilt derived from androcentric privilege, these voices echo the plaintive cries of women, the poor and people of color who in various ways have suffered the injustices of a white patriarchal social order. In what seems like a caricature of the plight of poor women of color, these men argue that they too have been triply oppressed. Male experience has been distorted by the pervasiveness of the "warrior psyche." In a sense, men are the first of the "war-wounded," for even though their culturally channeled "warrior energy" might leave the victims of violence in its wake, they have been robbed of their own humanity. And although their energies have been exploited by others, spokesmen for the movement claim that they have been unfairly condemned, especially by women, for doing what the culture has compelled them to do. It is a case, they argue, of "blaming the victim." As a result Keen claims that white males in particular have been the doubly victimized through "reverse discrimination." And finally whereas the battered women's movement has focused on women and children as the victims of male-initiated domestic violence, others in the men's movement assert that an alleged widespread battering of men by women has been shrouded in silence.

With a shrillness that recalls Peter Finch's middle-class lament in *Network*—"We're mad as hell and we're not going to take it anymore," Sam Keen declared that "[i]n both trivial and profound ways men have begun to claim victim status and have ceased to swallow the blame imputed to them by feminists and minorities."[15] (Despite the book's pretense to liberalism, it is noteworthy that Keen, either consciously or unconsciously, conflates the term "men" with white men.) First and foremost the position imposed on men by a patriarchal social order insists that they discipline the male body to assume the warrior role. This introjection of authoritarian controls not only distorts psychological experience, it also contorts men physically. Keen's description of this fearsome yet pathetic contemporary male—"shoulders back, chest out, stomach pulled in, anal sphincter tight, balls drawn up into the body as far as possible, eyes narrowed, breathing foreshortened and anxious, heart rate accelerated, testosterone in full flow"[16]—is instantly recognized by his audiences throughout the country.

It is this putting on of the modern image of manhood, what Keen calls "character armor," which seems so peculiarly heart-rending to many in the white middle and upper-middle classes. And it is not only for the purposes of serving in the armed forces, for the war is not only on the battlefields abroad. The war for men is a way of being, every day, in every walk of life. "Our fragile, tender, wild and succulent bodies are being deformed,"[17] he claims. What emerges from Keen's discussion is an acute sense of the vulnerability of men, physically and psychologically, in an alien environment. Here they must fight in order to defend themselves and those who depend upon them. Keen reflects this deep sense of betrayal, as if someone is responsible for putting men in this unwanted position. And the consequence of this sense of betrayal is a free-floating anger toward other men who are feared as competitors and toward the world in general. When that hostility is focused, it most often is directed toward those for whom, in a patriarchal social order, this man has responsibilty—the women who are closest to him. But whereas Robert Bly recognizes that this unchanneled "warrior energy" may have regrettable consequences, Keen seems to have little sympathy for the victims of male violence.

> Until women are willing to weep for and accept responsibility for the systematic violence done to the male body and spirit by the war system, it is not likely that men will lose enough of their guilt and regain enough of their sensitivity to weep and accept responsibility for women who are raped and made to suffer the indignity of economic inequality.[18]

Keen's deeply disturbing assertion seems to suggest that women are victims of battering and sexual violence because they are at least in part to blame for the oppression of men. In some sense rape is allegedly understandable, if not justifiable. Men must pay a physical price for assuming this unwanted role in modern society: increased likelihood of heart disease, stroke, cancer, and premature death. One researcher noted the male-to-female ratio of death by lung cancer is 6 to 1; cirrhosis of the liver and heart disease is 2 to 1; and sadly enough, suicide is 2.7 to 1. And on average women outlive men in this culture by some seven years.[19] Should it be surprising, he seems to ask, that women be visited with some retribution?

The animosity toward women is palpably present in Keen's work for it is not only women's traditional role that angers him but the new feminist woman, described in the most stereotypic fashion. "Sporting their newly acquired habit of aggression, credit cards and birth control pills,"[20] these women allegedly combine the worst of both old and new. The virtue of submissive respect for their men is replaced by an arrogant independence, and yet Keen seems to imply that men still have to pay the bill. Keen bristles at the very thought that these women are in any way oppressed. Echoing the attitude of sexist male radicals in the 1960s, he opines that women are simply not repressed like other minorities, be they blacks, Indians or Jews, or the poor of this world. The assertion that they suffer the ravages of a class-based animus is allegedly an insult to the truly oppressed. Their complaints are supposedly trivial compared to "real" suffering, and their protest amounts to an unwarranted whining.

This antipathy toward women is evident in a cartoon that appeared in *A Circle of Men: The Original Manual for Men's Support Groups* written by Bill Kauth, "co-founder of the new warrior training adventure." In place of the sexist silhouette of a naked woman on a rig's mud flaps appears the image of a male, arms and legs akimbo, seemingly flattened by—one as-

*Feminism beginning to work its way into every
crack and crevice of society.*

FIGURE 6.1   "Sally's Transport." "Feminism beginning to work its way into every
crack and crevice of society." Published in *A Circle of Men* by Bill
Kauth, Saint Martins Press, New York, NY. Reprinted by permission.

sumes—the truck itself, Sally's Transport (See Figure 6.1). The logo below—"feminism beginning to work its way into every crack and crevice of
society"—makes clear what can be inferred from the image: feminism is
the mirror image of male sexism. Feminists are therefore not the allies of
the men's movement but rather its enemies. As one correspondent wrote to
Man! Men, Relationships, Community, the mainstream women's movement
is less interested in equal rights than the most regressive elements of the
men's movement.[21] Keen scorns the goddess movement as merely a reversal of "genderal supremacy" in which women replace men as the dominant party. "Ideological feminism," as he calls it, is therefore an unjustifiable
political strategy cynically employed by feminists to exploit women's past
suffering for the purpose of unfairly discriminating against men. They allegedly use the same technique of scapegoating that men had so success-
fully employed in the past against women. Their egocentric self-interests
have supposedly had a substantially detrimental effect upon men in contemporary American culture.

Robert Bly argues that the present generation of middle-aged men, raised to manhood in the 1960s, has been unduly influenced by this "new distribution of 'yang' energy."[22] The feminist revolution has produced a generation of "soft men" who are no longer "life-giving." In short, they have been emasculated by women who have used their sexual wiles as well as their political energy to domesticate the "wild man" in every male. Contrary to statistical evidence which indicates that 2 to 8 million women each year in the United States are battered and that perhaps as many as one half of all women will suffer from domestic violence at the hands of their male partner at some time in their lives, Bly contends that the contemporary American male cannot stand up to women in fights. The "warrior energy" in the male psyche has receded, and men no longer can summon up enough of it "to defend their soul houses."[23] They are regarded as "wimps," who are "hen-pecked," in the archaic language of the 1950s, or "pussy-whipped," as it is often described within the men's movement itself. Some men, like Robert Moore, have even expressed concern that men are being battered by their female partners, although U.S. Department of Justice statistics indicate that such incidents constitute less than 5 percent of the total domestic violence figures.

THE POWERFUL FATHER HAS BEEN ALL BUT REPLACED BY THE POWERFUL MOTHER

Even though many in the men's movement direct their hostility toward feminists for their emphasis on power rather than merely equality, the ground of Keen's animosity seems to transcend particular women. His deep-seated fear lies in his relationship to woman *qua* "WOMAN" [*sic*], that is, as mythic archetype. Following in the footsteps of his mentor Paul Tillich, whom he regarded as his intellectual "savior," Keen employs German Romantic language to describe the power of woman. Like Tillich's definition of the holy, Keen's image of woman is as "the mysterious ground of our being that we cannot penetrate."[24] As in Schelling's description of the *Überseiende* ("God above God"), woman is the *Unvordenkliche,* the literally incomprehensible or "unthinkable," impervious to the *logos* of man. Keen claims that this archetypal woman, present in the male imaginary, exercises "mythic power" over men. As mother, she precedes language and therefore informs and shapes the male child and his world. Adult males may mistake her existence for "the real," but in one sense they must settle for the *maya* of maternal power. Since woman is the impenetrable, a man cannot return to the womb. He is abandoned in this world and must make the best of it. Hence woman's presence telegraphs a profound sense of danger, vulnerability, alienation, and meaninglessness, all of which a man cannot articulate. Words fail him. *"[T]he essence of the threat he feels from WOMAN,"* stresses Keen, *"lies in its vagueness."*[25] This threat is not merely psychological, he reasons, but rather ontological. The very existence of woman in the male imaginary necessitates the problematicization of what it means to be a man.

Although Keen argues that women experience meaning through childbirth, men have no such alternative. Meaning must be created by men themselves. Men are tempted to create that *raison d'être* magically by imagining the murder of woman. As related in the Hindu tale of the Baba Yoga, a particularly fearsome and ugly manifestation of female energy in the form of a boar, adolescent males fantasize killing the witch, but, like Bly, Keen warns that such a tactic is a waste of male energy. That hostility needs to be directed toward some male activity that ritually creates and inscribes the meaning of manhood in the soul of each male. Yet this primal insight which, according to both Keen and Bly, was recognized by our primitive forefathers, has been forgotten in modern Western cultures. In part it is because "[t]he powerful father has been all but replaced by the powerful mother."[26]

Whereas women (like "WOMAN") are blamed for what Keen regards as the lamentable condition of modern men, Bly believes that the responsibility must be equally shared by men and women. And although women share in the responsibility, Bly seems to argue that they cannot be blamed because their attempt to dominate men in modern society is biologically inscribed. If anyone is to blame, it is the men who allow women to emasculate them. Although Bly's analysis is peppered with biologisms concerning the foundation of the male psyche, the arrival of manhood, unlike womanhood, is not regarded as a natural phenomenon. Little girls allegedly become women of their own accord, but male children, Bly argues, need the assistance of their male elders. Virility is culturally produced through the initiation of pubescent boys into manhood by men. The discovery of the "Wild Man"— Bly's icon of masculinity—is therefore not reducible to an inner journey to uncover a preexistent reality but rather consists of an anagnoretic ritual of homosocial self-creation.

Bly believes, however, that those who fathered the present American generation of largely white, middle-aged, middle-class sons have failed in their obligation. The very transformation of human culture from "primitive" to modern societies has entailed a certain loss as well as innumerable gains. Modern industrial culture with its division of labor between home and workplace has lead to the decline of contact between fathers and sons. Whereas "primitive" cultures ensured the presence of the fathers to serve as models of virility for their sons, contemporary corporate America is marked by the absence of the father from the home. Male rites of passage in aboriginal cultures guaranteed that boys could be wrested away from the influence of their mothers, but in the modern setting no one is present to cut the mother's apron strings. As advocates for the men's movement read it, the problem faced by men in contemporary culture is not anxiety produced by too abrupt a separation from the mother, but rather the pain caused by the failure to separate from her at all. Corporate social organization, which causes the absence of the father from the home, thereby undermines the very aim of a patriarchal culture: the continued existence of a supposedly virile and dominant male.

Bly argues that contemporary men thirst for this "father substance." "It astounds me," writes Patrick Dougherty, a psychologist sympathetic to the men's movement, "how many men, and professionals who counsel men, honestly believe that a man can figure out who he is by being in a relationship with a woman."[27] According to the movement, manhood is learned through imitation. And neither mothers nor female partners can adequately make up for the legacy of the "absent father." Dougherty argues that this crisis is exacerbated by "the absence of the healthy male group" that initiates boys into men and from which the individuation process of the mature adult commences. Michael Meade depicts the collective effervescence of teenage males at rock concerts as an unconscious yet hopeless groping for the long-absent male ritual of initiation. But although the expression of this energy can take on relatively innocuous forms, Bly warns that, without recognizing the need for rituals of masculinity, we risk and have experienced destruction and suffering on a massive scale, for example, war, crime, domestic violence.

Bly's emphasis on the need for male rites of passage recalls Lionel Tiger's work *Men in Groups*. In the aftermath of the Second World War and the disastrous consequences of fascist Social Darwinism, Tiger hoped to restore the respectability and presence of biological insights to social theory. The phenomenon of men in groups, he argued, was not purely a cultural creation but was also the result of basic instinctual drives.

> [M]ale bonding as a biological propensity is not only a phenomenon unto itself, but that in part it is the very cause of the formation of those various male groups observable around us. . . . There may indeed be a bonding predisposition which preceded the group in time.[28]

Tiger speculates that "biological propensity" is related to the differentiation of brain processes between males and females. "Male bonding" developed as the brain evolved to adapt to the physical environment: hunting in groups was far more effective in securing food than hunting alone. Tiger suggests that this basic form of social organization has remained over the millenia as an instinctual and learned behavior down to the present day. The spokesmen for the men's movement, however, protest that there is a notable absence of such groups in contemporary America. And if men have an instinctual predisposition toward such bonding, then the lack of such groups is simply unnatural. Men are therefore not only alienated from each other; they are also estranged from their essence.

The purpose of the men's movement then is to restore to men what is rightfully their birthright: their manhood. Yet the memory of such rituals is allegedly lost, due in part to the demise of "mythological thinking" that Meade contends disappeared some seven hundred years past and Bly nearly a millenium ago. If boys are to grasp the meaning of the "wound" inflicted by the absence of their fathers—indeed, if they are to grasp the meaning of their meaning, they must live a narrative of transformation. In this respect the movement oddly mimes the sentiments of its analogue in the women's movement: "womanspirit." As the lesbian novelist Monique Wittig advised her sisters who wished to explore an anagnoretic feminist spirituality, "You say there are no words to describe this time, you say it does not exist. But remember. Make an effort to remember. Or, failing, invent."[29] The men's movement has been frequently ridiculed for its anachronistic and cross-cultural appropriation of male initiation rites, such as, drumming from African culture, smudging, talking sticks, vision quests from Native American cultures, chanting from Hindu culture, etc., with only superficial attention to authenticity and historical accuracy. They conjure up images of white, middle-class, middle managers, doffing their suits and ties for skewed Hollywood-influenced ideas of what a "primitive" drumming ritual might be. Yet, from the perspective of the men's movement, their experiments with these forms seem no more and no less justified than those associated with wicca and other types of women's spirituality rituals.

Bly attempts to recover/reinvent the ritual necessary for the maintenance of male culture by rereading the Germanic fairytale written down and interpreted by the Brothers Grimm in the nineteenth century. In this narrative of the transition from childhood to manhood, a golden ball belonging to the king's son rolls into the cage where lies imprisoned a "Wild Man." This creature who lived in the bottom of a lake had been captured by the king after several of his men had been lost, ostensibly eaten by the Wild Man. In return for the ball, the Wild Man makes the boy promise to steal the key to the cage, hidden under his mother's pillow. The boy does so, and accompanies the Wild Man into the forest, never to see his parents again. The Wild Man shows him a stream in which, entranced by his reflection, his hair falls, turning a golden color. They part company and the boy undergoes a series of trials as the son of a poor gardener and, with the Wild Man's help, a mysterious knight. A king's daughter falls in love with him, and upon catching her golden apple thrice, he becomes her betrothed, yet not before suffering a wound in his leg attempting to escape the king's men. Unmasked as the mysterious knight, the humble son of the gardener marries the king's daughter. The story ends with the return of the Wild Man who, freed from his enchantment by the boy's actions, reveals himself as a Great King, Iron John. As a sign of his gratitude, he gives all of his gold to the boy grown into manhood.

Bly's book is dedicated to unraveling this tale of transformation. It is the Wild Man who frees the boy from his childhood. Neither the father, who has imprisoned the Wild Man, nor the mother, who hides the key to his cage, can effect this liberation. Both seem to work actively against the boy's transition to manhood either by containing the Wild Man or refusing the boy access to him. In that the Wild Man is not a "preexistent reality" but rather a metaphor for the ritual of initiation itself, the narrative can be read as an artifact of an earlier culture that preserved the male rite of passage. "The Wild Man here amounts to an invisible presence, the companionship of the ancestors and the great artists among the dead."[30] Some men's circles have even created rituals for the invocation of the spirits of the ancestors— great men who are welcomed into the presence of the group and whom they would like to emulate. Michael Meade refers to the "herm" or gravestone, etymologically related to Hermes, the messenger of the gods, that denotes the entrance to the underworld of male ancestors. It is this passageway to the past that is reiterated in some of the rituals of the men's movement.

This legacy of male ancestors, signified by the Wild Man, teaches the boy about himself, to look into the very bottom of the male psyche (the stream), and in so doing, to discover his own sexuality (his golden hair)— clearly defined in the storyline as heterosexuality. The narrative suggests that the beautiful daughter of the king is the reward for the rejection of the mother. For only through the theft of the key under the mother's pillow is the Wild Man set free, and only through the Wild Man does the boy win the daughter's hand. In this respect, Bly suggests that the "Wild Man is nature itself."[31] The ritual is a conduit for the power that allegedly exists at the foundation of the male psyche that otherwise lies dormant and turns stagnant.

Although the "soft men" of the 1960s claimed to be more in touch with their emotions, it is Bly's opinion that these men repressed their own nature. Without the company of their elders, young men try to loose the Wild Man themselves, but it cannot be done alone. They suffer from self-inflicted wounds, aborted and futile attempts to plumb the depths of their psyches. Virtually every contemporary man, it is argued, bears the scars of these attempts that painfully discourage men from risking renewed efforts to contact their deeper selves. But whereas the structure of modern corporate society and the women's revolution coincided to produce this "unnatural" man, bearing the stigmata of alienation, the men's movement and its rituals supposedly allow men to express feelings which, like the Wild Man himself, would otherwise remain locked away.

Just as the Grimm Brothers' narrative of the Wild Man leads from his liberation to the wounding of the boy, so, too, does the ritual lead to the metaphoric wounding of the male. But although the wound endured by men in contemporary society from the absence of their fathers festers and is a source of great anguish, the wound of the male rite of passage functions as a "male womb." Bly specifically recognizes this wound as a "female opening," given the boy by the king's knights in the tale of Iron John and symbolizing the male ritual of self-creation and the discovery of the "Inner King." For, as a consequence of male culture, a man is born out of the male, rather than a female, body. Like the birth of Dionysus who, having been prematurely born, is sewn by Zeus into his own thigh and is later to be delivered whole and perfect, John Craig asked in *Wingspan,* "Was not the place I was in—that circle of men with the flow of brotherhood inside it—the male body, the male womb, where a new god could be born?"[32] As in the religious ritual of baptism by water or fire, unless a man be born again, he cannot enter the kingdom.

This act is the "clean break" from the mother that both Bly and Keen believe is necessary for the recovery of manhood in modern culture. "A man is fashioned by a process of subtraction, decision, abstraction, being severed from the 'natural' world of WOMAN,"[33] claims Keen. But the initiate's ritually inscribed separation from the mother is foreshadowed by the already gendered character of the rite itself. In order for the boy to separate himself from the mother, he must give himself to the homosocial community that is already separate from women and constitutes itself as this very separation. The initiation thereby both introduces the boy to manhood and recapitulates and resanctifies the social solidarity of the homosocial community. Both Keen and Bly argue that there is no place for women in this male ritual, and they would prefer that the men's movement not focus on questions about or concerning women. The boy's transition to manhood lies in his birth by the body of men who function as a "male mother." Like the "father" of the men's movement itself, Robert Bly, the "male mother" appears as a nurturing and caring parent, but not in concert with the biological mother. In the men's movement the biological and male mothers are conceived as competitors for the affection of the boy child. The appropriation or, better yet, theft of motherhood by the male mother (derived from aboriginal male suspicion and jealousy) negates the pivotal role of women in the reproduction of human culture and banishes them to the margins of homosocial community. Yet, although the male mimesis of the childbirth is culturally performed, Bly attempts to steal the natural authority of mothers which they derive from the physical act of giving birth.

The son does not receive a hands-on healing, but a body-on healing. His cells receive some knowledge of what an adult masculine body is. The younger body learns at what frequency the masculine body vibrates. It begins to grasp the song that adult male cells sing, and how the charming, elegant, lonely, courageous, half-shamed male molecules dance.[34]

Even granting Bly a certain latitude for poetic license, his metaphors smack of unwarranted essentialist claims. Yet it is clear that in his estimation a boy cannot physically become a "true" man without undergoing the male rite of passage.

Through the discovery of the Wild Man, that is, the community of men, a man receives the male wound/womb and gives birth to himself. He now stands together with his brothers wholly apart from women. The men's movement recognizes the phallus as the primal signifier of this noble autonomy. The newly born man/man born anew is the phallic principle. While the male psyche is informed by the seminal substance of the father, it is also protected by the collective force of the male community. And though the flaccid culture of "soft men" is a matter of shame, the new man is embodied in the erect phallus that Keen regards as "a natural object of worship."[35] Freed from the lack of self-confidence imposed by modern corporate culture and feminism, men enjoy the attributes of *homo erectus:* "intensity, shrewdness, desire to penetrate, liveliness, impulse, daring."[36]

Like the Latin *normalis,* meaning "perpendicular," the phallus rises from the ground of human culture to affirm the virtues of a phallic morality. The men's movement therefore aims at nothing short of the reappropriation of what was believed to have been lost—the phallus—as central to the male experience. The manual *A Circle of Men* recommends one exercise, titled "My Dick Speaks," in which men are encouraged to describe their experiences from the point of view of their penises, using pet names for the fetishized organ.[37] Although the culturally phallicized male has supposedly suffered from trauma at the hands of feminism and modern social organization, this ritual seeks to end wordless impotence by bringing men to speech. They are to articulate their phallic desires which have been silenced by incestual taboos. Men can be men once more. They can embrace a potent sexuality and recover the acumen and ferocity of the hunter. Their intuition and their thoughts will no longer be inhibited by the presence of the mother, and they will renew Western civilization with a reconfigured primitive virile asceticism in place of modern maternal domesticity.

IRON JOHN IS NO GIFT TO WOMEN

Not everyone, however, is nearly as optimistic about the men's movement as its progenitors. Although it may be rightfully argued that the parodies of the movement in the mass media distort its image, a close examination of its philosophical underpinnings produces a cause for concern. As drawn by Bly, Keen, and others, its conclusions are disquieting and its presuppositions do not seem to be markedly different from those which produce contemporary male territorial games.

What can be inferred from the men's movement's emphasis on the recovery of male ritual? Man *qua* man owes nothing to women. Man produces himself. He is *sui generis*. And like the holy, he is worthy of reverence and respect: sentiments to which he is entitled but which the present-day culture supposedly does not recognize. The role of woman in the creation of man is supposedly unmasked as *maya,* as illusion. Her presence is effaced in the male rite of passage. As if drawn from the writings of medieval theologians, the generation of man is seminally imprinted by the father and culturally shaped by the homosocial community. Woman as *mater* provides the material but not the spiritual reality of masculinity. Umbilical cord cut, this new man, like his primitive forefather, will stand erect in unity with his brothers, segregated, if not physically, then spiritually from his gender counterpart.

The polemical call for the anachronistic return of a homosocial world echoes the most regressive sentiments in American society that lament the loss of exclusively male preserves, (bars, clubs, associations). And members of the men's movement themselves trace their spiritual, if not historical, ancestry to the popularity of fraternal organizations in the nineteenth and early twentieth centuries, for example, Masons, Elks, Moose, Odd Fellows, etc.—organizations typically known for politically reactionary views toward women and other groups in American society. It is not just that the men's movement follows separatist sentiments, as some African-American and lesbian-feminist groups have in the past; it is that many voices in the men's movement, including the rank-and-file, hold women in particular responsible, if not to blame, for the plight of largely white, middle-class, middle-aged heterosexual males. As I have heard myself on numerous occasions, these men actually conceive of themselves as being victimized by "male-bashing" feminists as well as by members of minority groups. They protest their innocence, as if they were noncombatants in the "war between the sexes." The attacks seem to them to be unprovoked, yet these war crimes remain unpunished. Some declare that they are incensed by what appears to them to be misandry, while others, like Sam Keen, seem to hold forth a peace-offering. He urges men and women to end the "blame game," as if the casualties on both sides are comparable and a truce is the only reasonable course of action.

What seems clear is that, based upon the ideology of social contract theory and radical individualism, many white males in the movement do not see themselves as enjoying the privilege to which, in this society, their skin color and biological sex entitle them. They believe that those privileges are actually a cultural fiction propagated by those who wish to leverage race and gender for their own personal advantage. These men hold that, what others see as privilege, they see as a burden. They are victimized by the expectations that society assumes are commensurate with privilege. It seems that, as Barbara Ehrenreich concluded in her analysis of the last fifty years in America, many privileged white males now want to enjoy the advantages this society offers them without shouldering its concurrent responsibilities. In a reversal of 1950s American culture, we are now facing "the collapse of the breadwinner ethic." In the wake of the narcissism of the Reagan era, men are evincing a distinct "commitmentphobia."[38] They simply feel overwhelmed by responsibilities and unappreciated by their dependents and society-at-large. The Religious Right with its politics of nostalgia has attempted to reverse this trend—along with feminism, affirmative action, etc.; however, there is little indication that its campaign has been successful among mainstream white males. A recent ad for *Newsweek* seems to reflect this sentiment. Above photos of two of *Newsweek's* 1993 covers—one depicting a special ecologically oriented children's issue and the other carrying the image of Michael Douglas in the movie *Falling Down* (March 29, 1993)—read the following respective logos: "Save the Earth" and "Save Your Hide." The ad clearly knows its audience: white men who, beleaguered by rapid change, feel they are an endangered species. The Douglas cover is emblazoned with the headline, "White Male Paranoia: Are They the Newest Victim—Or Just Bad Sports?"

But there are some critics who argue that this privileged class of males cries wolf. "[T]he fact is," writes Jill Johnston, "that white men are not an oppressed group."[39] They are not even willing to recognize the consequences of exercising privilege: that the *ressentiment* of women and minorities is the cost of doing business as the power elite. As naive as it may sound, many of these men desire approval and want to be liked. The anger of women and people of color catches them by surprise, and the shock gives way to an intermittantly expressed hostility. Women are most often the subject of their attack, in part because publicly avowed expressions of racism are no longer as acceptable as twenty years ago, whereas sexist comments are largely met with tacit, if not vocal, approval in male company. If we can take these male theorists at their word, their animosity toward women is rooted in their anger toward their mothers. It was their mothers who supposedly denied them the key to the Wild Man's cage. It was their mothers who wanted to turn them into "mama's boys" by preventing them from joining the homosocial world. Yet it is this very model of dichotomous sexual roles that reveals the truly regressive nature of the men's movement. Women are regarded as embodying the domestic and the natural. (In this respect, the men's movement bears some similarity to the classic thesis indicting the patriarchal social order, first advanced by Sherry Ortner.[40]) Males, on the other hand, are regarded simultaneously as both "Wild Men" and culture-bearers. They use their "natural" energies of aggression and domination to tame nature, including women, in order to establish the household of a domestic psychic economy (*oikonomia*).

In belaboring the point of the domestication of women, however, the theorists of the men's movement seem somewhat behind the times. According to the U.S. Bureau of Labor Statistics, in the 1980s fewer than 10 percent of all families fit the description of the 1950s icon of domestic harmony: the wife as homemaker, caring for children, and the husband as breadwinner. Contemporary society is far more characterized by the two-income family with both partners, whether married or not, competing in the marketplace. Yet it is this very development that throws women into a double-bind. The domesticity of women is regarded with suspicion by men who view it through the lens of homosocial community, while women's participation in the workplace on an equal footing with men is viewed as an unwanted intrusion into a previously all-male preserve. Caught in this Catch-22 situation, women can't win. As much as it is alleged that the subject of females is excluded from these newly formed anagnoretic rituals of masculinity, the hostility toward women provides much of the energy that drives the movement.

Bly's disclaimers to the contrary, some theorists in the men's movement hold women at least in part responsible for the disappearance of the male rites of passage, the supposed *sine qua non* of manhood. The postmodern world is regarded as the consequence of domineering mothers and absent fathers and therefore the crisis of the unified subject is not universal but gender-specific. It is men who have faced the dissolution of subjectivity. Individual men live the legacy of maternal domesticity while simultaneously and futilely attempting to establish their masculine identity on their own. Keen laments the loss of an "organizing center" that plunges males into a "confusing plurality."[41] Postmodernism is born out of the failure of modernism, but, unlike other cultural theorists who see the postmodern era as an inevitable consequence of linguistic, philosophical, and political developments, the men's movement does *not* regard it as a *necessary* failure. Modernism with its bias toward the domination of the "real" may be redeemed, but its revitalization may only be achieved through a healthy dose of premodernism.

Like the nineteenth century *fin-de-siècle* artists, such as Gauguin, Rousseau, and later Picasso, who sought the regeneration of Western culture through exposure to African, Indian, and Polynesian cultures, so, too, does the men's movement wish to graft the modernist impulse to the supposed vitalism of aboriginial cultures. Reflecting the colonialist mentality of progressives from a previous era, theorists of the movement selectively appropriate the "primitive." But whereas the European avant-garde of a century ago drew from the imperial experience of their countries' colonial adventures, contemporary Americans consume the hyperreal images of these cultures, made available largely through the mass media. Insulated from the violence of the colonialist legacy, these theorists naively deem such adoption completely innocent, as if their appropriation of the "primitive" is any less offensive. It is clear, however, that these "rediscovered," yet decontextualized, rituals are not for the benefit of indigenous cultures but for the renewed virility of a Western patriarchal society in crisis. As in the nineteenth and early twentieth centuries when the European powers plundered their colonies in Africa, Asia, Latin America, and the Near East, the men's movement mines the postmodern legacy of colonialism for images that benefit the welfare of white males.

As a hybrid of "primitivism" and modernism, the movement is reminiscent of Durkheim's models of social solidarity in which Western society's organic solidarity is contrasted with the mechanical solidarity of primitive social orders. Although Durkheim espoused the alleged superiority of modern civilization's economic interdependence, he recognized the crisis in the social order brought about by the radical individualism or *différence* resulting from an ever-increasing division of labor. Specialization led to widespread *anomie* in urban centers. Primitive cultures, on the other hand, were modeled on *ressemblance,* in which members of the clan were characterized by similarity. Bound together under the sign of the clan's totem, individuals saw themselves mirrored in each other in a vision of infinite sameness. Although the social organization that produces organic solidarity eclipsed primitive economic arrangements, mechanical solidarity did not disappear completely. It is lodged in the psyche of modern Western culture. It is that supposed primitive vitalism that captured the imagination of late nineteenth-century progressive artists and intellectuals as well as proto-fascists, all of whom were highly critical of European bourgeois culture.

The reappropriation of the "primitive" is therefore fraught with danger. On the one hand, it disparages the integrity of indigenous ritual by appropriating it for the benefit of a class which has traditionally exploited these peoples. On the other hand, it reinforces an image of sameness—a visceral masculinity—in a postmodern era that has witnessed an increasing sensitivity toward and respect for cultural pluralism. Consciousness shaped by mechanical solidarity at its worst fears difference, and regards the Other as being mysterious and threatening. There seems to be little question that many voices within the movement regard females as the mysterious, the incomprehensible, the unfathomable, and the tenor throughout many of the discussions in men's groups evinces a deep anxiety about women. The men's movement might reinforce the bulwark of men's consciousness, but there is little doubt that many of these white males regard themselves as being under siege. Although the movement argues that its focus is on men, not women, Jill

Johnston had good reason to argue in her *New York Times Book Review* article that "Iron John is no gift to women."[42] The movement and its rituals allow men to express not only their vulnerability and loneliness but also their anger toward women. Although it might be argued that it is better to have men unleash their hostility in the context of a weekend wilderness ritual than in the form of battering, it is not at all clear that the men's movement can solve the problem of male violence.

These voices argue that ritual is conspicuous by its absence in modern culture and that modern man has lost the power to think mythologically. Imbued with a soulless rationalism, modern man has supposedly lost touch with his native wildness and has substituted an anaesthetized existence of corporate consumerism. Beseiged by women at home and in the workplace, he struggles to control his fate, but only ends up injuring himself. But are these contentions true? Has "contemporary man" lost the power to think mythologically? And are the male rites of passage notably absent from modern American culture?

In his classic work *Myth and Reality,* Mircea Eliade rejected the contention that mythological thinking died with the advent of the modern era.[43] On the contrary, eschatological myths are preserved in sources as widely diverse as Marxist utopian visions of the *Reich der Freiheit* to premillennialist hopes for the Second Coming. The mass media inundates the culture with mythological images. Newspaper comics, comic books, magazines, televised sports, and prime-time programming, not to mention movies, all provide mythic narratives of the battle between good and evil and include the trials and tribulations of the mythic hero, whether it be the likes of Rambo and the Terminator or innumerable private detectives and police inspectors. In a society in which the father is markedly absent from the home, mass culture becomes the means by which the image of masculinity is transmitted from generation-to-generation. Mythology becomes reality.

Jean Baudrillard contends that, in an economic and cultural system driven by consumption rather than production, reality has been effaced by cultural fictions. If history is based on a concept of the "real" derived from "natural" needs rather than culturally created ones, then postmodern America has dropped out of history. Our hypperreality is, by definition, mythological, and it is the only "reality" we know. Baudrillard, like his intellectual predecessor, Marshal McLuhan, contends that the epistemic constitution of the individual has changed. Rather than holding "contemporary man" estranged from mythological thinking, these theorists suggest that the postmodern subject is closer to the "primitive" than his immediate predecessor, "modern man." The icons of popular culture—from Madonna to Mickey Mouse—are the myths of this postmodern American society. Society is therefore planted thick with mythic images, whether found in television shows and movies or in churches, museums, sports stadiums, rock concerts, and dance clubs.

Although a plethora of mythic images dominate postmodern consciousness, spokesmen for the men's movement contend that American culture is
allegedly bereft of ritual. They suggest that men in contemporary society
have no way to share in the bonding of homosocial community and to effect
the necessary break with the mother. Yet, even Lionel Tiger's work on male
bonding, *Men in Groups,* which is so embraced by the men's movement,
belies this contention. In his chapter "Men Court Men: Initiations and Secret Societies,"[44] Tiger cites the phenomenon of the secret society, a predominantly male activity, in contemporary as well as "primitive" cultures.
These societies are most often associated with adolescence and schooling in
the form of initiations at military academies and the widespread presence of
fraternities on college campuses across the country. The activities of these
groups most often involve a hierarchy with the initiates or "pledges" at the
bottom, thereby establishing a liminal time-space continuum that the initiate
must traverse despite what is perceived to be considerable danger. The rituals of obeisance and humiliation are accompanied by other frequently
homoerotic elements, such as nudity and sexual stimulants, simulated sexual
acts, as well as blood and alcohol. These organizations have their analogues
outside of educational institutions through the continued presence of secret
societies in American culture (Masons, Shriners, Knights of Columbus, and
the American subculture of male bonding in bars throughout the country).

Although it may be true that the popularity of male secret societies has
declined in recent years, it can hardly be said that men have no vehicle to
express their longing for association with other males. The explosive popularity of American professional sports, that are a major component of mass
media entertainment, has more than taken up the slack. In a culture based
upon the consumption of images rather than in the production of work values
as the basis for male identity, televised sport becomes the means by which
a young boy learns how to be a man. Television viewing itself becomes the
ritual, inviting the mastery of a highly specialized body of knowledge, mimetic identification with sports figures as "role models," the use of sexually
charged language, and the segregation of males from those who are regarded
largely as outsiders and interlopers—wives, daughters, mothers, sisters. Even
in a generation of sons that was torn apart from their fathers over the Vietnam War, American sport became the means—in fact, in many households,
the only means—to overcome the generation gap. As a child and later as a
teenager, I remember how vehement political disagreements over conflicts
in Southeast Asia were all but forgotten when my father, uncles, male friends,
and coworkers would sit down in front of the television set to cheer on
Terry Bradshaw and the "Steel Curtain" of the Pittsburgh Steelers. The bonding
was immediate and deep: we were all on the same team, vicariously expe-

riencing the thrill of domination and commiserating with one another over our deeply painful defeats.

Although the men's movement suggests that violence against women may be a result of the failure of men to channel their "warrior energy" through male initiation ritual, the prevalence of male bonding in bars, college fraternities, military academies, fraternal organizations, sports viewing, and military service all suggest otherwise. Lionel Tiger argues that "[a]ggression-out results from the bonding of males." He concludes that men in groups either require a "preexistent object" for their aggression, or they must invent one. In either case, aggression is an essential characteristic of male groups, not a consequence of their absence. Whereas this aggression may, in some instances, be directed toward newly initiated members in a given male society, most often the object of aggression is gendered female. Despite the attempt of some men within the men's movement to heighten consciousness about sexist attitudes toward women, these new men's groups are not exempt from such aggressive outbursts. In her book *Backlash*, Susan Faludi noted that during one men's conference Robert Bly responded to a question about a woman's refusal to understand a man's emotional needs by advising, "Then you bust them in the mouth."[45] Bly's later disclaimer that he meant it figuratively does not dispel the statement's aggressive intent, conceived within the context of a homosocial environment.

WHAT WOMEN WANT IS TO STOP SERVING AS SCAPEGOATS

In his book *Fire in the Belly*, Keen argues that Freud's inquiry "What do women want?" has been more than adequately answered in the contemporary world as has been made abundantly clear to sensitive men. They want "justice, equality, respect and power." Keen suggests however that the real question of the modern era is what men want.[46] The men's movement seems to answer the question tautologically: men want to be men—something women, and particularly men's mothers, supposedly do not allow them to be. Despite the perfunctory manner in which Keen simultaneously acknowledges and dismisses the perennial Freudian inquiry that haunts modern patriarchal culture, it seems that the men's movement has missed the point. From the perspective of women whose bodies and souls have been ravaged by the misogynist violence of men, the utopian dreams of Enlightenment harmony seem a far cry from everyday reality. As the late Dorothy Dinnerstein declared in *The Mermaid and the Minotaur: Sexual Arrangements and Human Nature*, "[w]hat women want is to stop serving as scapegoats (their own scapegoats as well as men's and children's scapegoats) for human resentment of the human condition."[47]

According to Dinnerstein, the aetiology of misogyny can be traced to the early relationships of offspring with their mothers. The woman as mother is the subject of not only her child's love but also her child's hostility. The reasons for these ambivalent feelings are complex, yet the work of Nancy Chodorow, like that of Dorothy Dinnerstein, suggests that its origins stem largely from the gendered character of childrearing. Chodorow noted that whereas technology and science have given women far greater latitude in child-bearing, the twentieth century witnessed an increasing emphasis on the exclusive responsibility of women for childrearing. The division of home and workplace and the literature on raising children pressured women to become the primary caretaker of their children as a natural and healthy development. During the 1970s and 1980s, the economic pressures for survival among the lower classes and for the maintenance of a given standard of living among the middle classes brought more and more women into the workplace. With that development came an accelerated need for child care. But child care workers have been and continue to be overwhelmingly women. Despite the men's movement's lament that a generation of "soft men" now dote on their female partners, there is little indication that today's heterosexual couples significantly balance the gender responsibilities for childrearing any more than did previous generations. Although popular literature abounds with images of the "new father," Ronald F. Levant has reported numerous studies that belie this impression. These sociological studies indicate that while men may be spending 20 percent to 30 percent more time in household work, child raising, and other family responsibilities, their female partners typically spend two to three times as many hours in such activities.[48] Teresa Jump and Linda Haas cite other studies that indicate that when men do become involved in child care, they most often limit their participation to playtime and punishment, leaving the mundane activities of preparing meals, changing diapers, and bathing children to the mother.[49]

The legacy of childhood which so informs both the gender identity and individual personality of the adult therefore has a significant impact on attitudes toward females. Superimposed on the image of women are the ambivalent feelings of the child in each adult for its mother. Under the rubric of exclusively female child-rearing, the mother embodies the source of both pleasure and nourishment. The child feels a sense of completion and transcendence in her presence. In and through her is experienced a oneness with all life, a contentment and harmony unsurpassed in human existence. As Freud claimed in *Civilizations and Its Discontents,* the child experiences an "oceanic feeling" in the womb which s/he carries into the world, originally as an infant and even later as an adult. But this religious, almost mystical, feeling of oneness is balanced by the dread that accompanies the experience of religious awe for the *mysterium tremendum.* For simultaneously with this satisfaction is the recognition of a separate entity, a different yet awesome person who has and exercises the power to withhold pleasure and gratification of the child's needs. The child discovers what Dinnerstein refers the grief of infancy[50] in which the discovery is made that the child is not omnipotent and that others—like the mother who is the paradigm for the "Other"—may deny it sustenance and attention. In the eyes of the child, the mother may not appear to be sufficiently faithful, particularly if she takes tactile pleasure in others. The child becomes aware that life is shot through with anticipation of death through separation, denial, and pain and concludes that the source of this existential and inconsolable grief is the mother. The mother-child relationship is thereby characterized by both love and fear—a fear that may well turn into hatred. Persecutory anxiety may ensue, based upon the fear that the mother might retaliate against the child for harming the mother's breast. The child may resent the seeming omnipotence of the mother and consider her an ever-present threat to be wary of as well as a source of gratification to be loved.

The long-term impact of these childhood experiences has an asymmetrical effect depending upon the sex of the child. In that little girls at least have the possibility of becoming mothers, they identify with their mothers. Dinnerstein suggests that separation-anxiety is overcome in the imagination of both the girl-child and the adult daughter by taking the mother's place, thereby becoming the source of nourishment, gratification, and love. Her world is not fragmented and estranged, but reunited in the female imaginary through her isomorphic identification with the mother and in the act of childbearing. In the latter case, the girl child-become-mother outgrows the hostility she once felt toward her own mother. As a consequence, the pattern of social interaction exhibited by women tends to be more relational, caring, and "maternal." From this point of view, the maternal instinct is not a biological drive but rather the result of the gender-specific psychological matrix between the female caretaker and the little girl.

In sharp contrast to the men's movement theorists who hold that separation from the mother is far more difficult for little boys than little girls, the Chodorow/Dinnerstein approach suggests the very opposite. The establishment of a separate ego is far more difficult for girls than for boys, contributing to such gender-specific ailments as bulimia and anorexia. Hostility toward the female parent is instead directed toward the girl's own body as a surrogate for her mother. Little boys, on the other hand, have no such impediment to separation from the mother. They cannot surmount the resentment and hostility toward their mothers by identifying with them. They are both biologically incapable of taking their mother's place in childbirth and culturally discouraged from exhibiting the maternal characteristics of childrearing. On the contrary the hostility of little boys toward their mothers and little girls is encouraged as an acceptable gesture of identification with the masculine gender. Hence whereas little girls suffer from the difficulties of separating definitively from their mothers, little boys must deal with a separation that appears to be altogether too abrupt.

This abrupt separation does not sever the memory of the little boy from both its desire for and fear of the mother. The mother, and later the mother inscribed in every woman, is constituted as the Other to be both desired and feared. As the source of nourishment and oral/tactile pleasure, she is to be acquired and dominated. Dinnerstein theorizes that the masculinist obsession with a female partner's fidelity stems from the infant's fear that the mother might ignore his pleas for attention, that she must be withholding her love and attention in order to expend it elsewhere on someone else. This thought of abandonment and the anxiety produced by the delay of immediate gratification creates the desire to have exclusive control over a woman. The child's egocentric perspective manifests itself in the behavior of men who feel that, while women ought to attend to one manchild alone, men have no such comparable moral obligation of fidelity to women. Because the mother resisted the male child's continuous demands, the adult male ensures himself against the maternal power of his female partner by seeking other sources of immediate gratification. In light of the fantasized infidelity of the mother-woman, it seems only just to men who feel victimized by their mothers and women in general.

Written into the gender construction of women, the mother is frequently read as transsubjective, that is, she embodies nature itself. As the "semi-sentient she,"[51] the mother-woman is not regarded in the same way as other persons, that is, the male as the normatively human. She is the transcendent ground of life; her subjective identity rides the surface of this deeper reality—a reality that is transferred to women in general. Women are constructed as the wellspring from which a man satisfies his needs, both physical and emotional. Their subjectivity, their moral agency, is effaced. In this male imaginary, ethics is gender-specific. It is specifically a male activity. A woman's virtue is not her own but belongs to the man who possesses her, who imposes the code of fidelity on her behavior. From this masculinist perspective, a woman's nature is inherently transgressive. Because she is a mother, she is a whore. She is desirable, and unless controlled by a man, faithless. She is not a person, a moral agent, in the same way that a man is. As the embodiment of nature, she is both a depth to be plumbed, and a surface to be written upon. As a surface her body is to be scored with the images of the patriarchal social order: as wife, mother, mistress, or whore. Like the protagonist in the film *Tattoo,* a woman awakens to find—much to her horror—the masculinity of the culture writ large upon her body. Frequently such writing takes the form of bruises, scars, cuts, and wounds. Her blood, which symbolizes the life of the male child, is brought to the surface in the ritual of domestic violence. The resentment toward the mother for her power to gratify the manchild's needs as well as the anger generated by her suspected infidelities explodes in periodic assertions of male dominance. The inscription of these fears in the masculine psyche reinforces the presence of the mother in the life of the adult male. Hence, even though he does not identify with the mother, as does a female, and was abruptly separated from her as a child, he nonetheless feels as if she has not "cut the apron strings." The men's movement misinterprets the persistence of anxiety about women in general and the mother in particular as an indication of the failure to establish a separate male identity instead of the shortcomings of the masculinist psyche itself. From the perspective of the Dinnerstein/ Chodorow model, his uncertainties as a man are not rooted in the failure to separate but in the failure to resolve his ambivalent feelings toward his mother and women in general. Extrapolating from this model, the abhorrent consequences—male territorial games and the battering of women—are not attributable to some innate biological characteristic of males. On the contrary Dinnerstein finds the structure of the masculinist psyche a result of the attempt to escape the "female tyranny" of the mother.[52] But as in the case of the masculinist psyche, the tyrannical aspects of the mother are not inherent but rather are the legacy of what has become an almost exclusively female occupation in modern Western societies: childrearing.

This gendered division of labor has traditionally been defended as one founded on biological nature. Men, it is argued, simply don't share the maternal instinct. Lionel Tiger, for example, claimed that the "genetic packages" of male and female were developed along the lines of a gendered division of labor whereby men hunted cooperatively in groups and women bore and nurtured the offspring. This pattern became "'programmed' into the life cycle of the creatures."[53] Frequently women's birthing experience and role in early child care have resulted in the cultural inscription of a "maternal instinct" in women. And too often any female who does not exhibit maternal traits is deemed an oddity or, at worst, deviant. Nancy Chodorow, on the other hand, suggests that since no direct gene to behavior relationship can be proven, the gendered division of labor in childcare is a cultural pattern capable of being altered.[54]

But whether biological or cultural, it is widely thought that men are singularly ill-adapted for childrearing and that the image of grown males caring for infants is so incongruous as to be uproariously funny, as the mass popularity of the comedy *Three Men and a Baby* (1987) attests. Based on the successful French film *Trois Hommes et Un Couffin* (1985), the screenplay narrates the trials and tribulations of three successful bachelors who discover a baby left at their door in a upper-class Manhattan apartment building. The dialogue unveils their haplessness in the face of an alien creature:

Michael: Look, we've got to do something. One of us has to
    pick it up.
Peter: Well, it's not going to be me.
Michael: Now what? I don't know anything about taking care of
    babies.
Peter: Well, neither do I.
Michael: Look we got to do something.
Peter: Well be my guest.
Michael: Hey, it's not my responsibility.
Peter: It's not mine either
Michael: Don't yell at me Peter.
Peter: Well, it can't be that difficult. All we gotta do is feed it.
    Then it'll shut up.
Michael: I don't know what babies eat.
Peter: Soft stuff. We were babies once for God's sake. What did
    we eat?
Michael: I don't know. It couldn't have been very good. I can't
    remember.

The scene ends with Michael standing over the cradle, trying to placate a
now inconsolable baby by showing the child his "hairy chest." The film
seeks to exploit the widespread belief in popular culture that men are singularly unfit for any kind of child care. But some theorists like Sara Ruddick
claim that whereas historically women may have more experience mothering, there is nothing to prevent men from doing the same.[55] So why don't
they take more responsibility in child care? As M. Rivka Polatnick has bluntly
put it, "men (as a group) don't rear children because they don't *want* to rear
children."[56] Polatnick argues that it is simply a matter of the distribution of
power in a patriarchal society, and men by and large see child care as an
added responsibility they need not undertake. Yet Chodorow has reported
research that showed that maternal behavior was triggered in *both* men and
women by the presence of infants.[57] It is not that men are constitutionally
incapable of child care; it is a matter of convenience. But the price paid by
women and children for the convenience of uninvolved fathers is extraordinarily high.

    Dinnerstein and Chodorow conclude that even though misogyny may be
grounded in unresolved ambivalence of the male child for its mother, hostility toward and violence against women is not an inevitable outcome of
biology, but rather the consequence of the gendered division of labor in
childrearing. Women come to serve as a scapegoat for the frustrations that
children, both male and female, feel as a part of human existence. Denial,
separation, loss, and the anxiety that they induce are focused on the primary
caretaker of childhood whom it is believed has betrayed the trust of the
child. But whereas female children have the imaginary potential to over-

come this fear, due to their isomorphic identification with their mothers, male children have no such option. They feel compelled to act out this tension endlessly in periodic spasms of metaphoric and actual violence against women.

The intellectuals of the men's movement claim that the solution to the violent potential of "warrior energy" lies in the separation from women and the renewal of male identity in segregated men's groups. Yet this proposal does little to address the issue of the origin of male hostility. On the contrary, as a participant in the men's movement for the past two years, I have noted that many of these sessions become vehicles for the repetitive expression of clichéd images of women. Women are frequently depicted as being sources of love and gratification (mother) and as being unfaithful partners (whore). It is still not uncommon to hear a man opine that, while his female partner should observe fidelity, he feels no such obligation. "Scoring" women is still regarded as a preeminent sign of masculinity and social status in men's groups. On the other hand, women are also commonly perceived as a threat: either that they will withhold their "charms," which mystically enthrall and gratify men, or that they prey on them by using their allure to entrap men into marriage and family life. The men's movement therefore seems to be wrong-headed. Such segregated weekend workshops, drumming rituals, and wilderness experiences only reinforce hostility against the mother and women in general.

Yet there does seem to be a grain of truth in the lament of the men's movement about the "absent father" in modern-day society. The absence of the father *does* have a tangibly negative effect on the psychological development of the son but not because he no longer initiates the male child into male society. Feminist theorists like Dinnerstein, Chodorow, and Ruddick show that the father's lack of participation in early child care focuses the pleasures and frustrations of early life on the mother. She becomes the icon for the human condition and must bear the enormous—indeed crushing—weight of the male child's expectations and adoration, his fears and disappointments, and even his rage and his revenge. In the latter case, she is the object of undeserved hostility, in part because frustration is an inevitable aspect of the human condition and in part because this culture genders child care as a female task. Although we as human beings can do very little about the former, women need not be the scapegoat for the human condition. Increasingly feminist theorists have called for the participation of men, as partners with women, in the activities of childrearing.

"Male mothering" offers several advantages over the present custom of female caretaking. The participation of men in bottlefeeding, changing, touching, holding, and caressing the infant deflects the child's investment of affect in the mother as the sole provider of nourishment and oral/tactile gratification. It does not separate the male child from the mother but rather dispels the image of the mother as nature—an assumption that men carry into their adult lives with appalling consequences for women. *This* form of "male mothering"—and not that espoused by Robert Bly, et al.—therefore holds the potential to undermine the sexist dichotomy of woman as body, man as mind/spirit, which haunts Western consciousness and provides a way to restore subjectivity and moral agency to women in the eyes of the male child grown to manhood. Because women are not the only source of physical comfort, the father's participation in childrearing preempts the taboo surrounding other male bodies. Rather than regarding the touch of male flesh repugnant or a confusion of male identity, as homophobic men do, heterosexual males may experience a transvaluation of the male body so that it may be seen as a source of beauty and sublimated eros. The re-cognition of the male body suggests that heterosexual males may no longer feel so threatened by gay men, nor will men in general need to overinvest emotionally in the phallus as the means to overcome the alienation from the male body that they experience at a young age.

It is not only that bodies, male and female, will become transvalued through male caretaking of children. Because women would no longer be seen as the sole providers of gratification for the male child's needs, the adult male may feel less compulsion to abide by the double standard of fidelity that is common in patriarchal society. Jealousy and the desire to control the female partner—both widespread factors in domestic violence—may no longer have the same kind of cathected force behind them. Even the conception of nature itself may very well change—no longer looked upon as being a transsubjective entity to be exploited for the welfare of man but rather as a source of life to be respected as well as used in a responsible fashion. The rationale for wars fought for control of natural resources to meet the needs of patriarchal societies—be they for foodstuffs, raw materials, or energy sources, like oil—may give way to a more relational model of international cooperation, negotiation, and compromise. But perhaps most important of all, "male mothering" may unwrite the text of male hysteria that is played out metaphorically in male territorial games and physically in the abuse, torment, and even murder of women. Rather than being the sole object of displeasure, subject to the irrational wrath of men, women may be treated as persons who, like men, exercise power, respond to needs, and who sometimes cannot fulfill them. Although the change entailed by "male mothering" does not imply that the male child will no longer suffer from the frustrations of being human, he won't necessarily feel compelled to vent his rage on women alone. Rather than sharing common cause with the son in dehumanizing the wife-mother as the object of desire and fear, the father would share with the mother a human concern for the happiness and disappointments of their son.

Of course, the strategy of shared childrearing may well address the generations of males to come and may alleviate to certain degree the effect of misogynist culture on women in the future; however, it does little for men who today feel deeply estranged from both their mothers and women in general or for women who bear the markings of male violence on their bodies and in their souls. My own impression is that the men's movement gives us little insight into the meaning of our ambivalent relationships with mothers and fathers. And while it does provide some contact with other men beyond the back-slapping, towel-snapping bravado that typifies most male relationships, it offers no breakthroughs in understanding women.

Strangely enough it is common in the men's movement to hear men explain that women are their closest friends. They are as dependent upon their female confidants as they were on their mothers to nourish and support them emotionally. By and large, men speak of their deep estrangement from their fathers and other men. To sit in a men's group is to hear the lament of lost souls who feel that they are misunderstood and largely isolated. Yet they frequently feel that they know how to deal with other men—competitors in a hostile environment. They gird their loins daily to combat other males over issues of competition great and small, from sexual partners to rush-hour traffic. Social contact among men is most often mediated by buffers, such as beer and conversation about sports and sexual exploits, which cushion against possible friction. Most men's groups ban the consumption of alcohol at their meetings and prohibit the discussion of sports, if not sexual exploits, on the grounds that they are strategies of avoidance. When men actually start talking *to* each other instead of *about* their conquests and heroes, the effect is revelatory.

What amazes them is that beneath the armor of their competitor is a similar human being, equally as vulnerable. This euphoric breakthrough engenders an experience of sameness, of male bonding, which reinforces the solidarity of male identity as the binary opposite of female. For despite their dependence on female confidants, they regard women as alien to their experience and as interlopers to their newly found sense of male solidarity. After participating in men's conferences and a men's group over the last two years, I sense that stereotypical images of women are often used to strengthen the relationship among men in groups. To breakdown those stereotypes is to risk sacrificing their newly won sense of camaraderie—a high price to pay for men who, just so recently, have felt alone, even among family members and coworkers. Thus men in these groups frequently perpetuate the gender roles of women as caretakers and sexual objects. And in a male society infused with the ethos of competititon, men's groups sometimes shift the focus of mimetic rivalry from male competitors to women. Increasingly women are depicted as the aggressive rivals of white middle-class men who sense that women inspired by the feminist movement are resisting their "natural" roles. The hostility once directed toward the mother is thereby reawakened not only through the misogynist sexual domination of women but also through the denunciation of their emerging social autonomy. As a consequence females play the scapegoat either in their traditional stereotypical roles as mother/whore or in their newly won freedom as liberated women.

Although some women have been quite hopeful about the potential of the men's movement to help end sexism and male violence, others have articulated their own discomfort with the increasing popularity of men's groups modeled after *Iron John* and *Fire in the Belly.* In Kay Leigh Hagan's collection *Women Respond to the Men's Movement,* feminist activists and academics confess a nervousness and even a visceral sense of danger about a resurgent androcentric consciousness in a patriarchal social order. Despite the caricatures of the movement in the mass media, the clinical psychologist Laura S. Brown finds nothing funny here. Males who seek a renewed self-/gendered-consciousness at the expense of women can be deadly serious. And while the feminist theologian Rosemary Radford Ruether admits that consciousness-raising among men would be most welcome, she asks whether this is the men's movement that women really need.[58] Although the men's movement commenced as almost an auxiliary to the second wave of feminism in the United States, it seems that it has been captured and shaped by influential leaders who have little sympathy for or understanding of the plight of women.

If it is to redeem its original potential of liberating men from the sexist attitudes that distort their experience of the world as well as oppress women, a movement segregated from women seems inherently unsuitable to the task. Josef Breuer postulated a century ago that the resolution of hysteria might be found in what his patient Anna O. called the "talking cure." The resolution of male hysteria today may likewise be found in a "talking cure" that characterizes much of the spirit of the men's movement. However, according to the psychoanalytic paradigm, "working through" neuroses requires the transference of affect onto the analyst whose liminal role as both surrogate inside and observer outside the patient's fantasy provides the critical distance necessary for the patient's metanoia. In a men's group within the contemporary movement, no one plays this role.

If men in contemporary society are subject to unresolved anxieties over the mothers in women and the women in mothers, they cannot work through those conflicts by talking to each other. They require persons who stand outside their circle—persons who can both serve as surrogates for the figures that haunt their memories and daydreams and provide critical analysis of the material that they unearth from their experiences. In short, they need women. The proposal may appear incongruous. The presence of women in a men's group exploring its identity seemingly contradicts the movement's very rationale. Luce Irigaray admits that "her sex is heterogeneous to this whole economy of representation, but it is capable of interpreting that economy precisely because it has remained 'outside.'"[59] In a patriarchal culture, how many males could provide the perspective necessary to understand the dynamics of male hysteria? To analyze its effects on their own experience? To understand the experience of their female partners, siblings, friends, and even strangers?

Although the expression of long-suppressed emotions and frustrations in male-only groups is preferable to outbursts of violence in war, battering, and other sports, its course is frequently aimless. Granted that there is a certain satisfaction in "getting things off your chest"; however, without some sense of focus or guidance, these men—and I include myself—are no closer to addressing the origin of internal conflict that fuels the hostility and estrangement with which they have to struggle. Although the leading theorists of the movement have in many cases only managed to reiterate the animosity toward women and minority communities, I must respect the good faith intentions of many rank-and-file participants. Whether they are investment bankers or mail clerks, real estate speculators or salesmen, many are emotionally in pain and they don't know why. Focusing hostility on women through male bonding temporarily alleviates the anxiety, but it does not end it. On the contrary male solidarity frequently confirms the appropriation of mythological images of men as predators and women as prey. Male bonding is not the answer. The good intentions of those men attracted to the movement can only come to fruition despite the theorists of the men's movement, not because of them. Perhaps both Freud and Keen have posed the wrong questions. For to escape the cycle of male violence that plagues both sexes, it is not a question of what either women or men want. It is a question of what men need, and what men need is not their own movement. They need to take seriously the critiques of androcentric culture by the women's movement—something most men still refuse to do.

But most men refuse to do so because they are afraid. In a phallogocentric culture, which equates power and being with possession and control of the phallus, men in general and the men's movement in particular are still haunted by castration anxiety. They fear that the phallus/themselves will be silenced by women who are seeking to speak their own language, based on their own experiences and their own bodily suffering in a patriarchal social order. Many men prefer to hear themselves speak, echoed in the painful cries of the enemy. But this other language/language of the Other threatens the hold that men have on themselves. It is as if men must constantly remind themselves of their own phallic power—be it through male territorial games or men's movement exercises or the anagnoretic recollection of mythopoetic fantasy. Each provides an alternative way by which men constantly reaffirm that they are men, that the masculinist power is still there. Yet none of these strategies evinces the courage to which men lay claim. On the contrary true courage involves a "letting go" of the fears of women-mothers, of masculinist control, of phallic supremacy. It is a time for males to grow up and to respect the voices of women, but whether boys in an androcentric culture will have the maturity to become men, together with women in a liberated society, is open to question. The close of the century beckons millennial changes. Would that such a vision come to pass.

NOTES

1. Sigmund Freud, *Civilized Sexual Morality and Modern Nervousness, The Standard Edition of the Complete Psychological Works of Sigmund Freud*, ed. and trans. James Strachey (London: Hogarth, 1974), IX: 187.
2. Sigmund Freud, *On the Universal Tendency to Debasement in the Sphere of Love (Contributions to the Psychology of Love II), The Standard Edition*, XI: 183. "The main protective measure against such a disturbance [psychical impotence] which men have recourse to in this split in their love consists in a psychical debasement of the sexual object, the overvaluation that normally attaches to the sexual object being reserved for the incestuous object and its representatives. As soon as the condition of debasements is fulfilled, sensuality can be freely expressed, and important sexual capacities and a high degree of pleasure can develop."
3. Cf., e.g., Don Shewey, "Town Meeting in the Hearts of Men: Who's Afraid of Robert Bly? The Media, Women, Men Why? Because He—and Men Like James Hillman and Michael Meade—Might Just Change Things," *Village Voice*, February 11, 1992, 36.
4. John Craig, "Money, Media, Men Mulled in Minneapolis," *Wingspan: Journal of the Male Spirit* (December 1990–March 1991): 46.
5. Sam Keen, *Fire in the Belly: On Being a Man* (New York: Bantom, 1991), 38.
6. Robert Bly, *Iron John: A Book About Men* (New York: Random House, 1990), 179.
7. Klaus Theweleit, *Male Fantasies*. Volume I: *Women, Floods, Bodies, Histories*, trans. Stephen Conway (Minneapolis: University of Minnesota, 1987), 243.
8. Bly, *Iron John*, 234.
9. Ibid., 135.
10. Keen, *Fire in the Belly*, 219.
11. Comment by Keen at "Understanding Men" weekend workshop, March 14, 1992, New York, NY.
12. Keen, *Fire in the Belly*, 214.
13. Luce Irigaray, "La différence sexuelle," *Éthique de la différence sexuelle* (Paris: Les éditions de minuit, 1984), 20.
14. Bly, *Iron John*, 184. Bly recalls a Russian folktale entitled "The Maiden Tsar" in which a naive young man is put to sleep when a pin is slipped into his collar by his tutor at the behest of his stepmother. Bly interprets the story as a metaphor for the collusion of educators and the "Poisoned side of the Great

Mother" in suppressing the consciousness-raising of young men. Feminism and poststructuralism in the academy are therefore seen as collaborators in obstructing the young man's quest for "the real," that is the archetypal male (Wild Man/ Iron John).

15. Keen, *Fire in the Belly*, 206.
16. Ibid., 41.
17. Ibid., 62.
18. Ibid., 47.
19. Fred Leafgren, "Being a Man Can Be Hazardous to Your Health: Life-style Issues," in *Men in Conflict*, ed. Dwight Moore and Fred Leafgren (Alexandria, VA: American Association for Counseling and Development, 1990), 265.
20. Keen, *Fire in the Belly*, 213.
21. "Dialogue," *Man! Men, Community, Relationships*, 15 (Summer 1992), 58.
22. Bly, *Iron John*, 3.
23. Ibid., 149.
24. Ibid., 15.
25. Ibid., 16.
26. Ibid., 20.
27. Patrick Dougherty, "A Personal Perspective on Working with Men in Groups," in *Men in Conflict*, ed. Dwight Moore and Fred Leafgren (Alexandrea, VA: American Association for Counseling and Development, 1990), 170.
28. Lionel Tiger, *Men in Groups* (New York: Marion Boyars, 1984), xv.
29. Monique Wittig, *Les guérrillères*, trans. David Le Vay (New York: Avon, 1969), 89.
30. Bly, *Iron John*, 41.
31. Ibid., 224.
32. Craig, "Money," 3.
33. Keen, *Fire in the Belly*, 31.
34. Bly, *Iron John*, 93.
35. Keen, *Fire in the Belly*, 70.
36. Bly, *Iron John*, 121.
37. Kauth, *A Circle of Men*, 65.
38. Barbara Ehrenreich, *The Hearts of Men. American Dreams and the Flight from Commitment* (New York: Doubleday, 1983), 13 and 121.
39. Jill Johnston, "Why Iron John Is No Gift to Women," *New York Times Book Review*, February 23, 1992, 31.
40. Sherry Ortner, "Is Female to Male as Nature Is to Culture?" *Women & Values: Readings in Recent Feminist Philosophy* (Belmont, CA: Wadsworth, 1993), 59–72.
41. Keen, *Fire in the Belly*, 111.
42. Johnston, "Why Iron John Is No Gift to Women," 1.
43. Mircea Eliade, *Myth and Reality* (New York: Harper & Row, 1963).
44. Tiger, *Men in Groups*, 126–55.
45. Susan Faludi, *Backlash: The Undeclared War against American Women* (New York: Doubleday, 1991), 310.
46. Keen, *Fire in the Belly*, 5
47. Dorothy Dinnerstein, *The Mermaid and the Minotaur: Sexual Arrangements and Human Nature* (New York: Harper Collins, 1991), 234.
48. Ronald F. Levant, "Coping with the New Father Role," in *Men in Conflict*, ed. Dwight Moore and Fred Leafgren (Alexandrea, VA: American Association for Counseling and Development, 1990), 83.

49. Teresa L. Jump and Linda Haas, "Fathers in Transition: Dual-Career Fathers Particpating in Child Care," in *Changing Men: New Directions in Research on Men and Masculinity*, ed. Michael S. Kimmel (Newbury Park, CA: Sage, 1991), 99.
50. Dinnerstein, *The Mermaid and the Minotaur*, 60.
51. Ibid., 105.
52. Ibid., 187.
53. Tiger, *Men in Groups*, 44.
54. Nancy Chodorow, *The Reproduction of Mothering: Psychoanalysis and the Sociology of Gender* (Berkeley: University of California Press, 1978), 19.
55. Sara Ruddick, *Maternal Thinking. Towards a Politics of Peace* (New York: Random House, 1989), 41.
56. M. Rivka Polatnick, "Why Men Don't Rear Children: A Power Analysis," in *Mothering: Essays in Feminist Theory*, ed. Joyce Trebilcot (Totowa, NJ: Rowman & Allanheld, 1983), 23.
57. Chodorow, *The Reproduction of Mothering*, 27.
58. Laura S. Brown, "Essential Lies: A Dystopian Vision of the Mythopoetic Men's Movement," and Rosemary Radford Ruether, "Patriarchy and the Men's Movement: Part of the Problem or Part of the Solution?" in *Women Respond to the Men's Movement*, ed. Kay Leigh Hagan (San Francisco: Harper, 1992), 93–100 and 13–18.
59. Luce Irigaray, *This Sex Which Is Not One*, trans. Catherine Porter with Carolyn Burke (Ithaca, NY: Cornell University, 1985), 152.

INDEX

Ackerman Gary, 57
Adorno, Theodor, 113, 119
AIDS, 57, 69
alcohol abuse, 17–18, 167
American flag, 100
Americanism, 98–100, 102, 164
anti-Semitism, 114–15, 119
Arabs, 36, 46, 116
assault, 11, 65–66; aggravated, 8;
    simple, 9
Augustine, 23–24
authoritarian personality study: applied
    to the Gulf War, 112, 116–17, 120;
    analogous to "chauvinist mind,"
    119; authoritarianism, 113–14;
    criticisms, 115; ethnocentrism, 40,
    112, 116–17; personalization, 115,
    117, 135; sexuality, 114, 117, 120
'Aziz, Tariq, 35–36

Baghdad Conference, 35–36
Baker, James, 47
Bataille, Georges, 140, 161;
    automutilation, 149, 151; bodily
    fluids, 144, 146, 149; death,
    143–46, 149, 151; degradation, 142;
    heterology, 142; male orgasm, 142,
    144–47, 150; and Marxism, 141;
    and Nietzsche, 141; scotoma, 140,
    145, 152–53; "sovereign man," 143,
    146, 149; and surrealism, 140–41;
    war, 144–147, 149; women, 147,
    150–52
battered women, xv, 1, 8–9, 11–12,
    14–16, 25, 29: definition, 13;
    self-perception, 21
Battered Women's Scoreboard, 5
batterers: 14, 26, 28–29: fantasized
    infidelity of female partner, 21–22;
    26, 30; male self-image, 19–20;
    obsessive libidinality, 29;
    scopophilia, 28–30; women as
    mimetic rivals, ˙137

battering, xx, 26, 54; and alcohol/drug
    abuse, 17–18, 167; and children,
    9–10, 14; and class, 13, 15–16;
    definition of, 8; and education,
    15–16; emotional battering, 13–14;
    and football, 3, 5, 91, 104; and
    generational transmission, 17;
    incidence of battering, 5, 7–12;
    medical intervention, 12–13; murder,
    2, 9; of men, 185, 188; paternal
    authority, 24; physical battering, 8,
    12, 24, 29, 183, 204; and pregnancy,
    29; rape, 8, 167; as ritualized
    "sport," 19; spillover of violence,
    19, 31, 135, 137, 170; stress model,
    4; and torture, 25–26; and
    unemployment, 17; and war, 3, 6–7,
    18, 56
Baudrillard, Jean, 112
Benjamin, Walter, 86, 111
Bezymenski, Lev, 50
Bianchi, Eugene, 91
blood, 147; football players', 87,
    111–12; sacrificial victim's, 111,
    120, 137; women's, 136–37, 150,
    153–54, 167, 204
blood sport, xv, 81, 152–53
Bly, Robert, xix; biological
    essentialism, 183–84, 194;
    generation of "soft men," 188, 192,
    194, 202; "Great Mother," 184;
    "Iron John," 192–93; need for male
    ritual, 189, 191; "warrior energy,"
    183, 185–86, 188, 201, 207; "Wild
    Man," 188–89, 191–94, 196
Braun, Eva, 49
Breton, Jacques, 140
Breuer, Josef, 210
Bromberg, Norbert, 49
Brown, Laura, 210
Brownmiller, Susan, 55
Bush, Barbara, 100
Bush, George, 42, 100, 157; and

215